ALASKA

TRAVEL GUIDE 2024 - 2025

Everything You Need to Know, From Local Culture and History to Hidden Gems, Safety Tips, and Must-See Attractions for Every Traveler

FarFlung Folios

Copyright © by FarFlung Folios 2024.

All rights reserved.

Excerpts for brief quotations used in critical reviews and other non-commercial uses permitted by copyright law, no part of this publication may be copied, distributed, or transmitted in any way without the publisher's prior written consent, including by photocopying, recording, or other electronic or mechanical methods.

The use of any trademarks or brands mentioned in this book is solely for the purpose of clarification and is not intended to imply any affiliation with the respective owners of those marks or brands.

Table of Content

Introduction	11
Chapter 1	16
A Brief History of Alaska	16
Chapter 2	26
Alaska Native Cultures	26
Traditions, languages, and way of life	26
Art and Music: The influence of Native and modern art, and the vibrant music scene	31
Festivals and Celebrations: Annual events that showcase Alaskan heritage, such as the Iditarod and the Fur Rendezvous	37
Local Etiquette and Customs: What visitors should know about Alaskan customs and behavior	42
Chapter 3	48
Laws and Regulations	48
General Travel Laws	48
Local Laws to Know: Fishing, hunting, and camping regulations	52
Cannabis and Alcohol Laws: What's allowed in Alaska and where	56
Respecting Nature: Regulations about wildlife interactions, conservation, and park rules	62
Chapter 4	68
Essential Phrases and Language	68
Common English Phrases Used in Alaska	68
Alaska Native Words and Phrases: Learn some key words from Alaskan indigenous languages	73
Practical Phrases for Travelers: Handy phrases for communicating in hotels, restaurants, and while navigating the state	78
Chapter 5	83

Planning Your Trip   83
   Best times to visit based on weather, wildlife, and activities   83
   How to Get There: Flights, cruises, and road trips – the best options for reaching Alaska   87
   Traveling Within Alaska: Navigating Alaska by car, train, boat, or plane   93
   How to Prepare for the Climate: Packing lists for summer, winter, and year-round adventures   99

Chapter 6   103
Internet, Communication, and Navigation   103
   Staying Connected   103
   Local SIM Cards and Data Plans: Options for tourists to stay connected affordably   108
   Essential Travel Apps: Apps for maps, weather, navigation, and emergency contacts   113
   Using GPS in Remote Areas: Tips for using navigation tools off the beaten path   119

Chapter 7   125
Health and Safety   125
   Staying Healthy in Alaska   125
   Safety Tips for Outdoor Adventures: Precautions for hiking, wildlife encounters, and extreme weather   131
   Emergency Contacts and Resources: Hospitals, ranger stations, and emergency hotlines   136
   Travel Insurance: Why it's important and what to consider for Alaskan trips   143

Chapter 8   150
Accommodations   150
   Hotels and Resorts: The best options for luxury and mid-range travelers   150
   Hostels and Budget Stays: Affordable accommodations for backpackers and budget-conscious travelers   156

Cabins and Lodges: Rustic accommodations close to nature	161
Camping in Alaska: Campsites, RV parks, and wilderness camping options	165
Unique Stays: Igloos, yurts, and other one-of-a-kind Alaskan lodgings	170
Chapter 9	**175**
Getting Around Alaska	175
By Road	175
By Air: Regional flights and bush planes for accessing remote areas	180
By Train: The Alaska Railroad and scenic train routes	185
By Boat: Ferries, cruise lines, and sailing between towns and islands	190
Public Transport: Buses, shuttles, and other options for navigating cities and towns	196
Chapter 10	**202**
Top Destinations and Attractions	202
Anchorage	202
Juneau: Exploring the capital city – historic sites, whale watching, and more	207
Fairbanks: Northern lights viewing, outdoor adventures, and cultural experiences	213
Seward: Gateway to Kenai Fjords National Park	220
Denali National Park: A guide to experiencing the highest peak in North America	226
Glacier Bay National Park: Highlights and tips for visiting Alaska's famous glaciers	233
Off-the-Beaten-Path Locations: Lesser-known gems and hidden treasures throughout the state	237
Chapter 11	**244**
Wildlife and Nature Experiences	244

Wildlife Viewing 244
Birdwatching: Top birdwatching locations and what species to look for 250
Fishing in Alaska: The best spots for fishing and what you need to know about licenses 256
Hiking and Backpacking: Famous trails, safety tips, and gear recommendations 263
Northern Lights: Best places and times to witness the aurora borealis 269
National Parks and Wilderness Areas: Overview of Alaska's most breathtaking parks 275

Chapter 12 282
Free and Paid Attractions 282
Museums, scenic views, and parks that don't cost a dime 282
Paid Experiences Worth Every Penny: Guided tours, boat cruises, and wilderness safaris 287
How to Book Activities: Booking tips, best times, and operator recommendations 294

Chapter 13 301
Day Trips and Excursions 301
From Anchorage 301
From Juneau: Excursions to Mendenhall Glacier and nearby islands 307
From Fairbanks: Exploring the Arctic Circle, Chena Hot Springs, and more 313
Multi-Day Excursions: Guided trips for those looking for extended adventures 320

Chapter 14 326
Food and Dining 326
Must-Try Alaskan Dishes 326
Best Restaurants for Every Budget: Fine dining, casual eateries, and budget-friendly spots 332
Cafes and Breweries: Where to grab a coffee or

local brew	337
Local Markets and Food Trucks: Tasting Alaska's best street food and market finds	343
Chapter 15	350
Festivals and Seasonal Events	350
Winter Festivals	350
Summer Festivals: Music festivals, cultural fairs, and events celebrating Alaskan heritage	356
Autumn and Spring Events: Smaller festivals and off-season events worth attending	362
Chapter 16	369
Off-the-Beaten-Path Adventures	369
Remote towns, secret trails, and unique experiences	369
Backcountry Adventures: How to plan your wilderness explorations	374
Small Town Charms: Discovering Alaska's quaint villages and their local flavor	380
Cultural Immersion: Visiting native villages and learning about indigenous traditions	385
Chapter 17: Practical Travel Tips	390
Money and Costs: Budgeting tips and what to expect in terms of cost	391
Traveling with Kids: Family-friendly activities and accommodations	398
Solo Travel in Alaska: Safety tips and how to meet fellow travelers	405
Sustainable Travel: How to minimize your footprint and travel responsibly in Alaska	412
Chapter 18	420
Resources and Apps for Travelers	420
Chapter 19	427
FAQs	427
Common traveler concerns and expert answers	

427

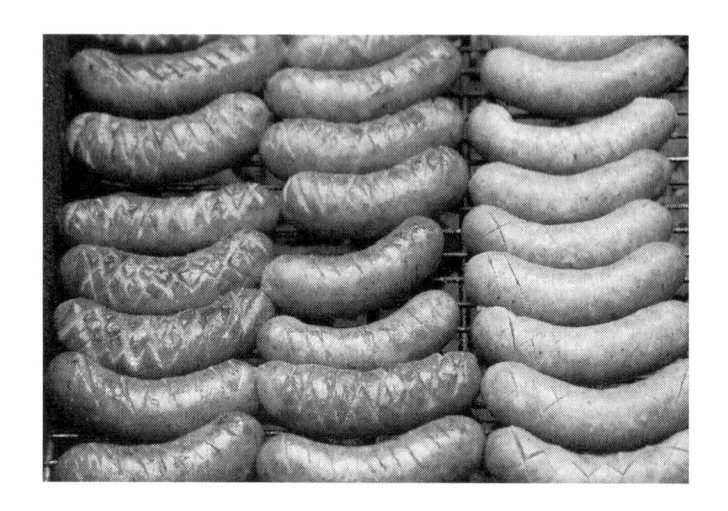

Introduction

As the largest state in the United States, Alaska offers something unique for every traveler who seeks both adventure and tranquility. Whether you're a nature lover eager to explore untouched wilderness, a culture enthusiast fascinated by the deep-rooted traditions of Alaska's native peoples, or someone simply looking to experience the beauty of this far-off land, Alaska is a destination that captivates all who visit.

Often referred to as "The Last Frontier," Alaska stands apart from any other place you may have visited. Its landscapes are vast, rugged, and unspoiled, with towering mountains, expansive forests, shimmering glaciers, and a coastline teeming with marine life. The natural beauty here can seem endless, whether you're cruising through the icy waters of the Inside Passage, hiking through the wilds of Denali National Park, or watching the northern lights dance across the sky on a cold winter night. In Alaska, every corner offers a view that can leave you speechless. The sheer scale of the state means that there's always something new to discover, whether it's a hidden waterfall, a quiet wildlife reserve, or a village tucked away in the wilderness.

Yet, there's more to Alaska than just its breathtaking landscapes. The state also boasts a rich and diverse culture. Alaska's history is deeply tied to the indigenous peoples who have lived here for thousands of years, and their traditions, art, and stories continue to be an important part of everyday life. Beyond the native culture, you'll also find influences from the Russian period, the Gold Rush era, and a modern-day spirit of resilience that defines the people who live here. From local art to traditional music, from festivals that celebrate Alaska's heritage to everyday life in small fishing villages, there's so much to learn about and appreciate in this state that is home to a truly unique blend of history and modernity.

But why visit Alaska? What makes it stand out among other travel destinations? First and foremost, Alaska is the ultimate destination for those seeking a deep connection with nature. Wildlife is abundant here, you might see bears fishing for salmon, whales breaching in icy waters, or bald eagles soaring overhead. For adventure seekers, Alaska offers world-class opportunities for activities like hiking, kayaking, dog sledding, and fishing. Whether you're looking for the thrill of conquering a mountain or the peace that comes with gliding through calm fjords, Alaska provides the setting for unforgettable experiences. The state's remoteness also makes it an ideal place to escape the busy pace of everyday life, offering the chance to reconnect with the natural world in ways that are hard to find elsewhere.

For those who enjoy learning and exploring cultures, Alaska offers insight into a world where tradition and nature are closely intertwined. Visitors can explore native villages, witness traditional crafts, and participate in local celebrations that honor the deep connection between the people and the land. And then there are the natural wonders that simply cannot be missed, like the northern lights, a once-in-a-lifetime spectacle for many, or the midnight sun, when daylight stretches well into the night during the summer months.

This guide you're about to read has been designed to make your journey to Alaska as smooth and rewarding as possible. We know that traveling to a place like Alaska can be both exciting and overwhelming, there's so much to see and do, and it's easy to wonder where to start. That's where this guide comes in. We've gathered all the important information you need, whether you're planning a short trip to one of the major cities or an extended adventure deep into the wilderness. From practical details like visa requirements and travel insurance to insider tips on the best times to visit and what to pack, this guide will help you prepare for every aspect of your journey.

You'll find information on how to get to Alaska and how to move around once you're here, whether you're traveling by car, train, plane, or boat. We've also included tips on public transportation and the best apps to use while traveling in Alaska. To make your trip as enjoyable and stress-free as possible, we'll guide you through the best places to stay, from luxury resorts to budget-friendly options, as well as give you suggestions for dining based on your taste and budget. And of course, no trip to Alaska would be complete without experiencing its unique attractions, so we've compiled a list of must-see sights, from the most famous tourist spots to hidden gems that only locals know about.

One of the most important things this guide will help you with is making the most of Alaska's natural beauty. We've dedicated sections to exploring Alaska's national parks, wildlife viewing opportunities, and adventure activities. Whether you want to hike along scenic trails, paddle through pristine rivers, or take in the views from a helicopter, this guide will show you where to go and how to plan these adventures. We also include tips for staying safe in Alaska's wild and often unpredictable environment, ensuring that you're well-prepared for the challenges that nature might present.

In addition to exploring the great outdoors, we've also highlighted Alaska's rich culture, art, and history. You'll discover local festivals that celebrate the state's diverse heritage, museums that tell the story of Alaska's past, and opportunities to interact with local artists and artisans. If you're interested in learning more about the native cultures that have thrived here for thousands of years, this guide will point you in the direction of cultural tours and events where you can experience the traditions and customs that are still alive today.

As you navigate this guide, you'll find that we've arranged the information in a way that's easy to follow. Each section focuses on a different aspect of traveling in Alaska, from the practical to the inspirational. We start by helping you plan the essentials, like how to get here, what to pack, and how to handle money matters. Then, we move on to the fun part, what to do, where to stay, and how to make the most of your time in this incredible state. Whether you're planning a short visit or a long adventure, this guide will be your companion, offering advice and recommendations every step of the way.

In short, this guide is packed with valuable information for anyone planning a trip to Alaska, whether it's your first visit or your tenth. We've carefully selected the details to ensure that you have everything you need to plan a smooth, enjoyable, and unforgettable experience. Alaska is a place that stays with you long after you've left, and we hope this guide helps you make the most of your time in this extraordinary land. Enjoy your journey to Alaska, you're in for a remarkable adventure.

Chapter 1

A Brief History of Alaska

The Indigenous peoples of Alaska have lived on this land for thousands of years, long before it became part of the United States or even before the arrival of European explorers. These early inhabitants are an essential part of Alaska's history, and their influence on the state's culture and way of life is still felt today. The rich traditions, stories, and ways of living passed down through generations provide a deep connection to the land and its natural resources. Understanding the Indigenous peoples of Alaska not only gives us insight into the past but also allows us to appreciate how their customs and values continue to shape the present.

The native peoples of Alaska are diverse, with several distinct groups spread across the state. Each group has its own language, traditions, and lifestyle, adapted to the specific environments they inhabit. The largest groups include the Inuit (often referred to as Eskimo), the Aleut, and the various Athabaskan peoples, among others. These groups are not homogenous; they have different histories and practices, but they all share a deep connection to the land, sea, and natural world around them. The Indigenous people of Alaska have always had a close relationship with nature, relying on the resources around them to survive in what can be one of the harshest environments in the world.

For thousands of years, these groups lived off the land and sea, developing methods of hunting, fishing, and gathering that were finely tuned to the seasonal rhythms of Alaska's climate. The Inuit, for example, lived primarily in the Arctic and sub-Arctic regions, where they became experts in hunting marine mammals like seals and whales, as well as caribou and fish. Their ability to thrive in such extreme conditions is a testament to their knowledge of the environment and their resilience. Similarly, the Aleut people, who lived on the Aleutian Islands, relied heavily on the sea for sustenance, becoming skilled boat builders and fishermen. Their small, nimble kayaks allowed them to navigate the often dangerous waters of the North Pacific, and they used harpoons and nets to catch fish, seals, and other marine life.

The Athabaskan peoples, who lived in the interior of Alaska, led a more land-based lifestyle, relying on hunting moose, caribou, and smaller animals, as well as gathering berries and other edible plants. They were also known for their expert craftsmanship, particularly in making tools and clothing from animal skins and bones. Their way of life was closely tied to the land and the changing seasons, as they moved with the migrations of animals and adapted to the cycles of nature.

One of the most important aspects of life for the Indigenous peoples of Alaska was their social and spiritual connection to the natural world. For many groups, the land, sea, and animals were not just resources to be used but were viewed as living entities with their own spirits and powers. This belief in the interconnectedness of all living things shaped their cultural practices and spiritual beliefs. Animals were often seen as spiritual guides, and hunting and fishing were done with great respect for the creatures being taken. Many groups practiced rituals to honor the animals they hunted, giving thanks for the food and materials they provided. This deep respect for nature has continued to influence Alaskan culture even as modern technologies and industries have changed the way people live and work.

Traditional art and storytelling were also central to the cultures of Alaska's Indigenous peoples. Art was often used to express spiritual beliefs and tell stories about the past. Carvings, masks, and other objects were created not only for practical purposes but also as a way to pass down important knowledge and cultural values. These art forms continue to be highly valued in Alaska today, with many artists drawing on traditional styles and techniques to create works that celebrate their heritage.

Storytelling was another vital tradition, with elders passing down myths, legends, and histories orally from one generation to the next. These stories often explained the origins of the world, the behavior of animals, and the relationships between people and the natural world. They were a way to teach younger generations about their history, culture, and the values that were important to their communities. This oral tradition is still alive today, with many Indigenous people working to preserve their languages and stories in the face of modern challenges.

The arrival of Europeans in Alaska in the 18th century brought significant changes to the lives of Alaska's Indigenous peoples. Russian explorers were the first Europeans to establish a presence in Alaska, followed later by American settlers after the United States purchased the territory from Russia in 1867. This period of colonization disrupted many aspects of Indigenous life, as new diseases, forced relocations, and changes to the environment due to commercial hunting and development took their toll on native populations. However, despite these challenges, the Indigenous peoples of Alaska have managed to maintain many of their cultural traditions and have played a crucial role in the state's modern history.

In modern times, the influence of Alaska's Indigenous peoples is still very much present. Many native groups have worked hard to protect their lands, languages, and cultures from the pressures of modernization and globalization. In 1971, the U.S. government passed the Alaska Native Claims Settlement Act, which granted Indigenous groups ownership of millions of acres of land and provided financial compensation for land taken from them. This landmark legislation helped to give Alaska's Indigenous peoples more control over their own futures, allowing them to maintain their cultural identity while also participating in the modern economy.

Today, many Alaskan communities continue to celebrate their Indigenous heritage through festivals, art, and cultural centers that educate visitors and locals alike about the history and traditions of the state's original inhabitants. In many parts of Alaska, you can still find people practicing traditional hunting and fishing techniques, making art using time-honored methods, and speaking in their native languages. The resilience and adaptability of Alaska's Indigenous peoples are a testament to their strength and the depth of their connection to the land.

The history of Alaska is shaped by various cultural and political influences, and one of the most significant periods in Alaska's past was its time under Russian control. The Russian era of Alaska began in the 18th century when Russian explorers arrived on its shores. Their presence marked the start of a period of colonization that would last for over a century, leaving a lasting imprint on the land and its people.

The first Russian explorers, led by Vitus Bering in 1741, were motivated by the desire to expand Russia's territory and access valuable resources, particularly furs. At the time, the fur trade was booming, and the sea otter pelts found in Alaska were highly sought after due to their warmth and softness. These furs were in great demand in Europe and Asia, and Russia saw an opportunity to establish a lucrative trading empire in Alaska. Russian fur traders, known as "promyshlenniki," began arriving in large numbers, establishing settlements along the coast. The Russians primarily focused on the Aleutian

Islands and the southern coast of Alaska, where sea otters were plentiful.

However, Russian colonization came at a cost to the Indigenous peoples of Alaska. The Aleut people, in particular, were heavily impacted by the Russian presence. Many were forced into labor to hunt sea otters, and the introduction of new diseases brought by the Russians led to a sharp decline in the native population. The Russians also imposed their own social structures on the Indigenous people, converting many to Christianity and disrupting traditional ways of life. Despite these challenges, there was also some level of cooperation between the Russians and certain Indigenous groups. The Russian Orthodox Church, for example, became a significant part of Alaskan culture, and many Indigenous people adopted the faith while incorporating aspects of their own beliefs into their practices.

The Russian-American Company, a government-chartered company, was established in 1799 to manage the Russian colony in Alaska. This company had a monopoly over the fur trade and played a central role in the administration of Russian Alaska. It was responsible for setting up trading posts and settlements, and it even governed the local population. The most significant of these settlements was Novo-Arkhangelsk, now known as Sitka, which served as the capital of Russian America. Sitka became the cultural and economic center of the colony, and it was here that Russian influence was most deeply felt.

Despite the initial success of the fur trade, by the mid-19th century, the Russian empire faced several challenges in maintaining its Alaskan colony. Overhunting had drastically reduced the sea otter population, which caused the fur trade to decline. Additionally, maintaining and protecting Alaska was expensive for Russia, which was already dealing with other geopolitical pressures, including the Crimean War and tensions with the British Empire. Russia began to view Alaska as a financial burden rather than an asset, and the government decided to sell the territory to the United States.

In 1867, the U.S. purchased Alaska from Russia for $7.2 million, a deal brokered by U.S. Secretary of State William H. Seward. At the time, many Americans ridiculed the purchase, calling it "Seward's Folly" or "Seward's Icebox," as they saw little value in acquiring what appeared to be a barren and frozen land. However, the acquisition would later prove to be a strategic and economic success for the United States. The formal transfer of Alaska from Russian to American control took place on October 18, 1867, in Sitka, and this date is still celebrated as Alaska Day.

The transition from Russian control to U.S. governance marked the beginning of Alaska's journey to statehood. For decades after the purchase, Alaska remained a distant and relatively undeveloped territory. It was governed by a series of military and civilian administrators, and its population consisted mostly of Indigenous people, Russian settlers, and a small number of American traders and missionaries. Alaska's vast and rugged landscape made it difficult to develop infrastructure, and for many years, it was seen as a remote and isolated outpost.

However, the discovery of gold in the late 19th century changed the fortunes of Alaska. The Klondike Gold Rush of 1896 brought a wave of prospectors, miners, and settlers to the region, leading to rapid population growth and the establishment of new towns and transportation routes. The gold rush also sparked increased interest in Alaska's natural resources, including its fisheries, timber, and minerals. Over time, Alaska became more economically integrated with the rest of the United States, and its strategic location made it increasingly important to national security, particularly during World War II when Alaska played a key role in the Pacific theater.

The push for Alaska's statehood gained momentum in the mid-20th century as more people recognized the territory's economic potential and strategic importance. In the 1950s, a movement for statehood emerged, driven by Alaskan residents who wanted greater representation and control over their own affairs. At the time, Alaska was governed as a U.S. territory, meaning it had limited political power and no voting representation in Congress. After years of campaigning, Alaska was finally granted statehood on January 3, 1959, becoming the 49th state of the United States.

Modern-day Alaska is a dynamic and important part of the United States. Its economy is diverse, with major industries including oil, fishing, tourism, and natural resource extraction. The discovery of oil at Prudhoe Bay in 1968 and the subsequent construction of the Trans-Alaska Pipeline in the 1970s transformed Alaska's economy. Oil revenues have become a significant source of income for the state, and Alaska's Permanent Fund, established in 1976, uses profits from oil production to provide annual dividends to residents. This unique fund has helped to stabilize the state's economy and provide benefits to its population.

Tourism is another major contributor to Alaska's economy. Each year, millions of visitors travel to Alaska to experience its stunning landscapes, wildlife, and outdoor activities. From cruises along the Inside Passage to hiking in Denali National Park, Alaska's natural beauty continues to draw people from around the world. The state's fishing industry is also a key economic driver, with Alaska producing some of the world's finest seafood, including salmon, halibut, and crab.

Alaska's population is relatively small compared to other U.S. states, with about 730,000 residents. The population is spread out across a vast area, and many people live in remote or rural communities. Anchorage, the state's largest city, is home to about 40% of the population, while other major cities include Fairbanks and Juneau, the state capital. Despite its small population, Alaska is incredibly diverse, with a mix of Indigenous peoples, descendants of Russian settlers, and people from all over the United States and the world.

In terms of its role in the United States today, Alaska remains an important part of the country's natural resource base, and its strategic location continues to be significant for national defense. Military bases in Alaska play a crucial role in U.S. operations in the Pacific and Arctic regions. Additionally, as concerns about climate change grow, Alaska's Arctic environment has gained attention for its vulnerability to warming temperatures and melting ice, raising important questions about the future of the state's ecosystems and way of life.

Chapter 2

Alaska Native Cultures

Traditions, languages, and way of life

Alaska is home to a diverse range of Native cultures, each with its own rich traditions, languages, and ways of life that have been passed down through generations. The Indigenous peoples of Alaska have lived on the land for thousands of years, long before it became part of the United States. They developed unique cultures shaped by the environment, geography, and climate of the vast region they inhabit. These cultures are as varied as Alaska's landscapes, but all share a deep connection to the land and natural resources, which continues to influence the daily lives of Alaska Natives today.

Alaska's Native peoples are made up of several distinct groups, each with its own language and traditions. The major groups include the Iñupiat and Yup'ik peoples of the Arctic and sub-Arctic regions, the Aleut or Unangan of the Aleutian Islands, the Athabaskan peoples of the interior, and the Tlingit, Haida, and Tsimshian peoples of the Southeast coastal areas. These groups are culturally and linguistically diverse, but they all have deep historical ties to Alaska and have adapted their lifestyles to the challenges of the region's often harsh environment.

One of the most important aspects of Alaska Native cultures is their connection to the land and sea. For thousands of years, Native peoples have relied on the natural resources around them for survival. This means that hunting, fishing, and gathering have long been central to their way of life. The Iñupiat and Yup'ik peoples, who live in the northern regions of Alaska, have traditionally hunted marine mammals like seals, walrus, and whales. These animals not only provided food but also materials for clothing, tools, and shelter. The Iñupiat and Yup'ik developed advanced hunting techniques and tools, including kayaks and harpoons, which allowed them to thrive in one of the world's most extreme environments. Their deep knowledge of the Arctic ecosystem has been passed down through generations, helping them live in harmony with nature.

In the interior of Alaska, the Athabaskan peoples have traditionally relied more on land animals, such as moose and caribou, as well as smaller animals like rabbits and birds. Fishing in Alaska's many rivers and lakes is also a major part of the Athabaskan way of life. The seasonal rhythms of the land dictated their movements, as many Athabaskan groups were semi-nomadic, moving from place to place in search of food. This close relationship with nature influenced not just their diet but also their spiritual beliefs and social structures.

The Tlingit, Haida, and Tsimshian peoples of Southeast Alaska developed a culture that was deeply connected to the ocean, forests, and rivers of their region. These coastal groups were expert fishermen, relying heavily on salmon, halibut, and other marine life for food. They also built large, sturdy wooden houses and canoes from the abundant cedar trees found in their region. The Tlingit, Haida, and Tsimshian are known for their elaborate totem poles, which are carved with images representing family histories, clan symbols, and spiritual beliefs. Totem poles are not just decorative objects but carry deep cultural significance, telling stories that are passed down through generations.

Language is a vital part of Alaska Native cultures, and there are many different Indigenous languages spoken across the state. However, like many Indigenous languages worldwide, some Alaska Native languages are endangered due to the impact of colonization and modernization. In the past, Native children were often forced to attend boarding schools where they were forbidden from speaking their languages, leading to a decline in fluent speakers. Despite these challenges, there has been a revival in recent years, with efforts to preserve and revitalize Native languages through education programs, language immersion schools, and community initiatives. These efforts are helping to ensure that the languages and the cultural knowledge embedded within them are not lost.

The social structure of Alaska Native groups often revolves around clans or extended family groups, with elders holding an important role as keepers of knowledge and traditions. Elders are highly respected, as they are the ones who pass down the oral histories, stories, and cultural practices that define the group's identity. Oral tradition is central to Alaska Native cultures. For thousands of years, history and knowledge have been passed down orally through stories, songs, and dances. These oral traditions contain important lessons about survival, respect for nature, and the relationships between people and the environment. Many of the stories are connected to the land, animals, and natural elements, reflecting the close relationship that Alaska Native peoples have with the world around them.

Art is another important aspect of Alaska Native cultures. Whether it is intricate beadwork, woven baskets, carved masks, or totem poles, Native art is deeply tied to cultural identity and spiritual beliefs. The designs and symbols used in these art forms often represent animals, natural forces, and ancestral spirits. In addition to being visually striking, Native art often serves a practical purpose as well. For example, clothing made by the Iñupiat and Yup'ik peoples is both beautiful and functional, designed to keep people warm in the freezing Arctic conditions. Similarly, the canoes built by the Tlingit, Haida, and Tsimshian peoples are not only finely crafted but also essential for travel and trade along the coast.

Trade was another important part of life for many Alaska Native groups, especially those living along the coast. Before the arrival of Europeans, Alaska's Native peoples had well-established trade networks that stretched across the region. Coastal groups like the Tlingit and Haida traded fish, sea otter pelts, and other goods with groups living farther inland. Trade allowed for the exchange of not only material goods but also ideas and cultural practices.

The spiritual beliefs of Alaska Native peoples are closely tied to the natural world. Many Indigenous groups believe that animals, plants, and even the elements like wind and water have spirits. This belief in animism shapes the way they interact with the world around them. For example, hunters often perform rituals to honor the spirit of the animal they have killed, showing respect for the life that was taken. This deep respect for nature is a common theme across Alaska Native cultures and has played a role in shaping modern conservation efforts in the state.

Despite the challenges of colonization, modernization, and the pressure to assimilate into mainstream American culture, Alaska Native cultures remain strong. In many parts of Alaska, Native peoples continue to practice their traditional ways of life, while also adapting to the realities of the modern world. Today, there are ongoing efforts to protect Native lands, preserve languages, and maintain cultural practices in the face of these challenges. Alaska Native organizations play an important role in advocating for the rights of Indigenous peoples, working to ensure that their voices are heard in decisions that affect their land and communities.

In modern Alaska, Native cultures are celebrated and play a significant role in the state's identity. Festivals like the Alaska Federation of Natives Convention and the Kivgiq (Messenger Feast) bring Native peoples together to celebrate their heritage through dance, music, and traditional games. These events are not only a way to preserve culture but also a means of educating younger generations and non-Native people about the rich diversity of Alaska Native traditions.

Art and Music: The influence of Native and modern art, and the vibrant music scene

Art and music are powerful expressions of culture, and in Alaska, both have long been integral to the lives of the Native peoples as well as the broader population that has developed over time. The state's artistic traditions are rich and varied, deeply rooted in the landscapes, history, and people who have called Alaska home for thousands of years. Today, Alaska's art and music scene is a vibrant blend of ancient traditions and modern creativity, where Native and contemporary influences come together to create something uniquely Alaskan.

Alaska's Native art is deeply tied to the spiritual and cultural traditions of the Indigenous peoples who have lived here for millennia. For these communities, art is more than just a form of expression; it plays a central role in their way of life, connecting them to their ancestors, their environment, and the spiritual world. Art in Native Alaskan cultures is often functional as well as decorative, with pieces like clothing, tools, masks, and totem poles serving both practical and ceremonial purposes. These artworks are filled with symbolism, reflecting the animals, natural forces, and spiritual beings that are central to the worldview of many Native Alaskan groups.

Totem poles, perhaps one of the most recognizable forms of Native Alaskan art, are a powerful example of this. Traditionally carved from large cedar trees, totem poles tell stories about the family or clan to which they belong. Each figure carved into the pole represents an important person, animal, or event in the clan's history. These poles are not simply decorative; they serve as visual records of ancestry, social status, and spiritual beliefs. They are often placed at the entrance of a family's home or within a village to commemorate important events or honor ancestors. The Tlingit, Haida, and Tsimshian peoples of Southeast Alaska are especially known for their totem pole carving, but similar carved art forms can be found throughout Alaska, each with its own regional style and meaning.

Mask-making is another important artistic tradition among Alaska Native cultures, particularly among the Yup'ik and Iñupiat peoples. Masks are often used in ceremonial dances and rituals, where they are believed to connect the wearer to the spirit world. Many masks are designed to represent animals or mythological beings, with each element of the mask carrying symbolic meaning. For example, a mask might feature multiple faces or exaggerated features to represent different spiritual forces or characteristics. These masks are typically made from materials available in the natural environment, such as wood, bone, feathers, and fur, and are often elaborately decorated. The use of these masks in dance is an expression of storytelling, with the movements of the dancers helping to bring the stories to life.

In addition to these traditional forms of visual art, Native Alaskan cultures are also known for their highly skilled craftsmanship in other areas, such as basket weaving and beadwork. Basketry, in particular, is a long-standing art form, with some Alaska Native weavers able to create baskets that are so finely woven they can hold water. These baskets are made from natural materials like spruce roots, grasses, and birch bark, and they often feature intricate patterns that are passed down through generations. Each basket tells a story, not only through the patterns and colors used but also through the purpose for which it was made, whether that be for gathering food, storage, or ceremonial use.

Beadwork is another important artistic tradition, particularly among the Athabaskan peoples of the interior. Beaded designs are often used to decorate clothing, footwear, and bags, and they often feature patterns that are inspired by the natural world, such as flowers, animals, and stars. The process of creating these beaded designs is painstaking and requires a great deal of skill, as each bead is sewn into place by hand to create the final design. These decorative items are often worn at important cultural events and ceremonies, where they serve as a visual representation of the wearer's identity and heritage.

While Native Alaskan art is deeply rooted in tradition, it continues to evolve in the modern world. Many contemporary Native artists draw on their cultural heritage while also experimenting with new materials, techniques, and themes. Some artists continue to create traditional art forms like totem poles, masks, and beadwork, while others have branched out into new mediums, such as painting, sculpture, and photography. These modern interpretations of Native art often explore themes of identity, survival, and the relationship between past and present. Through their work, these artists contribute to the ongoing story of Alaska's Native peoples, keeping their traditions alive while also addressing the challenges and opportunities of living in the 21st century.

Music, like art, has always been an important part of Alaska Native cultures, and it continues to play a vital role in both traditional and modern life. Traditional Native Alaskan music is closely tied to the rhythms of nature and the cycles of life. It is used to celebrate important events, tell stories, and connect with the spiritual world. Drumming and chanting are central to many ceremonial practices, with different rhythms and melodies used to convey specific meanings. In many Alaska Native cultures, music is not just something to listen to but is deeply intertwined with dance and storytelling. Songs are passed down from one generation to the next, preserving the oral history and cultural knowledge of the community.

The drum, in particular, is a powerful symbol in Alaska Native music. It is considered the heartbeat of the people, and its steady rhythm is believed to connect the human world with the spirit world. Drums are often made from animal skins stretched over wooden frames and are played with sticks or by hand. Different regions of Alaska have their own distinctive drumming styles, and the drums themselves are often decorated with symbols that represent the community or the performer's family. Drumming accompanies many different types of performances, from social dances to healing rituals, and it is a vital part of maintaining the cultural traditions of Alaska's Native peoples.

Chanting and singing are also key elements of traditional Native Alaskan music. Many songs are used to tell stories about historical events, spiritual journeys, or important life events such as birth, marriage, and death. The lyrics of these songs are often highly poetic, filled with references to nature, animals, and the spiritual world. In some cultures, the songs are accompanied by movements and gestures that help to illustrate the story being told. These songs are not only a way of passing down history but also a means of connecting with the past and maintaining a sense of cultural identity.

While traditional music continues to be a strong influence in Alaska, the modern music scene is also vibrant and diverse. In addition to traditional forms, Alaska is home to a wide range of musical genres, including folk, rock, jazz, and classical music. Many contemporary Alaskan musicians draw inspiration from the state's natural beauty, history, and cultural diversity. The music scene in cities like Anchorage and Fairbanks is particularly lively, with local musicians performing in venues ranging from small bars to large concert halls. Music festivals, such as the Alaska Folk Festival, showcase the talents of local and visiting artists and provide opportunities for people to come together and celebrate their shared love of music.

Some modern Alaskan musicians incorporate traditional Native elements into their work, blending ancient rhythms and instruments with contemporary styles like rock or hip-hop. This fusion of old and new creates a unique sound that reflects the complexity of Alaskan identity in the modern world. These artists use music as a way to explore their heritage while also engaging with the broader musical trends of the 21st century.

The influence of both Native and modern art and music in Alaska can be seen throughout the state, from the vibrant street art that adorns urban areas to the ceremonial songs and dances performed at cultural festivals. Art galleries, museums, and cultural centers provide spaces where both traditional and contemporary works are displayed, offering visitors a chance to experience the rich artistic traditions of Alaska firsthand. In recent years, there has been a growing interest in preserving and promoting Native Alaskan art and music, with efforts to support Indigenous artists and musicians through grants, exhibitions, and performances.

Festivals and Celebrations: Annual events that showcase Alaskan heritage, such as the Iditarod and the Fur Rendezvous

Alaska is a state that celebrates its unique heritage through a variety of annual festivals and events. These festivals not only bring communities together but also give visitors an opportunity to experience the state's history, culture, and connection to nature. From winter traditions that date back generations to modern celebrations of Alaskan resilience and adventure, the state's festivals showcase its rich cultural tapestry and deep ties to the land. Two of the most well-known and iconic Alaskan celebrations are the Iditarod Trail Sled Dog Race and the Fur Rendezvous, both of which highlight the state's history of endurance, survival, and celebration of the great outdoors.

The Iditarod Trail Sled Dog Race is one of Alaska's most famous and celebrated events. Held every March, this legendary race spans over 1,000 miles from Anchorage to Nome, crossing some of the most challenging and remote terrain in the world. The race commemorates the history of dog sledding in Alaska, which for centuries was the primary mode of transportation for Native peoples and settlers alike. In particular, it honors the famous 1925 serum run, when dog sled teams braved blizzards and treacherous conditions to deliver life-saving diphtheria serum to Nome, which was suffering from an outbreak of the disease. This heroic journey, often called the "Great Race of Mercy," captured the world's attention and remains a powerful symbol of Alaskan resilience and determination.

The Iditarod is much more than just a race it's a test of human and animal endurance, teamwork, and skill. Mushers, the people who drive the sleds, and their teams of dogs train year-round for this grueling event, which can take anywhere from 8 to 15 days to complete, depending on weather conditions and the speed of the teams. The Iditarod is famous for its unpredictable challenges: extreme cold, snowstorms, and even the occasional encounter with wildlife. The route traverses vast stretches of wilderness, with checkpoints set up in remote villages where mushers can rest and tend to their dogs. For many Alaskans, both participating in and following the race is a yearly tradition that connects them to the state's pioneering past.

The dogs, typically Alaskan huskies, are the true heroes of the Iditarod. Known for their incredible strength, endurance, and intelligence, these dogs are bred specifically for long-distance racing and are treated with the utmost care by their mushers. The bond between musher and dog is at the heart of the Iditarod, as both depend on each other to navigate the treacherous trail. The race celebrates this partnership, as well as the traditional way of life in rural Alaska, where dog sledding is still used for transportation in some areas.

For visitors, the Iditarod offers a chance to witness an event that is deeply embedded in Alaskan culture. The ceremonial start in Anchorage is a major event in itself, with mushers and their teams parading through the streets to the cheers of spectators. As the race progresses, fans can follow the action through live updates, and some even venture to remote checkpoints to watch the teams pass through. The Iditarod captures the spirit of adventure that defines Alaska, making it one of the most exciting and important events on the state's calendar.

Another major Alaskan festival that draws both locals and visitors alike is the Fur Rendezvous, often referred to simply as "Fur Rondy." This winter celebration takes place in Anchorage over several days in late February and early March, and it is one of the oldest and most beloved traditions in the state. The Fur Rendezvous began in the 1930s as a way for trappers and miners, who spent long winters isolated in the wilderness, to come together, trade goods, and enjoy some much-needed social interaction. Over time, it grew into a major community event, celebrating not only Alaska's history but also its unique culture of resilience in the face of harsh conditions.

Fur Rondy is packed with activities that showcase the rugged, adventurous spirit of Alaska. One of the most popular events is the World Championship Sled Dog Races, which, like the Iditarod, highlights the importance of dog sledding in Alaskan history. These races, however, are much shorter and faster, with teams racing through Anchorage on a compact course over the course of three days. It's an exhilarating event for spectators, who line the streets to watch the teams speed by. The fur trade, which played a crucial role in Alaska's early economy, is also honored at Fur Rondy through exhibitions and demonstrations of traditional trapping and fur handling techniques. Visitors can learn about the different types of fur-bearing animals native to Alaska, and see firsthand how trappers would prepare pelts for trade.

Fur Rondy is not just about the past, however; it also celebrates the fun and quirky side of Alaskan life. Events like the Running of the Reindeer, where participants race through the streets of downtown Anchorage chased by reindeer, highlight the state's playful and eccentric spirit. There are also snowshoe softball games, ice carving competitions, and the Outhouse Races, where teams race outhouse-shaped sleds down a snowy track. These lighthearted events are a reminder that, even in the depths of winter, Alaskans know how to have a good time.

In addition to these outdoor activities, Fur Rondy also offers plenty of opportunities for visitors to experience Alaskan culture through arts, crafts, and food. Local artisans showcase their work at markets, where you can find everything from traditional Native carvings to handmade jewelry and clothing. There are also food vendors offering Alaskan specialties, such as reindeer sausage, smoked salmon, and berry jams, giving visitors a taste of the state's unique flavors. Music and dance performances are also an important part of the festival, with both Native and contemporary artists taking the stage to entertain the crowds.

The Iditarod and Fur Rendezvous are just two examples of the many festivals that highlight Alaska's heritage and way of life. Throughout the year, communities across the state come together to celebrate their connection to the land, the changing seasons, and the cultures that make Alaska so special. These events serve as a way for Alaskans to honor their history, but they also offer a chance for visitors to experience the state in a way that goes beyond the typical tourist activities.

Alaska's festivals are deeply tied to the rhythms of the natural world, with many celebrations timed to mark significant seasonal changes. For example, the Midnight Sun Festival in Fairbanks celebrates the summer solstice, when the sun remains above the horizon for 24 hours, bathing the state in endless daylight. This event includes live music, food, and sports, and it gives Alaskans a chance to enjoy the brief but glorious summer season. Similarly, the Alaska State Fair, held in late August in Palmer, marks the end of summer and the beginning of harvest season, showcasing giant vegetables grown in Alaska's long daylight hours, as well as livestock, crafts, and local food.

In the winter months, communities across Alaska celebrate the return of the light after months of darkness with festivals such as Kivgiq, or the Messenger Feast, which is celebrated by the Iñupiat people of northern Alaska. This festival, held in February, brings together people from different villages to share food, dances, and stories, reinforcing the bonds between communities and ensuring that cultural traditions are passed on to younger generations. Kivgiq is a time of joy and renewal, as people celebrate the return of the sun and look forward to the warmer months ahead.

These festivals and celebrations offer a glimpse into the heart of Alaskan culture, where the natural world plays a central role in shaping the rhythm of life. Whether through the excitement of the Iditarod, the community spirit of Fur Rondy, or the joyful celebration of the Midnight Sun, Alaska's festivals remind both locals and visitors of the state's unique heritage, its connection to the land, and its enduring spirit of adventure. They are not just events on a calendar but are important cultural touchstones that reflect the resilience, creativity, and joy of the people who call Alaska home.

Local Etiquette and Customs: What visitors should know about Alaskan customs and behavior

When visiting Alaska, it is important to be aware of the local customs and etiquette, as they can differ from those found in other parts of the United States and the world. Alaska, being a vast and diverse state, is home to a wide range of cultural practices and behaviors that have developed over centuries, influenced by its Indigenous peoples, the rugged landscape, and the unique challenges of living in a remote and often harsh environment. For travelers, understanding and respecting these customs will not only help you blend in more easily but also enhance your experience by fostering positive interactions with locals.

One of the first things to understand about Alaska is the strong sense of community that exists, particularly in smaller towns and rural areas. Because many people in Alaska live in isolated communities, often far from large urban centers, there is a deep-rooted tradition of helping one another. This spirit of cooperation is essential for surviving the challenges that come with living in such a remote place. For example, it's common for people to assist strangers in need, whether it's offering a ride to someone stranded on the side of the road or helping a neighbor fix a broken generator. As a visitor, if you find yourself in a difficult situation, don't be afraid to ask for help—Alaskans are generally warm and willing to lend a hand. At the same time, it's important to offer help if you see someone who may need it, as this sense of mutual support is a core part of the social fabric in many areas.

However, while Alaskans are typically friendly and open, there is also a strong emphasis on personal independence and self-reliance. Many people move to Alaska to enjoy the solitude and freedom that comes with living in a place with such a low population density. This means that while Alaskans are happy to assist when needed, they also value their privacy and space. If you're visiting a rural or wilderness area, be mindful of the fact that people may prefer to keep to themselves. In some places, it's considered polite to announce your presence before approaching someone's home or property, especially if the area is remote. This can be as simple as giving a quick honk of your car horn or calling out from a distance, as many homes may not be easily accessible by road. Respecting people's privacy is an important part of fitting in with local customs.

Another key aspect of Alaskan culture is the close relationship that people have with the land. Alaskans are deeply connected to nature, and this connection is reflected in their customs and behaviors. The state's natural beauty is a source of pride for many residents, and there is a strong ethos of environmental stewardship. When visiting, it's essential to respect the natural environment and the wildlife that inhabit it. This means following Leave No Trace principles, which include packing out all of your trash, staying on designated trails, and avoiding disturbing wildlife. Many locals are passionate about protecting Alaska's pristine wilderness, so being mindful of your impact on the environment will go a long way toward earning respect from those you meet.

In addition to respecting the land, it's also important to understand that hunting, fishing, and subsistence living are integral parts of life for many Alaskans, particularly in rural areas and among Indigenous communities. For some people, these activities are not just recreational but are necessary for survival. Subsistence hunting and fishing, in particular, are vital for many Native Alaskan communities, who rely on local resources to provide food throughout the year. As a visitor, it's important to be aware that these practices are deeply rooted in cultural traditions and should be respected. If you're invited to participate in a hunting or fishing activity, be aware that there may be specific customs or rituals associated with it, and always ask questions if you're unsure about how to behave.

When it comes to social interactions, Alaskans tend to be straightforward and down-to-earth. In general, people are not overly formal, and you'll find that casual conversations are the norm, even in professional settings. Titles and honorifics are not commonly used, and most people will introduce themselves by their first names, regardless of their position or status. This informal approach to social interactions can make it easier for visitors to strike up conversations with locals, whether you're chatting with a store clerk, a fellow traveler, or someone at a bar. However, while the tone may be casual, it's still important to be respectful and avoid overly personal questions, especially with people you've just met.

In some Native Alaskan communities, there are specific social customs that visitors should be aware of. For example, when attending a cultural event, such as a potlatch or community gathering, it's customary to show respect by listening quietly and not interrupting when someone is speaking. In many Indigenous cultures, elders are highly respected, and their words carry great weight. If you have the opportunity to meet an elder, it's important to show deference, and you may want to offer a small token of appreciation, such as a gift or a kind word. In some cases, it may be customary to ask permission before taking photographs or participating in certain activities, so always be sure to check with your hosts if you're unsure.

It's also important to note that the pace of life in Alaska can be slower than what many visitors are used to, especially if you're coming from a major city. In smaller towns and rural areas, things may move at a more relaxed pace, and people tend to take their time with tasks and appointments. This can be particularly noticeable in services like dining, transportation, and repairs. Patience is key when navigating these situations, and understanding that this slower pace is part of the culture can help you avoid frustration. In general, it's a good idea to build some flexibility into your travel plans to account for delays or changes in schedule, especially if you're traveling to more remote areas where weather and other factors can easily disrupt plans.

Another aspect of Alaskan culture that visitors should be aware of is the significant role that Native Alaskan traditions play in the state's identity. Alaska is home to many Indigenous groups, including the Iñupiat, Yup'ik, Athabaskan, Tlingit, Haida, and Aleut peoples, each with its own customs, languages, and ways of life. These traditions are still very much alive today, and you may encounter them in a variety of contexts, from art and music to food and festivals. It's important to approach Native Alaskan cultures with respect and an open mind, recognizing that these communities have deep historical roots and a wealth of knowledge about the land and its resources.

While English is the dominant language in Alaska, you may also hear Native languages being spoken, particularly in rural areas and during cultural events. Learning a few words or phrases in a Native language, such as "Quyana" (thank you in Yup'ik) or "Gunalchéesh" (thank you in Tlingit), can go a long way toward showing respect for the local culture. However, it's important not to appropriate or misuse these languages, as they are deeply tied to the identity and history of the people who speak them.

Alaska's diverse population also means that you'll encounter a wide range of cultural practices and beliefs. In cities like Anchorage and Fairbanks, for example, there is a growing mix of cultures, with people from all over the world coming to live and work in the state. This diversity is reflected in everything from the food you'll find in restaurants to the festivals and events that take place throughout the year. As a visitor, being open and curious about the different cultures you encounter will enrich your experience and help you connect with the people who live here.

Chapter 3

Laws and Regulations

General Travel Laws

For U.S. citizens traveling to Alaska, the process is relatively straightforward. Since Alaska is part of the United States, U.S. citizens do not need a passport or visa to travel domestically within the country. This means that whether you are traveling to Alaska by plane, cruise, or road, you do not need a passport to enter or exit Alaska from another U.S. state. A government-issued ID, such as a driver's license or state identification card, is typically sufficient for air travel between the lower 48 states and Alaska. However, due to enhanced security measures, it is important to note that all travelers must comply with the REAL ID Act. Starting in May 2025, travelers will need to present a REAL ID-compliant driver's license or another acceptable form of identification, such as a passport, when flying domestically. It's a good idea to check with the Transportation Security Administration (TSA) or your state's motor vehicle department to ensure that your ID meets these new requirements before your trip.

For U.S. citizens traveling by land or sea, especially when driving through Canada to reach Alaska or taking a cruise that crosses international waters, a passport is required. If you're driving to Alaska via the Alaska

Highway, which runs through Canada, you will need a valid U.S. passport or a passport card to enter and exit Canada. A passport card is less expensive than a passport book and can be used for land or sea crossings between the U.S. and Canada, but it cannot be used for international air travel. Additionally, travelers may be asked to provide proof of sufficient funds and a return or onward ticket to demonstrate the intent to return to the U.S. after their stay in Alaska. If you're planning to take a cruise that departs from a U.S. port and stops in Canada or another country before arriving in Alaska, a valid U.S. passport is necessary.

For international travelers, the requirements to visit Alaska are similar to those for visiting any other part of the United States, but specific details can vary depending on your country of citizenship. Most international visitors to Alaska will need a valid passport and, in many cases, a visa or authorization under the U.S. Visa Waiver Program (VWP). The Visa Waiver Program allows citizens of certain countries to travel to the U.S., including Alaska, for tourism or business purposes for up to 90 days without obtaining a visa. Instead, eligible travelers must apply for an Electronic System for Travel Authorization (ESTA) before their trip. The ESTA is an online system that determines eligibility for travel under the VWP and must be completed at least 72 hours before departure. It's important to note that an approved ESTA is valid for multiple entries over a two-year period or until the traveler's passport expires, whichever comes first. Travelers from VWP countries should ensure they have a valid ESTA and passport when planning their trip to Alaska.

For citizens of countries not covered by the Visa Waiver Program, a visitor visa is required. Most tourists and business travelers will need to apply for a B-1 (for business purposes) or B-2 (for tourism purposes) nonimmigrant visa. The process for obtaining a U.S. visa involves completing an online application, paying a fee, and attending an interview at a U.S. embassy or consulate in your home country. Visa processing times can vary, so it's important to start the application process well in advance of your planned trip to Alaska. International visitors should also be aware that even with a visa, entry to the U.S. is not guaranteed. Upon arrival, U.S. Customs and Border Protection (CBP) officers will review your documents and may ask questions about the purpose of your visit, your travel plans, and your financial ability to support yourself during your stay.

In addition to passports and visas, international travelers should also be familiar with customs regulations and entry procedures when arriving in Alaska. Whether arriving by air, sea, or land, all travelers will need to go through customs inspection upon entering the U.S. Visitors are required to declare items they are bringing into the country, and certain goods may be subject to restrictions or taxes. This includes food products, plants, animals, and large amounts of currency. It's a good idea to review the U.S. Customs and Border Protection website for specific guidelines on what can and cannot be brought into the U.S., as well as the limits on duty-free items.

Travelers should also keep in mind that health and security measures may affect entry requirements. For example, during the COVID-19 pandemic, additional health screenings, testing requirements, or quarantine measures were implemented for international travelers entering the U.S. While many of these restrictions have been lifted or modified, it's still important to check for any updates or advisories before your trip, as the situation can change quickly. Health insurance is another consideration for international travelers. The U.S. does not provide universal healthcare, and medical services in Alaska, particularly in remote areas, can be expensive. It is highly recommended that international visitors purchase travel health insurance that covers medical emergencies, including evacuation, especially if they plan to visit remote or wilderness areas of Alaska.

For travelers transiting through other countries on their way to Alaska, such as those flying through Canadian airports, it's important to be aware of any additional entry or transit requirements. Canada, for example, requires most international travelers, including those passing through on their way to Alaska, to obtain an Electronic Travel Authorization (eTA) if arriving by air. Travelers should check the entry and transit rules of any countries they will be passing through to avoid any issues or delays during their journey.

Local Laws to Know: Fishing, hunting, and camping regulations

Fishing is one of the most popular activities in Alaska, attracting both local residents and visitors from all over the world. Whether you're interested in catching salmon, halibut, or other fish species, it's essential to be aware of the regulations that govern recreational fishing. Alaska's fishing regulations are designed to protect fish populations and ensure that fishing is done in a sustainable way. The Alaska Department of Fish and Game (ADF&G) is the agency responsible for managing the state's fisheries, and they set specific rules that vary depending on the species of fish, the location, and the time of year.

One of the most important things to know about fishing in Alaska is that you must have a valid fishing license if you're over the age of 16 and planning to fish. Licenses can be purchased online or at various authorized vendors throughout the state. There are different types of licenses available depending on whether you are a resident of Alaska or a non-resident, and the cost will vary accordingly. In addition to a standard fishing license, certain species of fish, such as king salmon, require an additional stamp or tag. It's crucial to check the specific requirements for the area you plan to fish in, as the rules may differ based on the region, the body of water, and even the size or age of the fish you're targeting.

Fishing regulations also include specific limits on the number and size of fish you can catch. These limits, known as bag and possession limits, are in place to prevent overfishing and to protect fish populations for future generations. For example, the bag limit for king salmon may be one or two fish per day in certain areas, while other species, like silver salmon, may have higher limits. It's important to familiarize yourself with these rules before heading out, as exceeding the legal limit can result in fines and penalties. Additionally, certain areas may have catch-and-release regulations, where fish must be released back into the water immediately after being caught. These regulations are often put in place to protect vulnerable fish populations, especially during spawning seasons.

Hunting is another major outdoor activity in Alaska, and it is subject to a different set of regulations that are strictly enforced to ensure the safety of both hunters and wildlife. Alaska is home to a wide variety of game species, including moose, caribou, bears, and waterfowl, making it a prime destination for hunters. However, just like with fishing, hunting in Alaska requires careful adherence to local laws. The Alaska Department of Fish and Game manages hunting seasons, permits, and quotas to maintain healthy wildlife populations and to prevent overhunting.

If you plan to hunt in Alaska, you must obtain the appropriate hunting license. Similar to fishing licenses, hunting licenses are available for both residents and non-residents, with different fees for each. In addition to a general hunting license, certain species, such as brown bears or mountain goats, require special permits or tags, which may be issued through a lottery system due to limited availability. Non-resident hunters are also required to hire a licensed guide if they plan to hunt certain species, such as bears or sheep, as this is mandatory for safety and conservation reasons.

Hunting seasons are strictly regulated, and they vary depending on the species and the region. For example, moose hunting season might open in one area in late August and last through September, while in another part of the state, the season may be different. It's crucial to know the exact dates for the species you plan to hunt, as hunting outside of the designated season is illegal. In addition to the season, there are also regulations regarding the type of hunting methods that can be used, such as restrictions on the use of certain firearms, traps, or baiting techniques. All hunters are required to follow these rules, and violations can result in severe penalties, including the loss of hunting privileges.

Another key aspect of hunting regulations in Alaska is the requirement for hunters to report their harvests. This helps the Alaska Department of Fish and Game track wildlife populations and ensure that hunting remains sustainable. After a successful hunt, you are typically required to fill out a harvest report and submit it to the department. In some cases, hunters are also required to bring in certain parts of the animal, such as the head or antlers, for biological inspection, which helps wildlife biologists monitor the health and size of the game populations.

Camping in Alaska offers some of the most breathtaking and remote experiences you can imagine, but it is also subject to specific regulations designed to protect the environment and ensure the safety of campers. Whether you're camping in a designated campground or setting up a tent in the backcountry, it's important to be aware of the rules that apply to the area you're visiting. In many national and state parks, as well as on federal lands, permits are required for camping. These permits help manage the number of visitors and ensure that fragile ecosystems are not overburdened by human activity.

One of the most important rules to follow when camping in Alaska is the Leave No Trace principle, which means that you should leave the environment exactly as you found it. This includes packing out all trash, avoiding damage to vegetation, and minimizing your impact on wildlife. In many parts of Alaska, especially in remote wilderness areas, campers are required to store food and garbage in bear-resistant containers. This is essential for both your safety and the safety of wildlife, as bears and other animals are attracted to human food, and feeding wildlife can have dangerous consequences for both animals and people.

In some areas, there may be restrictions on campfires, especially during dry seasons when the risk of wildfires is high. It's important to check the fire regulations before starting a fire, and if fires are allowed, be sure to use existing fire rings or portable stoves to minimize the impact on the environment. Campfires should always be fully extinguished before leaving the area, and never left unattended.

When camping in Alaska's wilderness, you also need to be prepared for the elements. The weather can be unpredictable, and temperatures can drop quickly, even in the summer months. It's important to pack appropriately, including warm clothing, rain gear, and a reliable shelter. Additionally, if you're camping in bear country, it's essential to know how to avoid encounters with bears and other wildlife. This includes making noise while hiking to alert animals to your presence, storing food properly, and keeping a safe distance if you encounter wildlife.

Alaska's camping regulations are designed to protect both campers and the environment, and following these rules ensures that the state's natural beauty can be enjoyed by future generations. Whether you're fishing in a remote river, hunting in the backcountry, or camping under the northern lights, understanding and respecting Alaska's local laws will help you make the most of your outdoor experience while preserving the wilderness for others to enjoy.

Cannabis and Alcohol Laws: What's allowed in Alaska and where

In Alaska, both cannabis and alcohol are legal for adult use, but there are specific laws and regulations governing how and where they can be consumed. These laws are designed to ensure that their use is safe, controlled, and does not interfere with public safety or the well-being of the community. Understanding the rules about cannabis and alcohol use in Alaska is important for both residents and visitors to ensure compliance with the law and to avoid potential legal issues.

Cannabis became legal for recreational use in Alaska in 2015, following a statewide ballot initiative known as Measure 2. This law allows adults aged 21 and older to possess, use, and purchase limited amounts of cannabis for personal use. Under Alaska law, individuals can legally possess up to one ounce (28 grams) of cannabis at a time. Additionally, adults are allowed to grow up to six cannabis plants in their private residence, with no more than three of those plants being mature at any given time. This provision allows for personal cultivation, as long as it is done on private property and is not visible to the public.

However, while cannabis is legal for personal use, there are still strict rules about where it can be consumed. Cannabis consumption in public places is illegal in Alaska. This includes parks, sidewalks, streets, and other areas that are open to the public. Consuming cannabis in a public space can result in a fine, and repeat offenses may lead to more severe penalties. Therefore, it's important for users to keep cannabis consumption to private residences or other private properties where it is permitted by the owner. Some designated cannabis lounges have also been opened in Alaska, allowing adults to legally consume cannabis in a social setting, but these establishments are still relatively rare and regulated closely by the state.

For visitors to Alaska, it is important to note that cannabis remains illegal at the federal level in the United States. This means that while it is legal to possess and use cannabis within the state of Alaska, it is still illegal to take cannabis across state lines, including traveling with cannabis on airplanes, even if you are flying to another state where cannabis is legal. Additionally, cannabis use is strictly prohibited on federal land, which includes many of Alaska's national parks and wildlife refuges. Since much of Alaska's land is federally owned, it's crucial for travelers to be aware of these boundaries and avoid consuming or possessing cannabis in federal areas. Violating federal cannabis laws can result in serious legal consequences, including fines and imprisonment.

For those who choose to purchase cannabis in Alaska, there are licensed dispensaries throughout the state where adults can legally buy cannabis products. These dispensaries are regulated by the Alaska Marijuana Control Board, which sets rules for how cannabis can be sold and what products are available. When purchasing cannabis from a dispensary, customers will need to show a valid government-issued ID to verify that they are 21 or older. Alaska's dispensaries sell a wide variety of cannabis products, including flower (the dried cannabis plant), edibles, concentrates, and topical products. Each of these products may have different potency levels, so it's important to read labels carefully and understand how different forms of cannabis affect the body. Edibles, for example, can take longer to produce effects compared to smoking or vaping cannabis, so users should consume them with caution, especially if they are new to cannabis or unfamiliar with the product.

As with alcohol, driving under the influence of cannabis is illegal in Alaska. It is considered a serious offense, and those caught driving while impaired by cannabis can face the same penalties as those driving under the influence of alcohol. This includes fines, license suspension, and potentially even jail time for repeat offenses. Law enforcement officers in Alaska are trained to recognize signs of cannabis impairment, and there are specific tests that can be used to determine if someone is driving under the influence of cannabis. For this reason, it's essential to avoid operating a vehicle if you have consumed cannabis, as the consequences can be severe.

In contrast to cannabis, alcohol has been legal for much longer in Alaska, though there are also specific laws that regulate its sale and consumption. The legal drinking age in Alaska, as in the rest of the United States, is 21. This means that it is illegal for anyone under the age of 21 to purchase, possess, or consume alcohol. Similar to cannabis, alcohol cannot be consumed in public places unless there is a special permit for an event, such as a festival or fair, where alcohol is allowed. Drinking alcohol in public parks, on sidewalks, or on beaches is generally prohibited, and violators may be subject to fines.

Alaska has a unique relationship with alcohol due to its remote communities and harsh climate. Some rural communities in Alaska have opted to ban alcohol entirely, a practice known as "local option." Under Alaska law, individual towns or villages have the authority to decide whether to allow the sale and importation of alcohol. Some communities have voted to become "dry," meaning that alcohol is completely prohibited, while others may be "damp," allowing possession of alcohol but not the sale of it. For travelers, this means that it is important to check the alcohol laws of specific communities before visiting, as bringing alcohol into a dry community can result in confiscation of the alcohol and legal penalties.

For those looking to purchase alcohol in Alaska, it can be bought at liquor stores, grocery stores (where permitted), and licensed bars and restaurants. The hours during which alcohol can be sold are regulated, and sales are typically allowed between 8 a.m. and 5 a.m., though local ordinances may impose additional restrictions on sale hours. Bars and restaurants that serve alcohol must also comply with strict rules about when they can serve alcohol, and it is illegal for establishments to serve alcohol to patrons who are visibly intoxicated. Alaska also has open container laws that prohibit having an open container of alcohol in the passenger area of a vehicle, even if the driver is not drinking.

One particularly important law in Alaska is related to driving under the influence (DUI). Alaska has strict DUI laws, and anyone caught driving with a blood alcohol concentration (BAC) of 0.08% or higher can be charged with a DUI. For commercial drivers, the legal limit is even lower, at 0.04%. DUI offenses are taken very seriously in Alaska and can result in hefty fines, license suspension, and even jail time for repeat offenders. Law enforcement in Alaska regularly conducts DUI checkpoints and patrols, especially during holidays and events where alcohol consumption is common. Because of the severity of the consequences, it is always recommended to arrange for a designated driver or use alternative transportation, such as a taxi or rideshare service, if you plan on drinking alcohol.

Alaska also has laws that address underage drinking and supplying alcohol to minors. It is illegal for anyone under the age of 21 to possess or consume alcohol, and providing alcohol to a minor is a serious offense that can lead to fines and even jail time. Establishments that sell alcohol are required to check the identification of anyone who appears to be under the age of 30, and failure to do so can result in penalties for the business. Additionally, there are laws that prohibit the possession of fake IDs, and anyone caught using a false ID to purchase alcohol can face legal consequences.

Respecting Nature: Regulations about wildlife interactions, conservation, and park rules

Respecting nature is a fundamental part of visiting Alaska. The state's breathtaking wilderness, diverse wildlife, and pristine ecosystems make it a destination like no other. However, these natural wonders are also delicate, and human interaction can have a significant impact if not approached with care and respect. Whether you are hiking through the state's national parks, observing wildlife in its natural habitat, or camping in remote areas, understanding and following the regulations about wildlife interactions, conservation, and park rules is essential to preserving Alaska's natural beauty for generations to come.

Alaska is home to a wide variety of wildlife, from majestic brown bears and moose to bald eagles and marine mammals such as whales and sea otters. While encountering wildlife is one of the highlights of visiting Alaska, it is critical to remember that these are wild animals that must be respected from a distance. Alaska's wildlife regulations are designed to ensure the safety of both the animals and the people who come into contact with them. The overarching principle is simple: observe wildlife from afar. Getting too close to wild animals can be dangerous, not only for the humans involved but also for the animals, who can become stressed or defensive when approached.

A key rule when it comes to wildlife interactions is maintaining a safe distance. For example, when observing bears, it is recommended to stay at least 300 feet away at all times. Bears are unpredictable and can become aggressive if they feel threatened, especially if they are with their cubs or near a food source. If you are in an area known for bear activity, it is important to make noise as you hike to avoid surprising a bear, as sudden encounters can lead to dangerous situations. Bear spray is also a recommended safety tool for anyone venturing into bear country, but it should only be used as a last resort if a bear approaches you aggressively. Knowing how to store food and dispose of trash properly is also critical in bear country, as leaving food or waste accessible can attract bears and lead to habituation, where bears lose their natural fear of humans and become more dangerous.

In addition to bears, many other animals in Alaska require careful and respectful observation. For instance, moose are large and seemingly slow-moving animals, but they can be very dangerous if approached too closely. Moose are known to charge when they feel threatened, especially during calving season or when they are defending their young. Always give moose plenty of space, and avoid blocking their path if they are moving toward you. If a moose feels trapped or cornered, it is more likely to act aggressively. The general rule of thumb for moose is to stay at least 75 feet away, but even greater distance is advisable if possible.

Alaska's marine mammals, such as whales, seals, and sea otters, are another major attraction for visitors. Whether you're on a boat tour or viewing them from the shore, it's essential to follow the regulations that protect these animals. In Alaska, federal laws, such as the Marine Mammal Protection Act, prohibit approaching marine mammals too closely, as this can disturb their natural behavior and cause stress. For instance, boats are required to maintain a distance of at least 100 yards from whales, and it's important to avoid making sudden movements or loud noises that could disrupt the animals. If a marine mammal approaches your boat, it is illegal to pursue or chase it; instead, you must allow the animal to pass and continue on its way without interference.

Alaska's parks and protected areas also have strict rules that visitors must follow to protect both the environment and the wildlife that live there. The state is home to some of the largest and most iconic national parks in the country, including Denali National Park, Glacier Bay National Park, and Kenai Fjords National Park. These parks are managed by the National Park Service and are dedicated to conserving the natural landscapes, ecosystems, and wildlife for future generations. When visiting any of these parks, it is important to familiarize yourself with the specific regulations for each area.

One of the most important rules to follow in Alaska's parks is the principle of Leave No Trace. This means that visitors must take all of their trash with them and avoid leaving any waste behind. Littering not only spoils the beauty of the natural environment, but it can also harm wildlife that may ingest it or become entangled in it. Pack out everything you bring in, including food wrappers, cans, and plastic waste. In some areas, you may even need to pack out human waste if you are camping in particularly sensitive ecosystems.

Another important aspect of respecting nature in Alaska is staying on designated trails and campsites. Many of Alaska's ecosystems are fragile, and even small disturbances can cause long-term damage. Hiking off-trail can lead to soil erosion, trampled vegetation, and the destruction of important habitats for wildlife. Similarly, setting up camp in undesignated areas can disrupt animal movements and negatively impact the environment. In most parks, camping is only allowed in designated areas, and you may need to obtain a permit if you plan to camp in the backcountry. These permits help park authorities manage the number of visitors in remote areas and ensure that human activity does not overwhelm the natural landscape.

Fishing and hunting are popular activities in Alaska, but they are also tightly regulated to ensure the sustainability of fish and wildlife populations. Fishing regulations, for example, set specific limits on the types and amounts of fish that can be caught, as well as when and where fishing is allowed. These regulations are carefully designed to protect fish populations, particularly during critical times such as spawning seasons. Overfishing can have devastating effects on both the environment and local economies that depend on sustainable fisheries. As such, it is essential for anglers to obtain the proper fishing licenses and follow all size and bag limits for the species they are targeting. Additionally, there are strict rules about the types of gear that can be used and how fish must be handled to minimize harm, particularly in catch-and-release fishing.

Hunting regulations in Alaska are similarly focused on conservation and the ethical treatment of animals. Hunting seasons and bag limits are established to prevent overhunting and to protect vulnerable species. Hunters must obtain the appropriate licenses and permits for the animals they intend to hunt, and they are required to report their harvests to the Alaska Department of Fish and Game. This helps the state track wildlife populations and ensure that hunting remains sustainable. In some cases, hunters may also be required to submit parts of the animal, such as the antlers or head, for inspection to help biologists monitor the health of the population. Hunting outside of the designated season, hunting without a license, or exceeding bag limits can result in significant fines and penalties.

In addition to these specific regulations, it's also important to respect the overall goal of conservation in Alaska. Much of the state's land is protected as wilderness, national parks, or wildlife refuges, and these areas are managed with the goal of preserving their natural state for future generations. This means that activities that may be allowed elsewhere, such as the use of motorized vehicles, may be restricted in these areas to minimize human impact. Similarly, noise pollution from things like drones or loud music can disrupt wildlife and detract from the experience of other visitors. In most parks and wilderness areas, drones are not allowed without special permits, and even in places where they are allowed, it is important to fly them responsibly and avoid disturbing animals or other people.

Chapter 4

Essential Phrases and Language

Common English Phrases Used in Alaska

When traveling to Alaska, it's helpful to be familiar with some common English phrases you might hear in daily conversations. While Alaskans speak the same English as the rest of the United States, there are certain expressions, terms, and ways of speaking that reflect the unique culture and lifestyle of the state. These phrases are often influenced by Alaska's rugged environment, its Native cultures, and the close-knit communities that exist throughout the state. Being aware of these common expressions can make interactions more fluid and help you feel more connected to the local way of life.

One phrase you'll likely hear in Alaska is "The Bush." In Alaska, "The Bush" refers to remote areas of the state that are not accessible by road. These areas are often only reachable by plane, boat, or snowmobile, and they include many of the smaller villages and rural communities scattered across the state's vast wilderness. Alaskans might say, "I'm headed out to the Bush" when they're planning to travel to one of these remote areas. Understanding this term is key, as it captures the sense of isolation and self-sufficiency that is common in many parts of Alaska.

Another common term is "The Lower 48," which is how Alaskans refer to the contiguous United States, meaning the 48 states that are all connected on the mainland. You might hear someone say, "I'm flying down to the Lower 48 for the holidays," which simply means they're traveling to one of the states that isn't Alaska or Hawaii. Because Alaska is so geographically distant from the rest of the country, this phrase is often used to differentiate between local life in Alaska and life in other parts of the U.S.

Similarly, the term "Outside" is used to describe anything or anyone from outside of Alaska. When Alaskans mention that something came from "Outside," they usually mean it came from another part of the country or world, outside of Alaska's borders. For example, "They brought in all the supplies from Outside" could refer to materials or goods that were shipped in from another state.

A common greeting or conversational question you might hear in Alaska is "How's the weather treating you?" Alaska's weather is notoriously unpredictable and can vary widely depending on where you are in the state. Asking about the weather is more than just small talk; it's a way of acknowledging the challenges that come with living in a place where conditions can change rapidly, especially in the winter months. In many parts of Alaska, surviving and thriving through the seasons depends on knowing and adapting to the weather, so it's often a central part of daily conversation.

When talking about time, especially in relation to daylight, you might hear people refer to "The Midnight Sun" or "The Dark." These phrases describe the extreme variations in daylight that Alaska experiences due to its northern location. In the summer, many parts of Alaska experience nearly 24 hours of daylight, which is known as "The Midnight Sun." On the other hand, in the winter, some areas experience long periods of darkness, which Alaskans may refer to as "The Dark." Conversations about light and dark are common, especially among locals who have adapted their daily routines to the unusual patterns of daylight.

Another phrase you might encounter is "break-up," which in Alaska refers to the time of year when winter snow and ice begin to melt and rivers and lakes start to thaw. Break-up usually happens in the spring, and it's a major event because it signals the end of winter's grip on the landscape. Alaskans often talk about how break-up is progressing, as it marks the transition into warmer months. You might hear someone say, "Break-up is early this year" or "It's going to be a slow break-up."

In daily conversations, Alaskans often refer to specific activities like "dipnetting" or "subsistence hunting." These terms relate to the ways many people in Alaska gather food. "Dipnetting" is a method of fishing that allows Alaskan residents to catch large amounts of salmon for personal use using a long-handled net. It's a practice that's important to many families, especially in rural areas, where they rely on it to stock up on fish for the winter. Subsistence hunting refers to the hunting practices of many Alaska Native communities, as well as other rural residents, who hunt animals such as moose, caribou, or seals to sustain their families. These practices are not just hobbies; they are a way of life and are often discussed in terms of necessity and respect for the environment.

Another common phrase you might hear is "snowmachine," which in Alaska is the preferred term for what is commonly called a snowmobile in the rest of the U.S. Snowmachines are an essential mode of transportation in many parts of Alaska, especially in areas where roads are not accessible during the winter months. You might hear someone say, "We took the snowmachine out to the cabin," meaning they used it to travel through snowy or icy terrain.

Alaskans also have unique expressions when it comes to outdoor activities and the natural landscape. "Glassing" refers to the practice of using binoculars or spotting scopes to scan for wildlife in the distance, often while hunting or hiking. You might hear someone say, "We spent the morning glassing for moose," which means they were looking through binoculars to spot animals. It's a term that highlights Alaska's rich wildlife and the importance of being aware of your surroundings when out in the wilderness.

A phrase that reflects Alaska's rugged and often remote terrain is "off the grid." This is used to describe living or traveling in areas without access to public utilities like electricity or running water. Many Alaskans live "off the grid" by choice, using solar panels, generators, and other means to power their homes in isolated locations. It's not uncommon to hear someone say, "We're building a cabin off the grid," indicating they are setting up a home far away from conventional services.

In conversation, you might also hear people referring to different types of weather in very specific terms. For example, "termination dust" is a term used to describe the first light snowfall that occurs in the fall, signaling the end of summer and the start of winter. "Termination dust" is often a conversation starter, as it's an indication that the long Alaskan winter is just around the corner. People might say, "I saw the termination dust on the mountains this morning," signaling that colder weather is approaching.

Alaska's landscape also influences local sayings, such as "sourdough," which has a double meaning. In its most basic sense, sourdough refers to the traditional bread starter used by early settlers, especially during the Gold Rush era. However, the term "sourdough" is also used to describe someone who has lived in Alaska for a long time and has become a seasoned resident. Being called a "sourdough" is a sign of respect, as it suggests that the person has weathered many of Alaska's challenges and is well-versed in the Alaskan way of life.

In contrast, a "cheechako" is someone who is new to Alaska or inexperienced in dealing with the state's unique environment. It's a term that originated during the Gold Rush and is still used today. Someone might jokingly say, "I felt like a cheechako when I saw my first moose," meaning they felt like a newcomer who was still learning the ropes of life in Alaska.

Lastly, when talking about distance or time, Alaskans often use a more relaxed approach, as travel in the state can be affected by weather and terrain. You might hear someone say, "It's just down the road," but in Alaska, this could mean anything from a mile to several hours of driving, depending on where you are. Alaskans are used to covering long distances to get to places, so "just down the road" can sometimes be a relative term.

Alaska Native Words and Phrases: Learn some key words from Alaskan indigenous languages

Alaska is home to a rich diversity of Indigenous languages that reflect the deep connection between Alaska Native peoples and the land they have lived on for thousands of years. These languages are not only a means of communication but also carry the cultural traditions, stories, and worldviews of the Native peoples who speak them. Learning a few key words and phrases from Alaska Native languages can offer a deeper understanding of the rich cultural heritage that has shaped the state and provide a meaningful way to connect with the people whose ancestors have inhabited the region for generations. It is important to note that Alaska is home to over 20 different Native languages, each with its own distinct vocabulary and grammar, making the state linguistically diverse and complex. However, by learning some common phrases and terms from different language groups, visitors can gain insight into the linguistic and cultural richness of Alaska's Indigenous communities.

One of the most widely spoken Alaska Native languages is Iñupiaq, the language of the Iñupiat people who live in northern and northwestern Alaska. A key phrase in Iñupiaq that is important to know is "Quyanaq," which means "thank you." This simple word reflects the importance of gratitude in Iñupiaq culture, where giving thanks is often expressed in daily interactions, especially in a subsistence lifestyle where people depend on one another and the land for survival. Using "Quyanaq" when speaking with Iñupiat people, even in an English conversation, is a respectful way to acknowledge this cultural tradition of gratitude.

Another useful word in Iñupiaq is "Umiak," which refers to a large, open boat traditionally used by the Iñupiat for hunting and transportation. The umiak was often constructed from driftwood and covered with seal or walrus skins, making it durable enough to navigate the cold waters of the Arctic. Understanding words like "Umiak" offers a glimpse into the practical aspects of life in the Arctic and how the Iñupiat adapted to their environment with ingenuity and resourcefulness.

In the Yup'ik language, spoken by the Yup'ik people in southwestern Alaska, one of the key words to learn is "Quyana," which also means "thank you." The similarity between this word and "Quyanaq" in Iñupiaq reflects the linguistic connections between some of the Native languages in Alaska, though each language has its own distinct features. Gratitude is an important concept across many Alaska Native cultures, and learning how to say "thank you" in Yup'ik is a simple but meaningful way to show respect when interacting with Yup'ik speakers.

Another interesting word in Yup'ik is "Qaspeq," which refers to a traditional piece of clothing worn by both men and women. A qaspeq is a lightweight, hooded garment often worn over other layers of clothing. It is typically made from cotton or other fabric and sometimes elaborately decorated with designs that reflect Yup'ik culture. The qaspeq is practical for the region's cool climate and also serves as a symbol of cultural identity. Understanding terms like "Qaspeq" helps to appreciate the ways in which language is intertwined with daily life and cultural expression.

The Athabaskan language family is another significant group of Native languages in Alaska, with several different languages spoken by various Athabaskan communities in the interior of the state. In the Gwich'in language, one of the Athabaskan languages, a word that reflects an important part of the culture is "Dinjii Zhuh," which means "the people" and is how the Gwich'in refer to themselves. Many Alaska Native cultures use terms for themselves that translate to "the people" in their respective languages, emphasizing their close-knit communities and their distinct identity. Knowing how a community refers to itself in its own language is a way of showing respect for that identity and recognizing the importance of self-naming.

In the Tlingit language, spoken by the Tlingit people of Southeast Alaska, a common greeting is "Wáa sá iyatee?" which translates to "How are you?" This phrase is a simple but important way to connect with someone in the Tlingit community and to show that you are making an effort to speak their language. The Tlingit language has a complex system of tones and sounds, making it challenging for outsiders to learn, but even small efforts to speak Tlingit are appreciated by the community.

Another important Tlingit word is "Lingít Aaní," which means "Tlingit land." This phrase is significant because it reflects the deep connection that the Tlingit people have to the land they have inhabited for thousands of years. Land is not just a place for the Tlingit; it is a living entity that is intertwined with their identity, culture, and spirituality. Using the phrase "Lingít Aaní" acknowledges the importance of land in Tlingit culture and the broader Native Alaskan worldview, where the land is treated with respect and care.

In the Alutiiq language, spoken by the Alutiiq people of the Kodiak Archipelago and the southern coast of Alaska, one of the key phrases is "Cama'i," which means "Hello" or "Welcome." This friendly greeting is commonly used in daily interactions and is a warm way to start a conversation with someone from the Alutiiq community. Knowing how to say "hello" in Alutiiq shows that you are making an effort to engage with the culture and language of the region.

Another notable word in Alutiiq is "Agnguutaq," which means "drum." Drumming plays a central role in many Alaska Native cultures, including the Alutiiq culture, where it is used in ceremonies, dances, and storytelling. The drum is more than just a musical instrument; it is a way of connecting with ancestors, celebrating cultural traditions, and communicating with the natural and spiritual world. Learning words like "Agnguutaq" highlights the cultural significance of music and dance in Alaska Native traditions.

In addition to these individual words and phrases from Alaska's Indigenous languages, it's important to understand that many Alaska Native languages have been passed down through oral traditions. Stories, histories, and teachings are often conveyed through spoken language, making these languages deeply connected to the cultural practices of storytelling, song, and ritual. By learning even a few words from these languages, visitors can gain a greater appreciation for the cultural and historical depth that each language carries.

It is also worth noting that many Alaska Native languages are considered endangered, as the number of fluent speakers has declined over the years due to historical factors such as forced assimilation and the suppression of Native languages in schools. Today, there are ongoing efforts to revitalize these languages through education programs, language immersion schools, and community initiatives. Learning even a few words or phrases from these languages not only helps visitors connect with the culture but also supports the broader movement to keep these languages alive for future generations.

Practical Phrases for Travelers: Handy phrases for communicating in hotels, restaurants, and while navigating the state

When traveling to Alaska, as with any destination, it's important to have a few practical phrases ready to help with basic communication. Whether you're staying in a hotel, dining at a local restaurant, or navigating unfamiliar areas, having the right words to ask questions or clarify information can make your trip much smoother and more enjoyable. While English is the primary language spoken in Alaska, travelers might find that certain situations, especially those involving logistics or unfamiliar locations, call for clear and concise communication. Understanding and using a few essential phrases can help bridge gaps and ensure you get the assistance or information you need.

When checking into a hotel, being able to communicate effectively with the staff is important to ensure that your stay is comfortable. One of the first things you may need to say is, "I have a reservation," which lets the front desk know you've already arranged your stay. Following that, you can say, "My name is..." and give them your full name so they can quickly locate your booking in their system. If you arrive without a reservation, you can ask, "Do you have any rooms available?" This question is straightforward and polite, making it easy for the staff to check their availability for the night.

During your stay, you might need to make specific requests, and knowing how to ask for what you need can make all the difference. If you find that you need something extra for your room, such as more towels or an extra pillow, you can ask, "Could I have some extra towels, please?" or "Could I have an extra pillow?" Being polite while making these requests ensures a better response from the staff. If there is an issue with the room, such as a malfunctioning appliance or a heating problem, you might say, "The heater isn't working," or "The TV isn't turning on." This kind of clear, direct communication makes it easier for hotel staff to understand and resolve the problem.

When checking out of the hotel, you might need to clarify specific details about your bill or payment. If you're unsure about any charges, you can ask, "Could you explain this charge on my bill?" This will help you understand the breakdown of costs and ensure there are no surprises. Additionally, if you need to leave your luggage at the hotel after checking out, you can ask, "Is there a place where I can store my luggage for a few hours?" Many hotels offer luggage storage for guests who need to explore the area before heading to their next destination, and this question is a simple way to confirm if that service is available.

In restaurants, knowing how to communicate effectively with the staff is just as important. When you first arrive, if the restaurant appears busy, you might need to ask, "Do you have a table for two?" (or the appropriate number for your group). If there is a wait, you can ask, "How long is the wait for a table?" This helps you manage your time, especially if you have other plans for the day. Once seated, asking for the menu is straightforward: "Could I see the menu, please?" If you have any dietary preferences or restrictions, it's always helpful to communicate these upfront. You might say, "I'm allergic to shellfish. Are there any dishes without shellfish?" or "Do you have any vegetarian options?"

While placing your order, clarity is key. A polite way to start is with, "I would like to order..." followed by the name of the dish. If you're unsure about a particular menu item, you can ask, "What's in the salmon special?" or "How is the halibut cooked?" This will help you make an informed decision. If you want something on the side, like an extra sauce or a specific preparation, you can say, "Could I have the sauce on the side?" or "Can you make that without onions?" Being clear about your preferences allows the restaurant to accommodate you more easily.

When the meal is finished, asking for the check is simple: "Could I get the check, please?" If you're dining in a place where tipping is customary, you might also ask, "Is the tip included?" to ensure you are following the correct etiquette. If you need to pay by a specific method, such as a credit card, you can ask, "Do you accept credit cards?" This will help avoid any confusion when settling the bill.

Navigating Alaska's vast and often rugged terrain requires good communication, especially when asking for directions or clarifying transportation details. If you're lost or unsure of your location, you can ask, "Could you tell me how to get to Denali National Park?" or "Which way to the nearest gas station?" Being specific about your destination helps others give more accurate directions. If you're taking public transportation, you might need to ask, "When is the next bus to Anchorage?" or "Does this train stop in Fairbanks?" Knowing how to phrase these questions ensures you get the information you need quickly.

When using rideshare services or taxis, you'll likely need to confirm that the driver knows your destination. You can say, "Could you take me to the airport, please?" or "How much will it cost to get to downtown?" If you're concerned about time, you can ask, "How long will the ride take?" This is especially helpful if you're in a hurry or trying to catch a flight. Understanding how to ask about both the fare and the duration of the ride will make your trip smoother and give you peace of mind.

In more remote areas, where there may not be as many services or amenities, you might need to ask about important local information, such as food availability or fuel. If you're in a small town and need to know where to find supplies, you can ask, "Is there a grocery store nearby?" or "Where can I get gas?" Since some rural areas of Alaska can be spread out with few facilities, these questions can help you locate what you need without wasting time searching on your own. It's always a good idea to be as specific as possible to avoid confusion, especially in areas with limited resources.

Lastly, when interacting with locals in Alaska, you'll find that people are generally helpful and willing to offer advice, but it's always appreciated when you are polite and clear in your communication. If you need help, you might say, "Could you help me with directions?" or "Do you know where I can find a good place to eat around here?" Simple, direct questions like these often lead to more detailed advice, as Alaskans are proud of their state and eager to share their knowledge with visitors.

Chapter 5

Planning Your Trip

Best times to visit based on weather, wildlife, and activities

Summer, particularly from June to August, is considered the best time to visit Alaska for most travelers. This period is often referred to as the high season for tourism, and for good reason. The weather is at its warmest, with temperatures in the southern coastal regions ranging from 60°F to 80°F (15°C to 27°C), while interior areas like Fairbanks can experience even warmer temperatures. In contrast, northern areas, such as the Arctic, remain cooler, but the conditions are still far more temperate than during the harsh winter months. The long daylight hours during summer, especially in places like Anchorage and Fairbanks, allow for more time to enjoy outdoor activities. In fact, many areas experience the famous "Midnight Sun," where daylight lasts for nearly 24 hours at the height of summer.

The extended daylight is one of the main draws for visitors in the summer. With almost constant sunlight, you'll have more time to hike, fish, kayak, and explore Alaska's natural beauty without worrying about nightfall. This is also the prime season for wildlife viewing, as many species are active during the summer months. Grizzly bears, black bears, moose, and caribou are often seen in the wild, particularly in national parks like Denali, Katmai, and Kenai Fjords. In addition, birdwatchers flock to Alaska to see migratory birds that visit during the warmer months. For marine wildlife, summer is also the best time to see humpback whales, orcas, and sea otters, especially along the Inside Passage and the Gulf of Alaska.

The summer months are also ideal for cruise travel, which is one of the most popular ways to see Alaska's coastal regions. Cruise ships operate from May through September, with the busiest times being in June, July, and August. During this period, travelers can enjoy glacier viewing, as well as stops in cities like Juneau, Ketchikan, and Skagway, where they can experience local culture, history, and wildlife excursions. Glacier Bay National Park and other fjord systems are particularly breathtaking during the summer, as the weather is clear and the glaciers are actively calving into the water.

However, summer is also the busiest time for tourism, so if you prefer smaller crowds and lower prices, you might want to consider visiting Alaska during the shoulder seasons. May and September, for example, are still excellent months to visit. While the weather can be cooler, especially in September, these months offer the advantage of fewer tourists. The wildlife viewing is still excellent, especially in September, as animals like bears and moose prepare for the winter months by actively feeding. Additionally, in late August and September, you'll start to see the northern lights reappearing as the nights grow longer. This can make for a spectacular bonus if you're visiting at the end of summer or the start of fall.

May, in particular, is an excellent time for those who want to experience Alaska's wilderness without the summer crowds. The days are growing longer, and although the temperatures are cooler, they are still comfortable for outdoor activities. By May, the snow has started to melt in most areas, making hiking trails more accessible, while rivers and lakes are thawing, allowing for fishing and boating opportunities. Many of Alaska's iconic attractions, such as Denali National Park, are starting to open for the season, but with fewer visitors compared to the peak summer months.

If you're interested in witnessing the dramatic transition from fall to winter, October can be a fascinating time to visit, but it's important to prepare for colder weather and the possibility of snow. By October, many of Alaska's tourist facilities begin to close, and some national parks become less accessible due to snow. However, if you're a photographer or someone who enjoys quiet, serene landscapes, October offers a chance to experience Alaska's beauty as the fall colors give way to the first snows. It's also a good time for northern lights viewing, as the longer nights provide the dark skies needed to see the auroras.

Winter, from November to March, is a magical time to visit Alaska if you're interested in snow sports, northern lights, and experiencing the state's rugged winter culture.

Alaska's winter months are characterized by long nights, cold temperatures, and plenty of snow, but for many visitors, these are the very reasons to visit. In areas like Fairbanks and parts of the Arctic, temperatures can drop well below freezing, often reaching -20°F (-29°C) or colder, especially in January and February. However, the cold brings with it the chance to engage in activities like dog sledding, snowmobiling, and ice fishing, all of which are integral to Alaska's winter way of life.

One of the main reasons people visit Alaska in the winter is to see the northern lights, also known as the aurora borealis. The auroras are most visible between September and April, but the peak viewing season is typically from late December to March, when the nights are longest and the skies are clearest. Fairbanks is one of the best places to view the northern lights, as it lies under the auroral oval, where the lights are most frequently visible. Many visitors come to Fairbanks in the winter specifically for aurora viewing, and there are several lodges and tours that cater to northern lights enthusiasts.

Winter is also a great time to experience Alaska's unique winter festivals, such as the Iditarod Trail Sled Dog Race, which takes place in March. The Iditarod is a world-famous dog sled race that runs from Anchorage to Nome, covering over 1,000 miles of harsh winter terrain. Attending the start of the race in Anchorage or cheering on mushers as they pass through small villages along the route offers a unique glimpse into Alaska's winter culture and its deep connection to dog sledding.

For skiing and snowboarding enthusiasts, Alaska offers excellent opportunities to hit the slopes. Resorts like Alyeska, located near Anchorage, provide world-class skiing, with deep powder and dramatic mountain views. Cross-country skiing and snowshoeing are also popular winter activities, with trails accessible throughout much of the state. Many Alaskans embrace the winter season and enjoy spending time outdoors despite the cold, so visitors can expect to see plenty of people participating in winter sports and enjoying the snowy landscapes.

Spring in Alaska, from April to early May, marks the beginning of the transition from winter to summer. This period, often referred to as "break-up," is characterized by the melting of snow and ice, as well as the return of migratory birds and other wildlife. Although the weather can be unpredictable, with occasional snowstorms still possible, spring offers a quieter time to visit. As the days get longer and the temperatures slowly rise, Alaska's landscapes begin to thaw, and signs of new life emerge. It's a great time to experience the state's natural beauty before the busy summer season arrives.

How to Get There: Flights, cruises, and road trips – the best options for reaching Alaska

Reaching Alaska is an adventure in itself, given its remote location and vast size. As the largest and northernmost state in the United States, Alaska is separated from the contiguous 48 states by Canada, making it accessible only by air, sea, or a long road journey. The method you choose to get to Alaska will depend on several factors, including your budget, the time of year, and how much time you have for travel. Whether you're flying, taking a cruise, or embarking on a road trip, each option offers a unique way to experience the journey to this breathtaking part of the world.

One of the most common and efficient ways to get to Alaska is by air. Flying is by far the fastest and most convenient way for most travelers, especially if you are coming from the continental United States, Canada, or international destinations. Anchorage, Alaska's largest city, serves as the primary air hub for the state and is home to Ted Stevens Anchorage International Airport (ANC). This airport connects Alaska with numerous major cities in the U.S., including Seattle, Los Angeles, Chicago, and Denver, as well as international locations like Canada and parts of Asia. For many travelers, flying into Anchorage is the easiest way to begin their Alaskan adventure.

Several major airlines offer regular flights to Anchorage, particularly during the peak summer travel season when demand is highest. Flights from the Pacific Northwest, particularly from Seattle, are the most frequent and often the most affordable. Seattle is a major gateway to Alaska, with multiple daily flights from airlines like Alaska Airlines, Delta, and United. Flight times from Seattle to Anchorage are generally around three and a half hours, making it a relatively short trip for most travelers. If you're flying from the eastern U.S., such as from New York or Washington D.C., expect longer flight times, typically around six to eight hours, with possible layovers in Seattle or other West Coast cities.

In addition to Anchorage, there are other airports in Alaska that serve as entry points for travelers, depending on where you plan to visit. Fairbanks International Airport (FAI) is another major airport located in the interior of Alaska, offering direct flights from several U.S. cities, as well as from international destinations. Fairbanks is particularly popular for travelers looking to explore Denali National Park or those hoping to see the northern lights during the winter months. Juneau International Airport (JNU) serves Alaska's capital city and is the primary gateway for visitors to Southeast Alaska, which is known for its beautiful fjords, glaciers, and wildlife. However, flights to Juneau often require a layover in Seattle or Anchorage.

For those looking to visit more remote areas of Alaska, such as small towns or villages in the Arctic or along the western coast, regional airlines provide flights from Anchorage, Fairbanks, or Juneau. These smaller planes, often operated by airlines like Ravn Alaska or Era Alaska, are essential for accessing communities that are not connected by road. Bush planes, a common sight in Alaska, also play a crucial role in reaching remote wilderness lodges or national parks that are otherwise inaccessible. While flying into these remote locations can be more expensive and weather-dependent, it offers a unique perspective of Alaska's rugged landscapes from the air.

Another popular way to travel to Alaska, particularly for those who want to experience the state's coastal beauty, is by cruise. Cruise travel is especially popular during the summer months, from May through September, when the weather is warmer, and the seas are calmer. Cruises to Alaska typically depart from cities along the West Coast of the United States and Canada, such as Seattle, Vancouver, and San Francisco, and they sail along the Inside Passage, a stunning route that winds through narrow fjords and past towering glaciers. The Inside Passage is one of the most scenic areas in Alaska, and a cruise offers the chance to see marine wildlife, such as whales, sea lions, and otters, up close.

Cruise ships often stop at several popular Alaskan ports along the way, including Juneau, Ketchikan, and Skagway. These stops allow passengers to disembark and explore local attractions, such as hiking trails, historic towns, or cultural centers that celebrate Alaska Native heritage. Some cruises also include visits to Glacier Bay National Park, where passengers can witness massive glaciers calving into the sea. Cruises vary in length, with most trips lasting between seven and fourteen days, though longer cruises are available for those who want to explore more remote areas of the Alaskan coastline.

Alaska's cruises are typically offered by major cruise lines like Princess Cruises, Holland America, and Norwegian Cruise Line, all of which have decades of experience operating in Alaska. Luxury cruise lines and smaller expedition vessels also offer more intimate and in-depth experiences, often focusing on wildlife viewing, kayaking, or visiting less-visited areas of Alaska's vast coastline. These smaller ships can access places that larger cruise ships cannot, offering a more personalized and adventurous experience.

For those who prefer to have full control over their travel schedule or want to experience the scenic beauty of North America on the way to Alaska, a road trip is another viable option. While driving to Alaska is a long journey, it can be one of the most rewarding, especially for travelers who enjoy the freedom of the open road and the chance to explore along the way. The most common route to drive to Alaska is the Alaska Highway, also known as the Alcan Highway. This historic road begins in Dawson Creek, British Columbia, and stretches more than 1,300 miles (2,100 kilometers) through the Canadian Rockies, across the Yukon, and into Alaska. The highway ends in Delta Junction, about 100 miles southeast of Fairbanks.

Driving the Alaska Highway offers an unparalleled opportunity to experience the wild, untamed landscapes of both Canada and Alaska. Along the route, travelers will pass through dense forests, mountain ranges, and remote towns, with opportunities to see wildlife such as bears, bison, and moose. The road is generally well-maintained, though travelers should be prepared for long stretches between services such as gas stations or restaurants, especially in the more remote sections. While the highway is fully paved, it can be rough in places, and certain sections may experience closures due to weather or construction, particularly in the spring and fall.

It's important to plan ahead when driving to Alaska, especially for those unfamiliar with the terrain. The journey can take several days, depending on where you're starting from, and it's recommended to carry extra fuel, food, and water, as well as a reliable spare tire and emergency supplies. Summer is the best time for a road trip to Alaska, as the weather is more predictable, and daylight lasts longer, allowing for safer driving conditions. Winter driving can be treacherous due to snow, ice, and limited daylight, so most people choose to avoid this route during the colder months unless they are experienced in winter travel.

For those who want to drive to Alaska but prefer a more leisurely pace, the Alaska Marine Highway System provides a ferry service that connects several coastal cities in Alaska with the mainland United States. The ferry system operates year-round and allows passengers to bring their vehicles onboard, making it possible to combine a ferry ride with a road trip. Ferries depart from Bellingham, Washington, and make stops in several Alaskan cities, including Ketchikan, Juneau, and Haines, before continuing on to more remote locations like Kodiak or Dutch Harbor. Traveling by ferry offers a slower, more relaxed way to reach Alaska, with the added benefit of scenic views of the coastline and the opportunity to spot marine wildlife.

Traveling Within Alaska: Navigating Alaska by car, train, boat, or plane

Traveling within Alaska offers a unique experience due to the state's vastness and the variety of terrains it covers. Alaska is the largest state in the United States, with over 660,000 square miles of land, much of which is wilderness and uninhabited. The state's geography ranges from rugged mountains and dense forests to tundra and coastline, making it necessary to use different modes of transportation depending on where you are and where you want to go. For travelers, navigating Alaska involves understanding how to get around by car, train, boat, and plane—each option offering distinct advantages depending on your itinerary and the areas you plan to visit.

Driving is one of the most common ways to explore parts of Alaska, especially for those who want to have the freedom to move at their own pace and access some of the more remote but accessible destinations. However, it's important to recognize that Alaska's road network is relatively limited compared to other states, particularly outside of the more populated regions. The main highways connect major cities such as Anchorage, Fairbanks, and Juneau to key areas, but many towns and villages in Alaska can only be reached by air or boat.

The primary highway system in Alaska includes the Alaska Highway, the Glenn Highway, and the Seward Highway, among others. The Alaska Highway (also known as the Alcan Highway) is a major route for those driving into Alaska from Canada, stretching from the U.S.-Canada border into the heart of the state. It is a well-traveled road that passes through stunning landscapes, including mountain ranges and vast stretches of wilderness. The Glenn Highway connects Anchorage with the interior of Alaska, passing by scenic spots such as the Matanuska Glacier, while the Seward Highway runs south from Anchorage to the coastal town of Seward, offering spectacular views of mountains, forests, and fjords along the way. These highways provide access to some of Alaska's most popular attractions, including Denali National Park, the Kenai Peninsula, and the coastal areas of Southcentral Alaska.

Driving in Alaska can be an adventure in itself, as the scenery is breathtaking, with opportunities to see wildlife along the roadside, such as moose, bears, and caribou. However, it's important to note that driving conditions can vary significantly depending on the season. In the summer months, from late May to September, the roads are generally clear and in good condition, making it an ideal time for road trips. Summer also offers long daylight hours, with some regions experiencing nearly 24 hours of sunlight, allowing for extended travel days. During the winter months, however, snow and ice can make driving more challenging, particularly in more remote areas where road maintenance may be less frequent. Travelers should be prepared for harsh winter driving conditions, including icy roads, snow drifts, and the potential for avalanches in mountainous areas. Winter tires and chains may be necessary, and it's a good idea to carry emergency supplies, such as food, water, and blankets, in case of breakdowns or road closures.

In addition to the main highways, many of Alaska's remote areas can be reached by gravel or dirt roads, such as the famous Dalton Highway, which runs north from Fairbanks to the oil fields of Prudhoe Bay on the Arctic Ocean. The Dalton Highway is one of the most isolated roads in the United States, with limited services along the way. It's primarily used by truckers and adventurous travelers who want to experience the remote beauty of Alaska's Arctic regions. If you plan to drive the Dalton Highway or other remote roads, it's essential to prepare carefully, as there are few places to refuel, and help may not be readily available in the event of an emergency.

For those who prefer not to drive or want to experience Alaska in a different way, the Alaska Railroad offers a scenic and comfortable alternative for getting around. The Alaska Railroad runs from Seward in the south to Fairbanks in the interior, passing through Anchorage and other key destinations along the way. The railroad is known for its breathtaking views of glaciers, mountains, and wildlife, and it is a popular choice for tourists who want to sit back and enjoy the journey without worrying about navigating the roads. The train makes stops at popular destinations like Denali National Park, where passengers can disembark to explore the park before continuing their journey.

The Alaska Railroad operates year-round, though the schedules and routes vary depending on the season. In the summer, the train offers more frequent service, with special sightseeing routes like the Denali Star, which connects Anchorage and Fairbanks, and the Coastal Classic, which runs between Anchorage and Seward. These summer routes are particularly popular with tourists, as they offer narrated tours and panoramic views from the train's large windows or observation cars. In the winter, the railroad continues to operate, though on a more limited schedule, offering a unique way to experience Alaska's snowy landscapes and possibly catch a glimpse of the northern lights during the longer nights.

Traveling by boat is another essential method of transportation in Alaska, especially for accessing the many coastal communities and islands that are not connected by roads. The Alaska Marine Highway System (AMHS) is a ferry network that serves as a lifeline for many of these remote communities, providing regular service to towns and cities along Alaska's coastline, including the Inside Passage, the Aleutian Islands, and the Gulf of Alaska. The ferries also connect Alaska with the mainland United States and Canada, with routes starting in Bellingham, Washington, and Prince Rupert, British Columbia.

The ferries offer both transportation and a scenic experience, as passengers can enjoy views of glaciers, fjords, and marine wildlife while traveling between ports. The ferry system is particularly popular with travelers who want to explore Southeast Alaska, including popular destinations like Juneau, Sitka, and

Ketchikan. Many ferries allow passengers to bring their vehicles on board, making it possible to combine a road trip with ferry travel. This is especially useful for those traveling to places like the Kenai Peninsula or Prince William Sound, where the roads do not connect all communities.

For travelers interested in exploring Alaska's coastal waters more intimately, there are also opportunities to take smaller boats or day cruises to visit specific areas, such as the Kenai Fjords, Glacier Bay, or Prince William Sound. These boat tours provide close-up views of glaciers, marine life like humpback whales and orcas, and the rugged coastline that defines much of Alaska's landscape. Many of these smaller boats can navigate into fjords and inlets that larger ferries or cruise ships cannot access, offering a more personalized experience of Alaska's natural beauty.

Given the vastness of Alaska and the limited road network, flying is often the most practical way to reach remote areas, especially in the northern and western parts of the state. Alaska has one of the highest numbers of small plane pilots per capita in the United States, and for good reason. Many communities in Alaska are not connected by road, and small aircraft are the primary means of transportation for both residents and visitors. Bush planes, which are small, rugged aircraft capable of landing on short airstrips or even gravel bars, are commonly used to reach remote villages, lodges, and wilderness areas.

Flying in Alaska offers a unique perspective of the state's vast and varied landscapes. Bush planes can take you deep into the backcountry, where you can access remote national parks like Gates of the Arctic or Wrangell-St. Elias, which are otherwise inaccessible by road. These flights often provide breathtaking aerial views of glaciers, mountains, and vast expanses of wilderness. Many travelers use bush planes to fly into hunting, fishing, or hiking destinations, or to reach isolated lodges that offer wildlife viewing and outdoor adventures.

In larger cities like Anchorage and Fairbanks, regional airlines operate regular flights to smaller towns and villages across Alaska. For example, Ravn Alaska and Alaska Airlines provide service to destinations like Bethel, Nome, and Kotzebue. These flights are essential for residents of these communities, as well as for tourists who want to experience the unique cultures and landscapes of rural Alaska.

How to Prepare for the Climate: Packing lists for summer, winter, and year-round adventures

uneven or muddy terrain. Many of Alaska's hiking trails are rugged, and it's not uncommon to encounter muddy conditions, especially after rain. Lightweight, moisture-wicking socks will help keep your feet dry and comfortable, even during long hikes. If you're planning more casual activities in towns or cities, you can also pack a pair of comfortable walking shoes or sneakers for easier terrain.

In terms of accessories, a hat for sun protection is important, as the long daylight hours and reflective surfaces, such as water or snow-capped peaks, can intensify the sun's rays. Sunglasses with UV protection are also essential, especially if you're spending time near glaciers or snowfields, where the sunlight can be particularly harsh on your eyes. A small daypack for carrying essentials like water, snacks, and extra layers is also useful for day trips and outdoor activities.

While summer offers milder conditions, Alaska's winter climate is a completely different experience, and preparation is even more critical. Winter temperatures can vary depending on where you are, but the interior of Alaska, around Fairbanks, often sees temperatures drop well below freezing, with lows that can reach -40°F (-40°C) or lower. Even coastal areas, which are somewhat moderated by the ocean, experience cold weather and frequent snowfall. If you plan to visit Alaska in the winter, you need to be prepared for extreme cold, especially if you'll be spending any time outdoors for activities like dog sledding, northern lights viewing, or cross-country skiing.

For winter travel, packing starts with a strong focus on insulation. Your base layer should be made of thermal, moisture-wicking material like merino wool or synthetic fabrics designed for cold weather. Avoid cotton, as it traps moisture and can leave you feeling colder. On top of the base layer, a heavy fleece or insulated jacket should be worn for added warmth. For outerwear, a down or synthetic insulated parka is crucial to protect you from the cold. Look for jackets that are windproof and water-resistant to handle both snow and windchill effectively. In particularly cold regions like Fairbanks or the Arctic, you might need additional insulation, such as down pants or insulated bibs, especially if you plan to be outside for extended periods.

Layering is just as important for your lower body in the winter. Thermal leggings or long underwear worn beneath insulated pants or snow pants will provide necessary warmth while allowing you to move freely. Snow pants are particularly useful if you'll be participating in outdoor sports or spending time in deep snow.

When it comes to footwear, insulated, waterproof winter boots are a necessity. The ground in Alaska is often icy or covered in snow during the winter, so your boots need to be able to keep your feet warm and dry. Look for boots with thick rubber soles that offer good traction to avoid slipping on ice. Pair these with thermal or wool socks, which will help retain body heat and keep your feet comfortable. In extreme cold, you may need to layer two pairs of socks for added warmth, but be sure that your boots have enough room to accommodate this without restricting circulation.

Accessories are equally important in winter conditions. A warm hat or beanie made of wool or synthetic materials is essential for keeping your head warm, as a significant amount of body heat can be lost through the head. A neck gaiter or balaclava is also recommended to protect your face and neck from the cold wind, particularly if temperatures drop below zero. Insulated gloves or mittens are crucial to prevent frostbite, and mittens tend to be warmer than gloves in extremely cold conditions. It's a good idea to carry hand warmers, which can be placed inside your gloves or boots for additional warmth on particularly cold days.

For year-round adventures, particularly if your trip spans multiple seasons, it's important to pack with versatility in mind. Layering is key, as it allows you to adjust your clothing to changing weather conditions. Even in the summer, Alaska's weather can be unpredictable, with sudden temperature drops, rain, or even snow at higher elevations. A typical packing list for year-round travel would include moisture-wicking base layers, mid-layers like fleece jackets, a waterproof shell, and a down jacket that can be worn when temperatures dip. You'll want to be prepared for both wet and dry conditions, so packing waterproof boots as well as lighter shoes for warmer days is a smart choice. Versatility in your gear allows you to switch between warm, cold, dry, and wet conditions as needed without overpacking.

In terms of additional gear, there are a few essentials that apply no matter the season. A good quality headlamp or flashlight is important, especially if you'll be visiting during the fall or winter months when daylight is limited, and darkness can last for much of the day. Even in the summer, a headlamp can be useful if you plan on camping or hiking late into the evening. Insect repellent is also a must for summer travelers, as mosquitoes can be a nuisance, particularly in wetland areas or near lakes and rivers. If you plan to be near glaciers or on the water, packing a waterproof dry bag to store electronics and important items is a good idea, as it protects your belongings from rain or splashes.

For those planning on camping or embarking on extended outdoor excursions, additional preparation is required. A four-season tent designed to handle wind and rain, as well as a warm sleeping bag rated for colder temperatures, is essential for camping in Alaska's wilderness. A reliable cooking stove, food storage that can keep animals away, and a GPS or map for navigation are all key items that can ensure your safety and comfort while exploring the remote areas of the state.

Chapter 6

Internet, Communication, and Navigation

Staying Connected

Staying connected while traveling in Alaska can be a unique challenge, given the state's vast wilderness, remote locations, and varying levels of infrastructure. Whether you are visiting one of Alaska's larger cities, like Anchorage or Fairbanks, or venturing into its more isolated areas, it's essential to understand the internet options, Wi-Fi availability, and mobile networks available in the state. With Alaska being the largest state in the United States and much of it being sparsely populated or completely uninhabited, the level of connectivity can differ significantly depending on where you are. Preparing ahead of time will ensure you can access the services you need while exploring this stunning and remote destination.

In Alaska's urban centers, such as Anchorage, Juneau, and Fairbanks, staying connected is generally straightforward. These cities have infrastructure that supports reliable internet and mobile networks, making it easy for travelers to access Wi-Fi, use mobile data, and stay in touch with family, friends, or work. Internet service providers like GCI, Alaska Communications, and HughesNet offer broadband and satellite internet to residents and businesses, meaning you'll find relatively fast and consistent internet service in hotels, restaurants, cafes, and other public places within these cities.

Wi-Fi is readily available in most hotels, where it is often included as part of your stay. Many accommodations, particularly chain hotels, offer free Wi-Fi for guests, though the speed and reliability can vary depending on the hotel and its location. In some places, you may encounter slower speeds, especially during peak usage times in the evening when many guests are online at the same time. Luxury hotels and business hotels often provide higher-speed internet as part of their service, and some may offer paid upgrades for faster or more consistent connections.

Restaurants, cafes, and coffee shops in urban areas also typically offer free Wi-Fi to patrons. National chains like Starbucks, as well as local coffee shops, tend to provide Wi-Fi access, which makes it easy to stay connected while grabbing a meal or a drink. If you're working remotely or need to catch up on emails during your trip, it's worth checking in advance whether your chosen cafe or restaurant has reliable Wi-Fi. Some libraries and community centers also provide free internet access, making them another option for travelers in cities who need to connect to the web.

In addition to Wi-Fi, mobile network coverage in Alaska's cities is relatively good. The major national carriers, such as AT&T, Verizon, and T-Mobile, all offer service in Alaska, though AT&T and Verizon tend to have the most extensive coverage. If you have a phone plan with one of these carriers, you should have no trouble staying connected in the major cities and along the primary highways that connect them. Most carriers offer 4G LTE service in populated areas, with AT&T and Verizon also rolling out 5G coverage in some parts of Anchorage and Fairbanks. However, it's important to remember that data speeds can fluctuate, and if many people are accessing the network at the same time, you may notice slower service.

However, once you leave the urban areas and venture into more remote regions of Alaska, staying connected becomes more complicated. Alaska's wilderness covers vast expanses of land with little or no infrastructure, which means that Wi-Fi availability is limited and mobile network coverage can be spotty or nonexistent. In smaller towns and villages, particularly those not connected to the road system, internet access may be slower and less reliable, and public Wi-Fi networks may not be as common. Many rural communities rely on satellite internet services, which tend to have slower speeds and higher latency compared to broadband services available in urban areas.

If you're planning to visit rural or remote parts of Alaska, such as the Arctic, the Alaska Peninsula, or some of the islands off the coast, it's important to plan ahead for limited connectivity. Mobile coverage in these areas is often sparse, especially if you're traveling into the backcountry or wilderness where there are no cell towers. Even major carriers like AT&T and Verizon have limited reach in these regions, and you may find that your phone loses signal altogether in certain locations.

For travelers heading into remote areas where mobile coverage is unreliable, satellite phones or personal satellite communication devices are often the best option for staying connected. Devices like Garmin's inReach or SPOT messengers allow you to send messages via satellite and provide GPS tracking, which can be essential for safety in remote areas. These devices work almost anywhere on the planet and are commonly used by hikers, campers, and adventurers who need to communicate in places without cell service. While satellite phones and communication devices tend to be more expensive than standard mobile phones, they offer peace of mind, particularly if you're exploring Alaska's more isolated regions.

Another consideration for travelers in Alaska is the availability of Wi-Fi and mobile coverage on cruises, ferries, and other forms of transportation. Many visitors to Alaska travel by cruise ship or use the Alaska Marine Highway System ferries to move between coastal towns and cities. On cruise ships, internet access is typically available, but it often comes at an additional cost and can be slower than what you might be used to on land. Cruise ships rely on satellite connections for internet service, which means the speeds are generally slower and more expensive than traditional broadband connections. If you need to stay connected during your cruise, it's a good idea to check with your cruise line about their internet packages and coverage areas before your trip.

Ferries on the Alaska Marine Highway System may also offer limited Wi-Fi, but it's not guaranteed and is usually slower and less reliable. In many cases, travelers on ferries rely on mobile networks when they are close to the shore, but as soon as the ferry moves into more remote waters, mobile coverage can drop off. If staying connected is important to you while traveling by ferry, it's worth downloading offline maps, books, and other content ahead of time to use while you're offline.

When traveling by car along Alaska's highways, mobile coverage is generally available along the main routes between Anchorage, Fairbanks, and the Kenai Peninsula, as well as along the Seward and Glenn Highways. However, there are still stretches of road, particularly in the interior and more rural areas, where coverage can be limited or absent altogether. If you're planning a road trip in Alaska, it's a good idea to carry a paper map or download offline maps to your phone in case you lose service while driving through more remote areas. Additionally, having a car charger or portable battery pack for your phone can be helpful in case you need to recharge your device while on the road.

In terms of international travelers visiting Alaska, it's important to check with your mobile carrier to see if your phone plan includes coverage in the United States. Many international carriers offer roaming plans that allow you to use your phone in the U.S., but these plans can come with additional fees, so it's important to understand the costs ahead of time. Alternatively, some travelers opt to purchase a prepaid SIM card from a U.S. carrier like AT&T or T-Mobile, which can provide temporary access to mobile data and calling services while in Alaska. If you have an unlocked phone, this can be a cost-effective option for staying connected during your trip.

For those who rely on regular internet access for work or communication, it's also worth considering portable Wi-Fi hotspots. These devices allow you to create your own Wi-Fi network using mobile data, and they can be useful if you're traveling in areas where Wi-Fi is not readily available but mobile coverage is present. Many carriers offer mobile hotspots, or you can rent a device for the duration of your trip. However, keep in mind that the same limitations apply, if you're in an area without cell service, your hotspot won't be able to connect.

Local SIM Cards and Data Plans: Options for tourists to stay connected affordably

When traveling to Alaska, staying connected is often a priority for tourists, whether for navigating, keeping in touch with family and friends, or sharing the experience on social media. One of the most affordable and convenient ways for international visitors to maintain communication during their trip is by purchasing a local SIM card and data plan. By using a local SIM card, travelers can access mobile networks, use data, make calls, and send text messages without incurring the often expensive international roaming charges associated with using a foreign SIM card abroad. Understanding the options available for purchasing a local SIM card and choosing the right data plan can help ensure that you stay connected affordably while traveling in Alaska.

Alaska, as part of the United States, operates on the same mobile network systems as the rest of the country, meaning that tourists can take advantage of the major U.S. carriers for SIM cards and data plans. However, it's important to note that due to Alaska's unique geography and sparse population, coverage can be more limited in remote areas compared to the rest of the U.S. As a result, choosing the right carrier and plan becomes crucial depending on where you plan to travel within the state.

The most widely available mobile carriers in Alaska are AT&T, Verizon, and T-Mobile. These major carriers provide relatively good coverage in the state's urban areas, such as Anchorage, Fairbanks, and Juneau, as well as along the major highways connecting these cities. However, coverage tends to drop off significantly in rural areas and especially in more remote regions where cell towers are sparse or nonexistent. Of the three, AT&T and Verizon tend to have the most reliable networks in Alaska, especially outside the larger cities.

For tourists who want to stay connected during their trip, the first step is to ensure that your phone is unlocked. An unlocked phone is one that is not tied to a specific carrier, allowing you to insert a SIM card from another provider. Most international visitors will need to confirm with their home carrier that their phone is unlocked before traveling, as some phones purchased through carriers are locked to that network for the duration of a contract. If your phone is locked, it may not be compatible with a U.S. SIM card, and you could face difficulties in accessing local networks. Once you've confirmed that your phone is unlocked, purchasing a local SIM card becomes an easy way to access the internet and make calls during your stay.

Upon arriving in Alaska, purchasing a local SIM card is relatively simple. SIM cards from the major carriers can be bought at mobile retail stores, electronics shops, or even at some airports and convenience stores. AT&T and T-Mobile offer prepaid SIM cards that are designed for short-term use, which are ideal for tourists. These prepaid SIM cards allow you to choose a plan that fits your needs without having to commit to a long-term contract. They typically include a combination of talk, text, and data, and the process of setting up the SIM card is straightforward: you simply insert the SIM card into your phone, follow the activation instructions, and your phone will connect to the local network.

AT&T is often considered one of the better options for tourists visiting Alaska, particularly those who plan to travel outside of the major cities. AT&T offers prepaid SIM cards that can be purchased for as little as $25 to $50, depending on the amount of data and services included. Their prepaid plans typically come with unlimited talk and text within the United States, and they offer a range of data packages to choose from. For example, you may find prepaid plans that offer 1GB, 5GB, or unlimited data per month, with prices increasing based on the amount of data you need. For most tourists, a plan with at least 5GB of data is recommended, especially if you plan to use GPS, social media, and other data-heavy applications regularly during your trip.

Verizon is another popular option for travelers in Alaska, known for its extensive coverage, particularly in more remote regions. Verizon also offers prepaid SIM cards with a variety of data plans that cater to tourists. While Verizon's prepaid plans tend to be slightly more expensive than AT&T's, they are often favored by those venturing into rural areas or national parks where other carriers might have less reliable coverage. Verizon's prepaid plans offer similar features, such as unlimited talk and text within the U.S., with data allowances that range from smaller packages to unlimited options. Tourists can purchase these SIM cards at Verizon stores or online, and activation is simple and quick.

T-Mobile is another carrier that provides prepaid options for tourists visiting Alaska, though its coverage is somewhat more limited compared to AT&T and Verizon, particularly outside the urban centers. However, for tourists planning to stay primarily in cities like Anchorage, Juneau, or Fairbanks, T-Mobile's prepaid SIM cards can be an affordable option. T-Mobile often offers competitive pricing, with plans that include unlimited talk and text and a range of data packages.

These plans can be purchased at T-Mobile stores or other authorized retailers. As with the other carriers, activation is straightforward and usually takes only a few minutes.

If you are looking for a more flexible or budget-friendly option, some tourists opt for MVNOs (Mobile Virtual Network Operators) that operate on the larger carriers' networks. MVNOs, such as Mint Mobile, Simple Mobile, or Cricket Wireless, often provide cheaper prepaid plans, making them a good choice for tourists who need basic connectivity at a lower cost. These carriers offer SIM cards that run on the same networks as AT&T, T-Mobile, or Verizon, but at a reduced price. You can purchase a prepaid SIM card from an MVNO online before your trip or at various retailers once you arrive in Alaska. MVNO plans tend to offer limited data packages, but for travelers who don't need heavy data usage, they can be a cost-effective option.

Once you've purchased your SIM card, data management becomes a key part of staying connected affordably. Even with a prepaid plan, data usage can add up quickly, especially if you're streaming videos, using GPS navigation frequently, or uploading large amounts of photos to social media. To make the most of your data, it's a good idea to download offline maps, travel guides, and other essential apps before your trip so you can access them without using mobile data. Google Maps, for instance, allows you to download maps of specific areas for offline use, which can be extremely helpful when driving through rural areas or using GPS in places with limited network coverage.

Additionally, take advantage of free Wi-Fi whenever it's available. Many hotels, cafes, and restaurants in Alaska's urban areas offer free Wi-Fi for guests, which can help you conserve your mobile data for when you're on the go. By downloading large files or doing data-heavy tasks while connected to Wi-Fi, you can stretch your prepaid data plan further and avoid the need to purchase additional data.

For international travelers, it's also important to note that most U.S. prepaid SIM cards and data plans do not include international calling or texting by default. However, some carriers offer add-ons or international packages that allow you to make calls or send texts to your home country at an additional cost. If you need to stay in touch with friends or family abroad, check with the carrier before purchasing your SIM card to see what options are available for international communication.

Essential Travel Apps: Apps for maps, weather, navigation, and emergency contacts

When traveling to a vast and remote destination like Alaska, staying prepared is essential for ensuring a smooth and enjoyable trip. While Alaska offers incredible opportunities for adventure, from hiking its rugged mountains to exploring its vast wilderness, it also presents challenges that require careful planning and reliable tools. In today's digital age, many of those tools come in the form of travel apps that can help you navigate, check the weather, find emergency contacts, and get updates on local conditions. Having the right apps on your phone can make all the difference, especially in a place as wild and unpredictable as Alaska. Here's a look at some of the most important travel apps that will enhance your experience and help you stay safe during your trip.

One of the most essential types of apps you'll need while traveling in Alaska is a reliable map and navigation app. Alaska's landscapes are vast, and many of the state's most beautiful and interesting destinations are far from well-marked roads. Whether you're hiking through a national park, driving along a remote highway, or navigating through small towns, having access to detailed maps can help prevent you from getting lost or taking a wrong turn.

Google Maps is a universally recognized and highly reliable app for navigation, and it's an essential tool for traveling within Alaska. Google Maps provides real-time driving directions, walking routes, and public transit information, which is especially helpful in cities like Anchorage or Fairbanks. It also offers offline maps, a feature that is extremely useful in remote areas where cell service may be spotty or nonexistent. Before heading out into areas with poor reception, you can download offline maps of the region, allowing you to access directions and landmarks even when you're off the grid. Google Maps also includes reviews and information about nearby restaurants, hotels, and attractions, making it a versatile app that can help you find what you need while on the road.

While Google Maps is widely used, many travelers who plan to spend more time hiking or exploring backcountry areas turn to apps like Gaia GPS or AllTrails. These apps are particularly useful for outdoor enthusiasts because they provide topographical maps, trail information, and GPS tracking, which can be invaluable when navigating the more remote parts of Alaska. Gaia GPS, for instance, offers detailed topographic maps that help hikers plan their routes and track their location in real-time. It's especially useful for backcountry hiking, as it includes information on elevation, terrain, and off-the-beaten-path trails. The app also allows users to download maps for offline use, which is crucial in areas without cell service. Gaia GPS has become a go-to app for adventurers who need reliable navigation in rugged, less-traveled landscapes.

AllTrails is another excellent app for those looking to hike in Alaska. It offers a comprehensive database of hiking trails, including user reviews, difficulty ratings, and trail maps. The app allows you to filter trails by length, elevation gain, and user ratings, helping you find the perfect hike for your fitness level and interest. AllTrails also offers the option to download trail maps for offline use, ensuring that you stay on track even when you lose service deep in the wilderness. Given that many hiking trails in Alaska lead into remote areas with little signage, having this app at your fingertips can provide peace of mind and keep you oriented.

In addition to maps and navigation, keeping an eye on the weather is crucial while traveling in Alaska. The state is known for its unpredictable and sometimes extreme weather patterns, where conditions can change rapidly. Whether you're hiking in the mountains or cruising along the coast, understanding the current and forecasted weather can make a significant difference in your safety and enjoyment of your trip.

The Weather Channel app is one of the most reliable and widely used weather apps available. It provides up-to-date weather forecasts, hourly updates, and severe weather alerts, which can be especially helpful if you're planning outdoor activities. The app includes detailed information about temperature, wind speeds, precipitation, and UV levels, allowing you to plan your day accordingly. In Alaska, where sudden storms or temperature drops are not uncommon, having this information at hand can help you adjust your plans and stay safe. The Weather Channel app also allows you to set alerts for specific locations, so you'll receive notifications if the weather changes in the area you're visiting.

Another useful weather app for Alaska is Windy. This app is particularly helpful for travelers who are interested in outdoor activities like fishing, boating, or kayaking, as it provides detailed information about wind speeds, cloud cover, and air pressure. Windy uses a visual, interactive map that shows current weather conditions in real-time, including wind patterns, temperature, and rain forecasts. This makes it an excellent tool for planning outdoor adventures where the wind can play a critical role in determining whether it's safe to be on the water or in the mountains.

For travelers who are interested in tracking the northern lights during their trip, apps like My Aurora Forecast are indispensable. Alaska is one of the best places in the world to view the aurora borealis, especially in winter, but seeing this natural phenomenon depends on a combination of factors, including solar activity and clear skies. My Aurora Forecast helps users track the likelihood of seeing the northern lights by providing real-time data on solar wind activity, aurora strength, and cloud cover. The app also offers long-term forecasts, so you can plan your aurora-viewing trip in advance and increase your chances of seeing this awe-inspiring light display.

In addition to navigation and weather apps, having quick access to emergency contacts and information is vital when traveling in Alaska, especially in remote areas where help may not be immediately available. Apps like Red Cross First Aid provide essential emergency response information that can guide you through basic first aid procedures in the event of an injury or medical emergency. The app offers easy-to-follow instructions for dealing with common emergencies like cuts, burns, hypothermia, or frostbite, which can be particularly useful in Alaska's outdoor environments. With built-in safety tips and emergency preparedness guides, Red Cross First Aid is a practical tool for anyone traveling in regions where access to medical care may be limited.

Another valuable app for emergency situations is Life360. This app allows travelers to stay connected with family and friends by sharing their location in real-time. Life360 is particularly useful for group travel, as it enables members of a travel party to keep track of each other's locations, ensuring that everyone stays safe and connected, even in large or unfamiliar areas. The app also includes a panic button feature, which can send an alert to designated contacts if you find yourself in an emergency situation. This feature is particularly useful for solo travelers or those exploring Alaska's more isolated regions.

For those venturing deep into the Alaskan wilderness, having a satellite-based communication tool is important for safety. Apps like Garmin's inReach work in conjunction with satellite communication devices, allowing you to send SOS alerts, share your GPS location, and send text messages even when you're far from cell service. This is a critical app for anyone planning extensive hiking, camping, or remote travel, as it ensures that you have a way to reach emergency services if something goes wrong.

Another helpful app for travelers in Alaska is Offline Survival Manual. This app provides a wealth of survival information, covering topics like how to build a shelter, find food and water, start a fire, and navigate in the wilderness. It's especially useful for travelers who plan to explore Alaska's vast backcountry, where getting lost or encountering harsh conditions is always a possibility. The app doesn't require an internet connection once downloaded, making it a handy resource for remote travel. While hopefully, you won't need to use it, having a guide to survival techniques in your pocket can offer reassurance when you're in unfamiliar terrain.

Using GPS in Remote Areas: Tips for using navigation tools off the beaten path

Using GPS in remote areas, especially in places like Alaska where much of the landscape remains untamed wilderness, requires careful planning and an understanding of the limitations and capabilities of your navigation tools. While GPS technology has made it easier for adventurers and travelers to explore off-the-beaten-path locations with greater confidence, relying solely on GPS without preparation can lead to problems, particularly in areas without cell service or in rugged terrain where signals can be blocked. To navigate successfully in these remote areas, it's important to know how to maximize the effectiveness of your GPS tools and be prepared for any potential challenges that may arise.

When traveling in remote areas, the first thing to understand is how GPS works and how it differs from using traditional map apps that rely on an internet connection. Global Positioning System (GPS) technology operates via a network of satellites that orbit the Earth, transmitting signals that are picked up by GPS receivers in your device. Unlike cellular signals, GPS signals are available virtually everywhere on the planet, including remote areas without cell service. This makes GPS an invaluable tool for navigation in the backcountry or in places far from cities and towns. However, GPS receivers must have a clear line of sight to the sky in order to accurately determine your location. Dense forest cover, mountains, or deep canyons can sometimes interfere with signal reception, which is something to keep in mind when venturing into more rugged areas.

One of the most important steps to take before using GPS in remote areas is to download offline maps to your device. Apps like Google Maps, Gaia GPS, and Maps.me offer the option to download maps for offline use, which is essential when traveling in places where you might lose cell service or data connectivity. By downloading maps ahead of time, you can still use your device's GPS functionality to track your location and follow routes, even when you're completely off the grid. This is especially helpful for remote hiking, backcountry driving, or wilderness camping. Keep in mind that offline maps often take up a significant amount of storage space, so it's important to have enough room on your phone or GPS device to store them.

Before setting out into a remote area, make sure you understand the terrain and the route you plan to follow. While GPS devices are extremely accurate in determining your location, they are only as useful as the maps you have loaded onto them. In places like Alaska, where there are vast expanses of wilderness with few established roads or trails, it's crucial to ensure that your maps are detailed enough to include the information you need. Topographic maps are ideal for remote travel because they provide information about the elevation, terrain features, and landmarks, helping you navigate more easily through unmarked or uneven areas. Apps like Gaia GPS and Topo Maps+ are popular choices for those heading into the wilderness, as they offer highly detailed topographic maps that can be downloaded for offline use.

When using GPS in remote areas, it's also important to save waypoints before you begin your journey. Waypoints are specific locations that you mark on your map before or during your trip, such as your starting point, significant trail intersections, a water source, or your intended destination. Marking these waypoints allows you to track your progress and retrace your steps if needed, which is especially helpful if you lose the trail or need to backtrack in unfamiliar terrain. Many GPS apps and devices allow you to create and save waypoints with a single click, and you can often label them with custom names, making it easier to identify important locations later on.

Another important consideration when using GPS in remote areas is battery life. Running GPS continuously on your smartphone or GPS device can drain the battery quickly, particularly if you are also using your device for other purposes, like taking photos or using other apps. To conserve battery life, it's a good idea to turn off non-essential functions like Wi-Fi, Bluetooth, and background apps that consume power. Some GPS apps offer the option to switch to "battery saver" mode, which limits the frequency of location updates to reduce power usage. Additionally, bringing a portable power bank or extra batteries is highly recommended for longer trips. These backup power sources can keep your device charged in case of unexpected delays or if you're traveling for multiple days without access to electricity.

In extremely remote areas, especially those with harsh weather conditions, it's important to have backup navigation tools in case your GPS device fails or loses signal. While GPS is incredibly helpful, it's never a good idea to rely on it as your sole means of navigation. Always bring a physical map and compass as a backup, and make sure you know how to use them. A map and compass don't require batteries, and they can be lifesaving tools if your GPS stops working, gets damaged, or runs out of power. Learning basic map-reading and compass skills before your trip will give you the confidence to navigate even if technology fails.

When you're navigating off the beaten path, it's also crucial to understand how to interpret the information your GPS device provides. GPS coordinates, for example, are expressed as latitude and longitude, which tell you exactly where you are on the Earth's surface. Many GPS apps and devices will automatically translate these coordinates into a position on your map, but it's helpful to familiarize yourself with reading coordinates directly, especially if you need to communicate your location to others or in case of an emergency. Knowing how to accurately pinpoint your location using coordinates can be incredibly valuable if you need to contact search and rescue services.

Weather can also play a significant role when using GPS in remote areas. Alaska, for instance, is known for its rapidly changing weather conditions, where a sunny day can quickly turn into rain or fog. Bad weather can make it difficult to see landmarks, obscure trails, and reduce visibility, which makes GPS even more valuable. However, extreme weather conditions like heavy rain or dense fog can sometimes interfere with GPS signals, especially in mountainous areas. If you're traveling in an area prone to unpredictable weather, it's essential to keep an eye on the forecast and plan accordingly. Some GPS apps, like Gaia GPS, even offer weather overlays, which can provide real-time weather updates and show how weather conditions may impact your route.

When traveling in remote areas, particularly for extended periods, it's important to share your travel plans and location with someone who is not on the trip. Apps like Life360 or Garmin's inReach allow you to share your real-time GPS location with family or friends, which is an extra safety precaution in case something goes wrong. Even if you're in a remote area without cell service, satellite communication devices like Garmin inReach or SPOT allow you to send your location via satellite and communicate with emergency services if needed. These devices are specifically designed for backcountry travel and are highly recommended for solo travelers or anyone venturing far from established roads or trails.

Chapter 7

Health and Safety

Staying Healthy in Alaska

Staying healthy while traveling in Alaska requires preparation, especially given the state's vast wilderness and its sometimes limited access to medical services. Alaska's unique geography, extreme weather conditions, and remote areas mean that travelers need to be mindful of their health and safety, particularly when venturing into the backcountry. Understanding how to access medical care, where to find pharmacies, and how to handle common health-related issues in the wilderness are all important aspects of ensuring a safe and healthy trip to this incredible destination. Whether you're visiting one of Alaska's cities or planning a long hike into the wild, knowing what resources are available and how to deal with potential medical issues will give you peace of mind and help you focus on enjoying your adventure.

In Alaska's larger cities, such as Anchorage, Fairbanks, and Juneau, medical facilities are similar to those found in the rest of the United States. Hospitals and urgent care centers are available in these cities, providing access to emergency services, general medical care, and specialized treatment. Anchorage, the largest city in the state, has the most comprehensive medical facilities, including the Alaska Native Medical Center and

Providence Alaska Medical Center, both of which provide a full range of medical services. If you encounter any medical emergencies while in Anchorage, these hospitals are equipped to handle everything from minor injuries to more serious conditions.

For non-emergency medical needs, urgent care clinics can be a good option for travelers who need treatment for things like sprains, minor infections, or common illnesses. Urgent care centers are typically faster and more affordable than hospital emergency rooms and can handle many medical concerns that don't require immediate emergency care. If you're staying in one of Alaska's larger cities, it's worth noting the location of the nearest urgent care center, just in case you need it during your trip.

Pharmacies are also widely available in urban areas. In cities like Anchorage, Fairbanks, and Juneau, you'll find chain pharmacies such as Walgreens and CVS, as well as smaller local pharmacies. These pharmacies stock over-the-counter medications, first-aid supplies, and prescription medications, making it easy to purchase any necessary health products during your stay. If you have a pre-existing medical condition that requires prescription medication, it's a good idea to bring enough medication to last for the duration of your trip, as it can sometimes be difficult to refill prescriptions quickly in smaller towns or rural areas.

For travelers who are venturing into more rural parts of Alaska, access to medical facilities becomes more limited. Many small towns and villages in Alaska do not have hospitals or urgent care centers. Instead, they may have small health clinics or community health centers that provide basic medical services. These clinics are typically staffed by nurse practitioners or physician assistants and can handle routine medical needs or provide initial care for injuries. However, they may not be equipped to handle serious medical emergencies. In such cases, patients may need to be transported by air to larger hospitals in Anchorage or Fairbanks. Given the remoteness of many of these communities, it's important to be aware that medical evacuation services, while available, can be expensive and time-consuming.

If you're traveling to one of Alaska's more remote areas or participating in wilderness activities such as hiking, camping, or fishing, it's essential to be prepared with basic wilderness first-aid knowledge. In the wilderness, even minor injuries or illnesses can become serious if not treated promptly, and getting help can take hours or even days, depending on your location. For this reason, having a well-stocked first-aid kit and knowing how to use it is crucial.

Your wilderness first-aid kit should include items such as adhesive bandages, gauze pads, antiseptic wipes, medical tape, tweezers, and scissors. It's also important to pack supplies for treating more serious injuries, such as a sterile dressing for larger wounds, a triangular bandage for making a sling, and an emergency blanket to prevent hypothermia. If you're planning a multi-day trek or camping trip in a remote area, consider including a splint in case of bone fractures, as well as medications for pain relief, allergies, and gastrointestinal issues.

When it comes to treating injuries or illnesses in the wilderness, the key is to remain calm and assess the situation. Minor injuries like cuts, blisters, and sprains are common in the backcountry and can usually be treated on-site with the supplies in your first-aid kit. For cuts and scrapes, clean the wound thoroughly with antiseptic wipes and cover it with a sterile bandage to prevent infection. For blisters, it's best to avoid popping them if possible; instead, cover them with a blister pad or bandage to protect the area from further irritation. Sprains and strains can be treated with the RICE method: rest, ice (if available), compression, and elevation. In remote areas where access to ice is limited, simply immobilizing the affected area and reducing movement can help alleviate pain and prevent further injury.

More serious injuries, such as deep cuts, broken bones, or severe allergic reactions, require immediate attention and may necessitate evacuation. If you or someone in your group experiences a major injury in a remote area, it's important to stabilize the person as best as you can and contact emergency services. Many wilderness travelers carry satellite communication devices, such as a Garmin inReach or SPOT, which allow them to send SOS messages and provide their exact GPS location to rescuers. These devices are highly recommended for anyone traveling far from established roads or trails, as they can make the difference in an emergency situation where there is no cell service.

Alaska's climate also presents its own set of health challenges, particularly for travelers who are not accustomed to cold weather or the state's rapidly changing conditions. Hypothermia is a serious risk in Alaska, especially in the winter months or in areas near glaciers and bodies of water where temperatures can drop quickly. Hypothermia occurs when the body loses heat faster than it can produce it, causing body temperature to drop to dangerously low levels. Early signs of hypothermia include shivering, confusion, slurred speech, and fatigue. If left untreated, hypothermia can be life-threatening.

To prevent hypothermia, it's essential to dress in layers and stay dry, as wet clothing can accelerate heat loss. In cold environments, always have a warm hat, gloves, and a waterproof outer layer to protect yourself from wind and rain. If someone in your group shows signs of hypothermia, it's important to act quickly. Move the person to a sheltered area, remove any wet clothing, and warm them up gradually by providing dry clothing, blankets, and warm fluids if possible. Avoid applying direct heat, such as a hot water bottle, as this can cause shock to the body.

Another cold-related health concern is frostbite, which occurs when skin and underlying tissues freeze due to exposure to cold temperatures. Frostbite typically affects the extremities, such as fingers, toes, ears, and nose. The affected area may feel numb and appear white or grayish in color. If you suspect frostbite, it's important to warm the affected area slowly, using body heat or warm (not hot) water. Avoid rubbing the skin, as this can cause further damage. In severe cases, frostbite can lead to permanent tissue damage, so it's important to seek medical attention as soon as possible.

While cold weather is a primary concern in Alaska, the summer months present different challenges, particularly for those traveling in mosquito-prone areas. Alaska is known for its large mosquito population, especially in wetland areas or near lakes and rivers. Mosquito bites can be more than just an annoyance—they can lead to infections if scratched excessively. To protect yourself from mosquitoes, it's a good idea to use insect repellent containing DEET or picaridin, wear long sleeves and pants, and consider using a mosquito net when camping.

Finally, staying healthy in Alaska means taking care of your general well-being during your trip. Make sure to stay hydrated, especially if you're participating in strenuous outdoor activities, and pay attention to signs of fatigue or dehydration. The long daylight hours in the summer can sometimes disrupt sleep patterns, so it's important to ensure you get enough rest to avoid exhaustion. If you're traveling in areas with limited access to clean water, consider bringing a water filter or purification tablets to ensure that your drinking water is safe.

Safety Tips for Outdoor Adventures: Precautions for hiking, wildlife encounters, and extreme weather

When preparing for outdoor adventures in Alaska, whether hiking, camping, or exploring the wild landscapes, safety must be your top priority. Alaska's stunning wilderness, rugged terrain, and abundant wildlife make it a dream destination for outdoor enthusiasts, but they also present unique risks that need careful consideration. The combination of unpredictable weather, remote locations, and encounters with wildlife requires a thoughtful approach to safety. Whether you're a seasoned adventurer or a first-time visitor, understanding the precautions necessary for hiking, dealing with wildlife encounters, and coping with extreme weather can help ensure that your experience is both safe and enjoyable.

One of the most important aspects of staying safe while hiking in Alaska is to plan thoroughly before setting out. The state's wilderness areas are vast, and many trails lead into remote regions with little or no signage, services, or cell reception. Before starting your hike, it's essential to research the area thoroughly. Know the length and difficulty of the trail, the terrain you'll encounter, and the expected weather conditions. It's also a good idea to familiarize yourself with any potential hazards specific to the region, such as steep drop-offs, river crossings, or unstable ground.

One of the first steps in planning a safe outdoor adventure is to tell someone about your plans. Always inform a friend, family member, or park ranger about your intended route, expected return time, and any alternate plans you might have. This ensures that someone knows where you are in case you don't return as scheduled, which is particularly important in Alaska, where many hiking trails lead deep into isolated areas. Leaving a detailed itinerary behind can be a lifesaving measure if you become lost or injured.

Bringing the right gear is also essential for a safe outdoor adventure in Alaska. Even for short hikes, you should carry basic supplies such as a map, compass or GPS device, plenty of water, snacks, a first-aid kit, and layers of clothing suitable for changing weather conditions. One of the most important pieces of gear to bring is a quality rain jacket or waterproof shell, as Alaska is known for sudden rainstorms, especially in coastal regions. Being wet can quickly lead to hypothermia, even in relatively mild weather, so staying dry is a key part of staying safe. Additionally, make sure to wear sturdy, waterproof hiking boots, as Alaska's trails can often be muddy, rocky, or uneven, and wet feet can lead to blisters and discomfort.

While hiking, always be aware of your surroundings. In Alaska, it's common to encounter wildlife, including large animals such as bears, moose, and wolves. Bear encounters are a particular concern, especially in areas known for high bear activity. Both black bears and grizzly bears are native to Alaska, and hikers should always be prepared to avoid surprising or provoking them. One of the most important safety measures when hiking in bear country is to make noise. Bears are naturally shy and will usually avoid humans if they know you're approaching. Talk loudly, clap your hands, or wear bear bells to alert animals to your presence as you move through dense forest or around blind corners where visibility is limited.

If you do encounter a bear while hiking, the way you respond depends on the situation. If the bear hasn't noticed you, the best course of action is to slowly and quietly back away, giving the bear plenty of space. If the bear does notice you, remain calm and do not run. Running can trigger a bear's instinct to chase, which is something you want to avoid at all costs. Instead, stand your ground, wave your arms to make yourself look bigger, and speak to the bear in a calm, firm voice. If the bear approaches, be prepared to use bear spray, a highly effective deterrent. Bear spray should be carried in an easily accessible location, such as on your belt or backpack strap, and you should know how to use it before you go hiking.

Another important safety tip in bear country is to practice proper food storage and waste management. Bears have an extremely sensitive sense of smell and are often attracted to food and garbage left by campers or hikers. If you're camping, make sure to store all food, trash, and scented items like toiletries in bear-proof containers or bear canisters. These canisters are designed to be carried in your backpack and are essential for preventing bears from getting into your supplies. At camp, never leave food unattended, and always clean up thoroughly after meals to avoid attracting wildlife. It's also recommended to cook and store food away from your sleeping area, at least 100 yards away, to reduce the risk of a bear coming near your tent at night.

Encounters with moose, while generally less dangerous than bear encounters, also require caution. Moose are common in many parts of Alaska, particularly near rivers and lakes, and they can be surprisingly aggressive if they feel threatened. Moose are most likely to charge when they are startled, particularly if they have calves with them. If you see a moose while hiking, it's best to give it a wide berth, moving slowly and quietly away from the animal. Never approach a moose, and be especially cautious during the fall rutting season when males can be more territorial.

In addition to wildlife, the weather in Alaska can pose significant risks, particularly if you're unprepared for sudden changes. Alaska's weather is famously unpredictable, and it's not uncommon for a sunny day to turn into rain, snow, or heavy winds within a few hours. Always check the weather forecast before heading out and be prepared for a variety of conditions, regardless of the season. Even in summer, temperatures can drop quickly in the evening or at higher elevations, so it's essential to pack warm clothing and extra layers, even if the day starts off mild.

Hypothermia is one of the most serious risks associated with outdoor activities in Alaska, especially for those who are not accustomed to cold or wet conditions. Hypothermia occurs when your body loses heat faster than it can produce it, leading to dangerously low body temperatures. Early signs of hypothermia include shivering, confusion, slurred speech, and fatigue. To prevent hypothermia, it's important to stay dry and avoid prolonged exposure to cold temperatures or wind. If you get wet, change into dry clothes as soon as possible, and keep moving to generate body heat. If you're camping, make sure to bring a high-quality sleeping bag rated for cold temperatures, and sleep on an insulated pad to keep yourself warm and off the cold ground.

If you suspect that someone in your group is developing hypothermia, it's important to act quickly. Move the person to a sheltered area, provide them with dry clothing, and offer warm fluids if available. Wrap them in blankets or a sleeping bag, and if possible, insulate their body from the ground using extra clothing or a sleeping pad. In severe cases, medical attention may be required, so it's important to assess the situation and be prepared to call for help if necessary.

Navigating Alaska's terrain can also present challenges, especially in mountainous regions where the risk of avalanches, rockfalls, or river crossings may be present. When hiking in areas with steep or unstable terrain, always pay attention to trail conditions and watch for signs of loose rocks, mudslides, or other hazards. In mountainous areas during the winter or spring, be aware of avalanche risks, which can be triggered by changes in temperature, new snowfall, or even the movement of hikers. If you're traveling in avalanche-prone areas, consider bringing avalanche safety gear such as a beacon, probe, and shovel, and make sure you know how to use them.

For those hiking or camping near rivers or lakes, water safety is another important consideration. Many of Alaska's rivers are fast-moving and extremely cold, even in the summer, so it's important to be cautious when crossing or walking near them. Never attempt to cross a river without assessing its depth and current speed. If the water is fast-moving or higher than your knees, it's usually best to find an alternate route or wait until the water level drops. Cold water immersion can lead to hypothermia quickly, so always be cautious when near water.

Emergency Contacts and Resources: Hospitals, ranger stations, and emergency hotlines

When traveling in Alaska, especially in remote or wilderness areas, having access to emergency contacts and knowing where to turn for help in case of an emergency is essential. Alaska's vast size and limited infrastructure, particularly outside the major cities, make it crucial for visitors to be prepared and aware of the resources available to them. Whether you're facing a medical emergency, getting lost on a hike, or dealing with a wildlife encounter, knowing where to find the nearest hospital, how to contact ranger stations, and what emergency hotlines to call can save valuable time and potentially lives. Being well-prepared in this regard is not just about having peace of mind; it's about being responsible in a state where help may be far away and difficult to reach.

Alaska's medical infrastructure is concentrated in its urban centers, such as Anchorage, Fairbanks, and Juneau, which serve as the primary hubs for emergency and hospital services. Anchorage, being the largest city in the state, has the most comprehensive medical facilities. The Providence Alaska Medical Center in Anchorage is the largest hospital in the state, providing emergency care, surgery, and specialized medical services. It is well-equipped to handle a wide range of medical emergencies and offers 24-hour care. Another major medical facility in Anchorage is the Alaska Regional Hospital, which also provides a full suite of emergency services and is staffed with highly trained medical personnel.

In Fairbanks, the Fairbanks Memorial Hospital serves as the primary healthcare facility for the region, offering emergency services and medical care for residents and visitors alike. For those in Alaska's capital city, Juneau, the Bartlett Regional Hospital is the main medical facility providing emergency care. These hospitals are located in the more populated parts of Alaska, and their emergency departments are fully capable of treating a wide variety of conditions, from trauma to illness.

However, if you're traveling outside of these cities and into more rural or remote areas, it's important to be aware that medical facilities may not be readily available, and in many cases, patients need to be transported by air to reach a hospital.

In smaller towns and villages, healthcare options are more limited, often consisting of community health clinics rather than fully equipped hospitals. These clinics can provide basic medical services and handle minor injuries or illnesses, but they are not equipped to deal with serious trauma or life-threatening conditions. For travelers in rural areas, it's important to know the location of the nearest clinic or health center in case of a medical emergency. Many small towns in Alaska rely on the services of regional health corporations that operate these clinics, such as the Yukon-Kuskokwim Health Corporation or the Southeast Alaska Regional Health Consortium.

When traveling in more remote parts of Alaska, such as the Arctic, the Aleutian Islands, or the Interior, emergency medical services are often provided by air ambulance services. In cases where ground transportation is not possible due to the terrain or distance, patients may need to be evacuated by helicopter or fixed-wing aircraft to a hospital in Anchorage, Fairbanks, or another regional medical center. Air medical services like LifeMed Alaska and Guardian Flight are commonly used for medical evacuations in the state. These services can be lifesaving, but it's important to be aware that air ambulance transport can be expensive, particularly for those without adequate health or travel insurance. Many travelers to Alaska opt for travel insurance that covers emergency medical evacuations to ensure they are financially protected in case of an emergency.

In addition to hospitals and clinics, ranger stations play a crucial role in ensuring the safety of visitors to Alaska's national parks and wilderness areas. Alaska is home to some of the most remote and wild national parks in the United States, including Denali National Park, Wrangell-St. Elias National Park, and Gates of the Arctic National Park. Ranger stations in these parks are staffed by park rangers who can provide valuable information about trail conditions, wildlife safety, and weather forecasts. They are also the first point of contact in case of an emergency in the park.

If you're planning to hike, camp, or engage in other outdoor activities in one of Alaska's national parks, it's a good idea to stop by a ranger station before setting out. Rangers can provide important safety advice, issue backcountry permits, and help you plan your trip based on current conditions. In an emergency, such as getting lost, a serious injury, or an encounter with dangerous wildlife, park rangers are trained in search and rescue operations and can coordinate efforts to find and assist you. Many parks have designated backcountry patrols, and rangers in these roles can be instrumental in providing emergency assistance.

Emergency hotlines are another critical resource for travelers in Alaska, particularly for those in remote areas where local services may be limited. In the event of an emergency, calling 911 is the standard protocol in Alaska, just as it is in the rest of the United States. When calling 911, it's important to provide as much information as possible about your location, particularly if you are in a remote area with no clear landmarks. In many parts of Alaska, cell phone service may be limited, especially in wilderness areas or on remote highways, so it's important to note that 911 may not always be reachable by cell phone. In such cases, satellite communication devices, such as a Garmin inReach or a SPOT messenger, are invaluable tools for contacting emergency services.

For those venturing into Alaska's backcountry or more isolated regions, having a satellite phone or personal locator beacon (PLB) can be a lifesaving investment. These devices allow you to send distress signals or communicate with search and rescue teams even in areas without cell phone reception. Many outdoor enthusiasts carry these devices for peace of mind, as they provide a direct line to emergency services, even in the most remote parts of the state. If you trigger an SOS alert with a satellite device, rescue teams will be dispatched to your GPS location, making it much easier for them to locate you in case of an emergency.

In addition to 911 and satellite emergency services, there are several other important hotlines to be aware of when traveling in Alaska. Poison control, for example, is an essential resource for anyone who may ingest something harmful while hiking or camping. The national Poison Control hotline is 1-800-222-1222, and it operates 24/7, providing advice on how to handle exposure to poisonous plants, animals, or chemicals. This is especially important in Alaska, where there are many wild plants and berries that can be mistaken for edible varieties but are toxic if consumed.

For those visiting coastal areas or engaging in activities on the water, the U.S. Coast Guard plays a critical role in emergency response. Alaska's waters are known for being cold and unpredictable, and boating or fishing accidents can occur quickly. The U.S. Coast Guard provides search and rescue services for those in distress on the water, and they can be contacted via VHF marine radio on Channel 16. If you are planning to spend time on a boat or kayak, it's important to have a working marine radio and know how to contact the Coast Guard in case of an emergency.

Another valuable resource in Alaska is the Alaska State Troopers, who are responsible for law enforcement and search and rescue operations across the state. Given Alaska's vast size and limited infrastructure, the State Troopers often cover large areas that include remote villages, highways, and wilderness regions. They can assist with a wide variety of emergencies, from lost hikers to vehicle accidents. The Alaska State Troopers can be reached via their local offices, or you can contact them through 911 for emergencies.

Mental health support is another critical aspect of staying healthy and safe while traveling. If you or someone in your travel party experiences a mental health crisis, Alaska's Careline is a resource available to provide support. The Careline Crisis Intervention hotline is 1-877-266-HELP (4357), and it operates 24/7, offering confidential support for people in emotional distress or those experiencing suicidal thoughts. Mental health crises can occur in response to the stresses of travel, isolation, or unexpected challenges, and having access to this kind of support can be an important part of staying safe while on the road.

Finally, it's important to familiarize yourself with the region-specific resources available in the areas you plan to visit. For example, if you're traveling along Alaska's highways, keep in mind that many stretches are extremely remote, with no gas stations, rest areas, or cell service for miles. The Alaska Department of Transportation provides real-time road conditions through its 511 hotline, which can give you updates on road closures, weather conditions, and any hazards you might encounter during your drive. This service is especially useful during the winter months when snow and ice can make driving more dangerous.

Travel Insurance: Why it's important and what to consider for Alaskan trips

Travel insurance is one of the most important yet often overlooked aspects of planning a trip to Alaska. Given Alaska's unique geography, unpredictable weather, and the nature of outdoor adventures that many travelers seek, having comprehensive travel insurance can provide a safety net that protects you from unexpected events, whether it's a medical emergency, trip interruption, or a need for evacuation from remote wilderness areas. In such a rugged and vast environment, where infrastructure can be sparse and distances between towns or medical facilities can be vast, travel insurance becomes a crucial tool for ensuring peace of mind and financial protection.

Alaska is known for its wilderness, extreme conditions, and outdoor opportunities that range from hiking and kayaking to skiing and dog sledding. These activities, while thrilling, come with inherent risks, and accidents or emergencies can happen even to the most prepared travelers. From sudden weather changes that cause flight cancellations to injuries that require evacuation from remote areas, travel insurance is essential for managing the unexpected. Travelers visiting Alaska often underestimate how isolated some parts of the state are. Unlike traveling in the continental United States or Europe, where help is often nearby, many areas of Alaska are only accessible by boat, plane, or on foot. If something goes wrong, the costs of medical care, evacuation, or trip changes can add up quickly.

One of the primary reasons travel insurance is so important for trips to Alaska is the potential for medical emergencies. Alaska's wilderness and outdoor activities can sometimes lead to injuries or health issues, and while the state does have excellent medical facilities in larger cities like Anchorage, Fairbanks, and Juneau, the reality is that in more rural or remote areas, medical care can be limited. In case of a serious injury or illness, evacuation to a hospital may be necessary, and this can often involve a costly airlift or transportation via a small plane. Medical evacuations, particularly from remote wilderness areas, can cost thousands or even tens of thousands of dollars. Without travel insurance, these expenses fall directly on the traveler.

Even for those with existing health insurance, it's important to note that many health plans, especially those based outside the United States, do not cover medical evacuations, and some may not cover out-of-network care in Alaska's remote regions. Travel insurance can fill in these gaps, ensuring that you're covered for medical expenses, hospital stays, and emergency evacuations, regardless of where you are in Alaska. If you're planning to engage in high-risk activities like glacier hiking, backcountry skiing, or bear viewing in remote regions, making sure your travel insurance includes coverage for adventure sports and evacuations is crucial.

Beyond medical coverage, another key aspect of travel insurance for an Alaskan trip is protection against trip cancellations or interruptions. Alaska's weather is notoriously unpredictable, and it's not uncommon for flights, ferries, and other forms of transportation to be delayed or canceled due to bad weather. This is especially true in the winter months, when snowstorms can cause major disruptions to travel plans, or in the summer, when fog can delay flights in and out of remote towns. If you've booked expensive excursions, cruises, or tours, a last-minute cancellation can lead to significant financial losses. Travel insurance with trip cancellation and interruption coverage ensures that you can recover non-refundable costs if your trip is delayed or canceled due to weather, illness, or other unforeseen events.

Trip interruption insurance also covers situations where you need to cut your trip short because of an emergency back home, such as a family illness or a natural disaster. In these cases, travel insurance can reimburse you for the unused portion of your trip, as well as any additional costs associated with rebooking flights or transportation to get home sooner than expected. For travelers visiting Alaska on a longer trip, particularly those exploring multiple destinations or engaging in activities with multiple bookings, trip interruption coverage offers an extra layer of protection.

For those traveling to Alaska by cruise, which is a popular way to explore the state's coastline, travel insurance is equally important. Cruises can be affected by mechanical issues, weather delays, or even outbreaks of illness on board. If your cruise is delayed, canceled, or rerouted, travel insurance can reimburse you for the costs of missed excursions, additional accommodations, or other expenses incurred due to the disruption. Many cruise lines offer insurance packages through third-party providers, but it's important to review the details carefully to ensure that the coverage is comprehensive and meets your needs.

Another factor to consider when purchasing travel insurance for an Alaskan trip is baggage loss or delay. Given the distances and remote nature of many destinations in Alaska, baggage can sometimes be delayed, especially if you are taking connecting flights through smaller airports. For example, if your luggage is delayed while you're on a remote fishing trip or wilderness lodge excursion, you may need to purchase replacement gear or clothing to continue your activities. Travel insurance with baggage delay or loss coverage can help reimburse you for the cost of these essential items. Similarly, if your baggage is lost entirely, the insurance will cover the cost of replacing your belongings.

For those bringing expensive equipment like cameras, drones, or outdoor gear, it's also important to check whether your travel insurance offers coverage for lost, stolen, or damaged personal belongings. Alaska's outdoor adventures often involve activities like kayaking, fishing, or hiking in rugged terrain, where there's a higher risk of damage to gear. Comprehensive travel insurance will cover these losses, ensuring that you're not left with the financial burden of replacing expensive equipment.

When choosing travel insurance for your trip to Alaska, there are several key factors to consider. First and foremost is the level of medical coverage offered. As mentioned earlier, Alaska's remote locations can make medical evacuations necessary, and these can be extremely costly. Look for a policy that offers at least $100,000 to $500,000 in medical coverage, depending on the nature of your trip and the activities you plan to undertake. Policies that include emergency medical evacuation coverage are essential for anyone venturing into Alaska's more isolated regions.

Another important consideration is whether the policy includes coverage for high-risk activities. Many standard travel insurance policies exclude coverage for activities like heli-skiing, glacier hiking, or mountaineering, all of which are popular in Alaska. If you're planning to engage in these types of activities, make sure to choose a policy that specifically includes coverage for adventure sports. Many insurance providers offer add-ons or specialized policies that cater to adventure travelers, ensuring that you're protected during more high-risk excursions.

When reviewing policies, pay close attention to the fine print regarding trip cancellation and interruption coverage. It's important to understand what types of events are covered and under what circumstances you can file a claim. For example, while many policies cover cancellations due to illness or severe weather, some may not cover changes due to minor delays or less extreme weather conditions. Be sure to select a policy that matches the level of coverage you need based on the time of year you're traveling and the specific risks associated with your trip.

It's also a good idea to check whether the travel insurance policy offers 24-hour emergency assistance. This can be particularly important in Alaska, where medical or logistical help may not always be immediately available. A good travel insurance provider will have a 24/7 helpline that can assist you in finding the nearest hospital, arranging medical evacuations, or coordinating alternative travel plans if your trip is interrupted. Having access to this kind of support can make a huge difference in a stressful situation, especially when you're far from major cities or traveling through areas with limited infrastructure.

For international travelers visiting Alaska, it's essential to confirm that the travel insurance policy offers worldwide coverage, including coverage within the United States. Not all international insurance policies automatically cover travel to the U.S., and it's important to ensure that you're fully covered during your time in Alaska. Additionally, make sure that your travel insurance includes adequate liability coverage, especially if you're planning to rent a car, RV, or boat during your trip. Liability coverage protects you in case of accidents or damage caused to others, and it's a key component of a comprehensive travel insurance plan.

Chapter 8

Accommodations

Hotels and Resorts: The best options for luxury and mid-range travelers

When it comes to selecting accommodations in Alaska, travelers are met with a range of options that cater to different needs, preferences, and budgets. Whether you're seeking a luxurious experience amidst breathtaking natural surroundings or prefer comfortable and reliable mid-range accommodations, Alaska offers an array of hotels and resorts that ensure a memorable stay. The state's unique geography, where major cities are separated by vast stretches of wilderness and small towns, means that finding the right place to stay often depends on the kind of experience you're looking for. This guide will cover some of the best options for luxury and mid-range travelers, helping you navigate the choices available, from high-end resorts to more affordable yet comfortable hotels.

For travelers seeking luxury, Alaska offers a variety of upscale hotels and resorts, many of which are set in pristine locations that allow guests to experience the beauty of the state in style and comfort. Luxury in Alaska doesn't just mean high-thread-count sheets or spa services although those are available but often also includes private excursions, guided wilderness experiences, and exclusive access to remote locations. These luxury accommodations frequently combine the rustic charm of Alaska's wilderness with modern conveniences, creating a perfect blend of adventure and relaxation.

One of the most iconic luxury options in Alaska is the Alyeska Resort, located in Girdwood, about 40 miles southeast of Anchorage. Nestled in the Chugach Mountains, the resort is renowned for its breathtaking views and year-round outdoor activities. In the winter, Alyeska is a premier ski destination, offering some of the best skiing and snowboarding in Alaska, while in the summer, guests can hike, bike, or take the scenic tram to the top of Mount Alyeska for panoramic views of the surrounding area. The resort itself offers luxurious rooms and suites, many of which feature stunning views of the surrounding mountains or Turnagain Arm. In addition to its outdoor activities, Alyeska Resort is known for its top-notch dining experiences, including the award-winning Seven Glaciers Restaurant, which sits at the top of the tram and offers fine dining with spectacular views.

Another excellent luxury option for those looking to combine nature and comfort is the Tutka Bay Lodge, located on a remote stretch of Kachemak Bay near Homer. This boutique lodge is only accessible by boat or floatplane, adding to the sense of exclusivity and adventure. Tutka Bay Lodge is known for its personalized service, gourmet cuisine, and immersive outdoor experiences, such as kayaking, bear viewing, and guided hiking. The lodge has just a handful of cabins, each tastefully designed with a blend of rustic elegance, offering a peaceful retreat surrounded by Alaska's wild beauty. Tutka Bay Lodge is particularly popular with couples seeking a romantic getaway or travelers looking for a once-in-a-lifetime adventure in a remote but luxurious setting.

For travelers seeking a high-end experience in Alaska's interior, the Chena Hot Springs Resort is an excellent choice. Located about 60 miles from Fairbanks, this resort offers a unique combination of natural hot springs, upscale accommodations, and access to the northern lights. Chena Hot Springs is famous for its geothermal pools, where guests can relax in naturally heated waters while surrounded by Alaska's stunning wilderness. In the winter, the resort is one of the best places to view the aurora borealis, thanks to its remote location and minimal light pollution. The resort also offers a range of luxury cabins and rooms, many of which feature private hot tubs or fireplaces. For those interested in eco-tourism, Chena Hot Springs is home to a renewable energy project, including a geothermal power plant, making it an ideal choice for environmentally conscious travelers.

While Alaska offers several high-end resorts and boutique lodges, there are also plenty of mid-range hotels that provide excellent accommodations for travelers who want comfort without breaking the bank. Many of these mid-range options are located in the state's larger cities, such as Anchorage, Fairbanks, and

Juneau, but they still offer convenient access to the wilderness and outdoor activities that draw people to Alaska in the first place.

In Anchorage, one of the best mid-range hotel options is the Hotel Captain Cook. This historic hotel is a local favorite, offering a blend of traditional Alaskan charm and modern amenities. Located in the heart of downtown Anchorage, the Hotel Captain Cook is within walking distance of shops, restaurants, and attractions like the Anchorage Museum and the Tony Knowles Coastal Trail. Despite its central location, the hotel also offers sweeping views of the surrounding mountains and Cook Inlet. Rooms are comfortable and well-appointed, and the hotel features several on-site dining options, including fine dining at the Crow's Nest. For mid-range travelers who want to experience a touch of luxury while staying within budget, the Hotel Captain Cook is an excellent choice.

In Juneau, the Silverbow Inn is a standout option for mid-range travelers. This boutique hotel is located in the heart of downtown Juneau, just steps from the waterfront and the Alaska State Capitol. The Silverbow Inn combines modern comforts with a quirky, artistic flair, making it a popular choice for travelers looking for something unique. Each room is individually decorated with a blend of contemporary and Alaskan styles, and the hotel offers a complimentary breakfast each morning featuring local ingredients. In addition to its great location, the Silverbow Inn is known for its rooftop hot tub, where guests can relax while taking in views of the mountains and the Gastineau Channel.

For those exploring Fairbanks, the Pike's Waterfront Lodge is a fantastic mid-range option. Situated along the Chena River, just minutes from downtown Fairbanks, this lodge offers comfortable accommodations with a touch of Alaskan charm. Pike's Waterfront Lodge is especially popular during the winter months, as it offers excellent views of the northern lights right from the property. The lodge features cozy rooms and cabins, many with river views, and offers amenities such as a sauna, fitness center, and outdoor fire pits. Pike's also has an on-site restaurant, Pike's Landing, which serves hearty Alaskan fare like salmon and king crab, making it a great choice for travelers who want to experience local cuisine without venturing too far from their accommodations.

In addition to hotels in the larger cities, there are also mid-range lodges and inns located in some of Alaska's more remote but popular destinations. For example, in Seward, the Harbor 360 Hotel is a well-regarded option for travelers visiting Kenai Fjords National Park. Located right on the waterfront, Harbor 360 offers comfortable rooms with views of the harbor, Resurrection Bay, and the surrounding mountains. The hotel is an ideal base for exploring the park's glaciers and wildlife, and it offers convenient access to boat tours, fishing charters, and hiking trails. Guests can enjoy the indoor pool and hot tub after a day of exploring, and a complimentary breakfast is provided each morning.

Another great mid-range choice in a more remote area is the Denali Bluffs Hotel, located near Denali National Park. This hotel offers rustic but comfortable accommodations with beautiful views of the Alaska Range. The Denali Bluffs Hotel is a popular choice for visitors to Denali who want to stay close to the park's entrance while enjoying modern comforts. The hotel offers shuttle service to the park and nearby attractions, and guests can relax after a day of exploring with a meal at the on-site restaurant, which specializes in local Alaskan ingredients.

For travelers looking to explore Alaska's coastal regions, the Lands End Resort in Homer is a mid-range option that offers stunning ocean views at an affordable price. Located at the end of the Homer Spit, the resort offers direct access to the beach and provides breathtaking views of Kachemak Bay and the surrounding mountains. Rooms range from standard options to oceanfront suites, and the resort features an on-site restaurant, the Chart Room, which serves fresh seafood and other local dishes. The Lands End Resort is a great choice for travelers who want to experience Homer's natural beauty while staying in comfortable and reasonably priced accommodations.

Hostels and Budget Stays: Affordable accommodations for backpackers and budget-conscious travelers

When traveling to Alaska, a destination known for its breathtaking wilderness and vast open spaces, finding affordable accommodations can significantly impact how much you get out of your trip. For backpackers and budget-conscious travelers, it's especially important to choose accommodations that are not only affordable but also strategically located near the activities and sights you want to explore. Thankfully, Alaska offers a wide range of options for those seeking budget stays. From hostels in the cities to more rustic lodges and inns in smaller towns, you can find accommodations that offer comfort, convenience, and access to Alaska's incredible outdoors without straining your wallet. By understanding what different places have to offer, their price ranges, and how to reach them from major transportation hubs, you can ensure that your trip stays within budget while providing an enriching experience.

One of the best-known options for affordable accommodations in Anchorage is the Alaska Backpackers Inn. This hostel is popular with solo travelers and backpackers who are looking for budget-friendly lodging in the state's largest city. Located just a short walk from downtown Anchorage, it provides easy access to local attractions, such as the Anchorage Museum, and restaurants, as well as public transportation for exploring the surrounding areas. The Alaska Backpackers Inn offers a variety of room types, ranging from dormitory-style bunk beds to private rooms, making it suitable for both solo travelers and small groups. The dorm rooms are the most budget-friendly option, with prices generally starting around $30 per night, depending on the season. Private rooms offer more privacy at a higher cost, typically around $70 to $90 per night. The hostel features a shared kitchen, which allows guests to cook their meals, reducing the need to eat out frequently, and a communal lounge area where travelers can connect and share experiences. From Ted Stevens Anchorage International Airport, the hostel is about a 15-minute drive, and you can easily reach it by taking a taxi, rideshare service, or public bus. Booking can be done through popular hostel booking sites, such as Hostelworld, or directly on the hostel's website.

Another excellent budget option in Anchorage is the Bent Prop Inn & Hostel of Alaska. Situated in the heart of downtown Anchorage, this hostel is a convenient choice for travelers who want to be close to the city's main attractions without paying for an expensive hotel. The Bent Prop Inn offers both dormitory beds and private rooms, making it suitable for various types of travelers, whether you're traveling solo or with a small group. Dormitory beds are usually priced between $35 and $45 per night, while private rooms can range from $80 to $100, depending on the season. The hostel provides free Wi-Fi, a communal kitchen, and a comfortable lounge where guests can relax after a day of exploring. Its central location makes it easy to walk to many of Anchorage's popular spots, including local cafes, shops, and parks. To get to the Bent Prop Inn from Anchorage International Airport, you can take a taxi or rideshare service, which takes about 15 minutes. Public transportation is also an option, with bus routes connecting the airport to downtown. You can book your stay at Bent Prop Inn through major booking platforms, or by calling the hostel directly to check availability.

Fairbanks, Alaska's second-largest city, also offers great options for budget-conscious travelers. Billie's Backpackers Hostel is a standout choice for those visiting this northern hub. Known for its warm, welcoming atmosphere and rustic charm, Billie's Backpackers Hostel is a favorite among budget travelers looking to explore Fairbanks and its surrounding areas. The hostel provides dormitory-style accommodations with shared bathrooms, and the rates are typically around $35 to $45 per night, depending on the time of year. One of the highlights of Billie's Backpackers Hostel is its large common area, where travelers can gather to share meals and stories. There's also an outdoor space for enjoying Alaska's long summer days or relaxing in the crisp winter air. The hostel is located near the University of Alaska Fairbanks, making it an excellent base for exploring the city's cultural attractions, such as the Museum of the North. During the winter months, Billie's Backpackers Hostel is a great spot for viewing the northern lights, as the area is relatively free from light pollution. To reach the hostel from Fairbanks International Airport, it's a short 10- to 15-minute drive via taxi or rideshare. Booking at Billie's can be done through hostel booking websites or by contacting the hostel directly.

If you're heading toward Denali National Park, there are budget accommodation options that provide close access to this incredible wilderness without the hefty price tag of more upscale lodges. One such option is the Denali Mountain Morning Hostel and Cabins, located near the park's entrance. This rustic but comfortable hostel offers both private cabins and shared dormitory-style accommodations, with prices for dorm beds typically starting around $35 per night and private cabins ranging from $80 to $120, depending on the season. This hostel is particularly popular with adventurous travelers looking to explore Denali's vast landscapes on a budget. The hostel's communal spaces, including a shared kitchen and cozy lounge, create a social atmosphere where guests can connect with others and plan hikes or wildlife tours. The hostel provides a shuttle service to the park entrance, making it easy to access Denali's famous bus tours and backcountry trails. To get to the Denali Mountain Morning Hostel, most travelers fly into Fairbanks or Anchorage and take a bus or train to the park's entrance. The hostel provides detailed directions on its website, and booking can be done directly through their online reservation system.

Further south, in Seward, which serves as a gateway to Kenai Fjords National Park, budget travelers can find affordable accommodations at the Moby Dick Hostel & Lodging. This simple but well-maintained hostel is located near the waterfront, offering easy access to boat tours, kayaking trips, and hikes in the nearby park. The Moby Dick Hostel features dormitory rooms starting at $30 to $40 per night, as well as private rooms for around $70 to $90. The hostel has a shared kitchen, which allows guests to prepare their own meals and save on dining expenses, and a communal living area where travelers can relax after a day of outdoor adventures. Seward is a popular destination for budget-conscious travelers who want to explore Alaska's fjords and glaciers without spending a fortune on accommodation. To reach the Moby Dick Hostel from Anchorage, many travelers take the scenic Alaska Railroad, which runs daily routes between the two cities, or drive the roughly 2.5-hour journey along the Seward Highway. Booking the hostel can be done through online platforms or by contacting the hostel directly.

For travelers seeking even more remote and rustic experiences, Alaska offers public-use cabins managed by the Alaska State Parks and the U.S. Forest Service. These cabins are often located in breathtaking locations along rivers, lakes, or in the middle of vast wilderness areas. They offer basic amenities, such as bunk beds, a wood stove, and an outhouse, but the real appeal is the chance to stay in remote, pristine areas at an affordable price. Prices for these cabins are generally low, typically ranging from $25 to $75 per night, depending on the cabin's location and size. These cabins must be reserved in advance, and many are accessible only by hiking, boat, or floatplane, adding an adventurous element to your stay. Travelers looking for a truly off-the-grid experience can book these cabins through the Alaska

State Parks or U.S. Forest Service websites. It's important to plan carefully, as many of the cabins are in remote locations that require detailed logistics to reach, including renting boats or arranging transportation with local operators.

Cabins and Lodges: Rustic accommodations close to nature

One of the most well-known and highly regarded places for rustic accommodations is Denali Backcountry Lodge, located deep within Denali National Park. This lodge offers guests a chance to stay in cozy cabins surrounded by stunning views of mountains and wilderness, while also providing access to some of the best hiking and wildlife viewing opportunities in Alaska. The Denali Backcountry Lodge is located about 92 miles inside the park, and to get there, guests must take a guided bus trip along the Denali Park Road, which is an adventure in itself. The lodge offers both private cabins and common areas where guests can relax, dine, and share stories of their experiences. Prices for stays at the Denali Backcountry Lodge typically range from $600 to $800 per night, depending on the season and the type of accommodation. The lodge is all-inclusive, meaning that meals, guided hikes, and other activities are included in the price. To reach Denali Backcountry Lodge from Fairbanks or Anchorage, most travelers take the Alaska Railroad or drive to the park entrance, from which the lodge arranges transportation deeper into the park.

Bookings can be made directly through the lodge's website or by contacting Denali National Park lodges.

For travelers seeking a more remote and off-the-grid experience, the Kachemak Bay Wilderness Lodge, located across Kachemak Bay from the town of Homer, is an excellent choice. Accessible only by boat or floatplane, this lodge offers an unparalleled opportunity to disconnect from the modern world and immerse yourself in Alaska's wild beauty. The lodge features rustic yet comfortable cabins with views of the bay or the surrounding forest, and it provides a range of activities, such as kayaking, hiking, and wildlife viewing. The lodge's intimate size ensures a peaceful experience, with a focus on personalized service and local, organic meals. Prices for a stay at the Kachemak Bay Wilderness Lodge are generally between $500 and $700 per night, including meals and activities. To get there, travelers typically fly into Anchorage, then drive or take a shuttle to Homer, where the lodge provides transportation across the bay. Booking can be done directly through the lodge's website or by contacting the lodge for more information about available dates and packages.

Further south, in the heart of the Kenai Peninsula, the Kenai Fjords Glacier Lodge offers a unique lodge experience set within the Kenai Fjords National Park. This eco-lodge is the only accommodation within the park, and it provides guests with a front-row seat to stunning glaciers, fjords, and abundant wildlife, including seals, sea lions, and whales. The lodge's rustic cabins are comfortable and thoughtfully designed, blending into the natural surroundings while offering guests modern comforts, including private bathrooms and electricity. Prices for a stay at Kenai Fjords Glacier Lodge typically range from $700 to $900 per night, with all meals, guided tours, and activities included in the price. To reach the lodge, travelers fly into Anchorage and drive or take a shuttle to Seward, where they board a boat for a scenic cruise through Resurrection Bay to the lodge. The lodge can be booked through Alaska Wildland Adventures, a company that operates the lodge and offers a variety of tour packages.

For travelers looking to experience Alaska's famous interior, the Borealis Basecamp near Fairbanks offers a rustic but luxurious experience, combining the charm of a cabin stay with the chance to view the northern lights in comfort. The Borealis Basecamp features dome-shaped cabins with large, clear windows that allow guests to stargaze and watch the aurora from the warmth of their beds. While the basecamp is remote and surrounded by wilderness, it also provides a range of amenities, including private bathrooms, cozy furnishings, and a dining area where guests can enjoy meals made from local ingredients. Prices range from $400 to $700 per night, depending on the season and the specific cabin type. The basecamp is located about 25 miles from Fairbanks, making it accessible by car or shuttle from Fairbanks International Airport. Travelers can book their stay directly through the Borealis Basecamp website or by contacting their booking office for more details.

Another great option for travelers seeking a remote but comfortable cabin experience is the Tonglen Lake Lodge, located just outside the entrance to Denali National Park. This lodge offers individual cabins that blend rustic charm with modern amenities, providing a peaceful retreat after a day of exploring the park's wilderness. The cabins at Tonglen Lake Lodge feature handcrafted furniture, private decks, and beautiful views of the surrounding forest and mountains. Prices for a stay at Tonglen Lake Lodge typically range from $350 to $500 per night, depending on the season and cabin type. The lodge also offers an on-site cafe that serves locally sourced meals, as well as yoga classes and art workshops, making it a perfect choice for travelers who want to combine adventure with relaxation. To reach Tonglen Lake Lodge, travelers usually fly into Fairbanks or Anchorage and take a train, shuttle, or drive to Denali National Park. Booking can be done through the lodge's website or by contacting the lodge directly to inquire about availability and packages.

In addition to these lodges and cabins, there are many public-use cabins scattered throughout Alaska's state parks and national forests. These rustic cabins provide a more rugged experience, often located in remote areas that are accessible only by hiking, boating, or flying in. Public-use cabins are typically very basic, with minimal amenities, such as wood stoves, bunks, and outhouses, but they offer a unique way to experience Alaska's wilderness on a budget. Prices for public-use cabins are generally affordable, ranging from $25 to $75 per night, depending on the location and size of the cabin. These cabins can be booked through the Alaska State Parks website or the U.S. Forest Service, and reservations should be made well in advance, especially during the summer months.

Camping in Alaska: Campsites, RV parks, and wilderness camping options

Camping in Alaska is a truly unique experience that offers a chance to immerse yourself in some of the world's most untouched and awe-inspiring natural landscapes. Whether you're pitching a tent in a designated campsite, parking your RV in a scenic park, or embarking on a wilderness camping adventure, Alaska provides a wide range of options to suit every kind of traveler. For those seeking to experience the state's pristine beauty up close, camping offers not only a cost-effective way to explore Alaska but also an intimate connection with its mountains, forests, glaciers, and wildlife. Whether you are a seasoned camper or someone just looking to try it for the first time, knowing where to camp, what amenities are available, and how to book your stay will help you make the most of your Alaskan adventure.

One of the most accessible and popular places to camp in Alaska is Denali National Park. With its iconic views of Denali (Mount McKinley), the tallest peak in North America, and a vast expanse of wilderness, this park draws adventurers from around the world. The park offers several developed campgrounds, including the Riley Creek Campground, which is located near the park entrance. Riley Creek is a great option for campers who want to explore the park while still having access to basic amenities such as running water, flush toilets, and a visitor center. The campground can accommodate both tent campers and RVs, with designated sites for each. Prices for camping at Riley Creek range from $15 to $28 per night, depending on the site type. To reach Riley Creek, travelers typically fly into Fairbanks or Anchorage and then drive or take the Alaska Railroad to the park entrance. The campground is just a few minutes from the park's visitor center, making it a convenient option for those looking to explore Denali's vast network of hiking trails and wildlife viewing areas. You can reserve a spot at Riley Creek Campground through the Denali National Park website or by calling the park directly.

For those who want to combine the beauty of Alaska's coast with the convenience of a well-maintained campground, the Seward Waterfront Park in the town of Seward is a fantastic choice. Situated along the shores of Resurrection Bay, this campground offers stunning views of the bay, mountains, and glaciers. It's a prime location for those who want to explore Kenai Fjords National Park, take a boat tour to see wildlife and glaciers, or enjoy a day of fishing. The Seward Waterfront Park is a simple but well-organized campground that provides basic amenities such as restrooms and potable water. The sites are open and spacious, with options for both tents and RVs. Prices are affordable, ranging from $20 to $40 per night, depending on the type of site and whether it includes electrical hookups. To reach Seward Waterfront Park, most travelers fly into Anchorage and then drive the scenic 2.5-hour journey along the Seward Highway, one of the most beautiful drives in Alaska. While reservations are not required for the park, it's a good idea to arrive early during the summer months to secure a spot, as the campground operates on a first-come, first-served basis.

If you're looking for a more remote camping experience but still want the comfort of a designated campground, the K'esugi Ken Campground in Denali State Park is an excellent option. This campground offers a more rustic feel than those found in Denali National Park, but it still provides basic amenities such as vault toilets, fire pits, and picnic tables. The highlight of K'esugi Ken is its incredible views of Denali on clear days, as well as its access to the park's extensive network of hiking trails. Camping here costs around $16 to $20 per night, making it a very affordable option for those who want to explore the Alaskan wilderness without venturing too far off the beaten path. To reach K'esugi Ken, travelers usually fly into Anchorage and drive about two hours north along the George Parks Highway. The campground is well-signed and easy to find, offering both drive-in sites and walk-in tent sites for those who prefer a bit more solitude. Reservations can be made through the Alaska State Parks website, though some sites are available on a first-come, first-served basis.

For campers who are traveling by RV and want to experience Alaska's rugged coastline, the Homer Spit Campground in the town of Homer is a wonderful choice. Located on the narrow strip of land known as the Homer Spit, this campground offers direct access to the beach, as well as stunning views of Kachemak Bay and the surrounding mountains. It's a great base for exploring Homer's art galleries, fishing charters, and wildlife tours. The Homer Spit Campground has sites for both tents and RVs, with full hookups available for RV travelers. Prices range from $35 to $45 per night, depending on the site type and amenities. While the campground is popular with RVers, tent campers are also welcome, and the open layout provides plenty of space to enjoy the views. To get to the Homer Spit Campground, most travelers fly into Anchorage and then drive about 4.5 hours along the Sterling Highway, passing through the scenic Kenai Peninsula. Reservations can be made through the campground's website or by calling ahead, as it can fill up quickly during the summer months.

For those seeking a true wilderness camping experience, backcountry camping in Wrangell-St. Elias National Park is hard to beat. This massive park, the largest in the United States, offers endless opportunities for adventurers to explore glaciers, mountains, and vast, untouched wilderness. Unlike designated campgrounds, backcountry camping in Wrangell-St. Elias requires a higher level of preparation and self-sufficiency, as there are no facilities, and campers must pack in and pack out all their gear and supplies. The cost for a backcountry permit is free, but campers must check in with a ranger station before heading out. While there are no marked campsites, some of the most popular areas for backcountry camping include the Nabesna and McCarthy Roads, which offer access to some of the park's most remote and beautiful landscapes. To get to Wrangell-St. Elias, travelers usually fly into Anchorage and then drive or take a shuttle to the park's entrance points at either Nabesna or McCarthy. Because this is a true wilderness experience, it's important to be prepared with bear-proof food containers, proper camping gear, and knowledge of Leave No Trace principles. Detailed maps and permits can be obtained at the park's visitor centers or ranger stations.

Camping in Alaska offers a unique way to connect with nature, whether you're staying in a well-maintained campground or venturing into the wilderness. The state's campgrounds and RV parks provide a variety of options for travelers looking to experience its stunning landscapes while enjoying the basic comforts of a campsite. Meanwhile, for the more adventurous, wilderness camping in the state's vast parks offers a once-in-a-lifetime chance to truly get away from it all. Booking a campsite in Alaska is typically straightforward, with many locations offering online reservation systems through the National Park Service, Alaska State Parks, or directly through the campground's website. Whether you're planning to camp near the coast, in the interior, or deep in the wilderness, the right preparation and understanding of the area can make your

Alaskan camping experience one that you'll never forget.

Unique Stays: Igloos, yurts, and other one-of-a-kind Alaskan lodgings

In a state as wild and unique as Alaska, the lodging options are equally extraordinary. Travelers looking to experience Alaska in a way that goes beyond the traditional hotel or cabin stay will find a wealth of one-of-a-kind accommodations that enhance the experience of exploring the Last Frontier. From staying in cozy yurts surrounded by wilderness to sleeping under the northern lights in an igloo-shaped lodge, these unique stays offer the chance to connect with Alaska's natural beauty in a setting that is as memorable as the adventures themselves. Whether you're looking to sleep in a handcrafted treehouse, a traditional yurt, or an ice-like igloo, there are a variety of options that cater to different tastes and budgets, ensuring that your stay in Alaska is unlike anything you've experienced before.

One of the most unusual and sought-after stays in Alaska is the Borealis Basecamp, located just outside Fairbanks. This unique lodging experience allows guests to sleep in clear-roofed igloo-shaped domes, offering an unobstructed view of the stars and, if you're lucky, the northern lights. These domes are equipped with modern amenities such as heating, private bathrooms, and comfortable beds, allowing you to enjoy the natural beauty of the Alaskan wilderness without sacrificing comfort. Borealis Basecamp is particularly popular during the winter months, when guests can witness the aurora borealis from the warmth of their dome. Prices for a stay at Borealis Basecamp typically range from $400 to $700 per night, depending on the season and type of dome. To reach the basecamp, most travelers fly into Fairbanks International Airport, which is about 30 minutes away by car. Borealis Basecamp offers shuttle services from the airport or Fairbanks, and you can book your stay directly through their website or by contacting them for more information about availability and packages.

For those looking to experience the traditional Alaskan wilderness in a more rustic setting, Mongolian-style yurts provide an ideal mix of simplicity and comfort. Across Alaska, there are several yurt accommodations that allow guests to immerse themselves in nature while staying in a cozy, eco-friendly space. One standout option is the Aialik Bay Yurt in Kenai Fjords National Park, accessible only by boat or kayak from the town of Seward. Surrounded by glaciers and wildlife, this off-the-grid yurt offers an intimate and adventurous way to explore the park. Guests need to be prepared for a more rugged experience, as the yurt does not have running water or electricity, but it is equipped with a wood stove, bunk beds, and cooking utensils. Prices for a stay at the Aialik Bay Yurt are around $125 per night, making it an affordable option for adventurous travelers. Getting to the yurt requires a boat ride from Seward, which is accessible by car or train from Anchorage.

Reservations can be made through local tour operators or the Alaska State Parks website.

Another unforgettable option for unique stays in Alaska is the Treehouse at Eagle's Nest in Homer. This handcrafted treehouse is built among the treetops, offering panoramic views of Kachemak Bay and the surrounding mountains. Designed with rustic charm and thoughtful craftsmanship, the treehouse features a cozy loft bed, a small kitchenette, and an outdoor deck where guests can take in the views and the sounds of nature. The treehouse is perfect for couples or solo travelers looking for a quiet retreat with easy access to hiking, kayaking, and wildlife viewing. Prices range from $150 to $250 per night, depending on the season. Homer is accessible by car or shuttle from Anchorage, a drive of about 4.5 hours along the scenic Sterling Highway. To book the Treehouse at Eagle's Nest, travelers can use popular vacation rental platforms or contact the property directly for more information on availability.

For an Alaskan experience that combines luxury with immersion in nature, the Sheldon Chalet offers a one-of-a-kind stay atop a glacier in Denali National Park. This remote lodge is accessible only by helicopter and offers sweeping views of Denali and the surrounding mountains. The Sheldon Chalet provides guests with an unparalleled sense of isolation and adventure, while still offering high-end amenities such as gourmet meals, private guides, and luxurious bedding. The chalet accommodates up to 10 guests at a time, making it an intimate and exclusive experience. Prices for a stay at the Sheldon Chalet are in the luxury range, typically starting at around $2,300 per night, per person, but this includes meals, guided activities, and transportation from Anchorage. The adventure of arriving at the Sheldon Chalet by helicopter, combined with its unique location atop a glacier, makes it a bucket-list destination for travelers looking to experience Alaska in a completely unique way. Reservations can be made through the Sheldon Chalet website, and trips are often booked well in advance due to its exclusivity.

For travelers seeking an authentic backcountry yurt experience that's both affordable and comfortable, the K'esugi Ken Yurt in Denali State Park offers a great option. These yurts provide a more comfortable camping experience while allowing guests to enjoy the spectacular views of Denali and the surrounding wilderness. The yurts are equipped with wooden floors, bunk beds, and a wood stove, making them suitable for year-round stays. K'esugi Ken is particularly popular with hikers, as the park's trails offer easy access to some of the best hiking routes in the area. Prices for the yurts range from $80 to $120 per night, making it an affordable and memorable option for travelers seeking a balance between rustic and comfort. To get to K'esugi Ken, travelers typically fly into Anchorage and drive about two hours north along the George Parks Highway. The yurt sites can be reserved through the Alaska State Parks website, and it's recommended to book well in advance, especially during the summer months.

These unique stays offer travelers a chance to experience Alaska in a way that goes beyond the ordinary. Whether you're sleeping in a cozy igloo dome under the northern lights, relaxing in a treehouse with sweeping views of the ocean, or staying in a remote yurt deep in the wilderness, these accommodations are designed to enhance your connection with Alaska's natural beauty. Booking these stays is typically straightforward, with many properties offering online reservation systems or direct booking options through their websites. Whether you're seeking a once-in-a-lifetime luxury experience or a more affordable adventure close to nature, Alaska's unique lodgings provide a memorable and deeply immersive way to experience the state's incredible landscapes and wildlife.

Chapter 9

Getting Around Alaska

By Road

Traveling by road in Alaska is one of the best ways to experience the state's vast, awe-inspiring landscapes at your own pace. Renting a car or an RV offers the freedom to explore remote areas, scenic byways, and national parks that may not be accessible by other means. Whether you are driving along the iconic Seward Highway or venturing into the more rugged interior, being behind the wheel allows you to stop whenever a stunning view, a wildlife sighting, or an interesting roadside attraction catches your eye. However, driving in Alaska requires some special considerations, from understanding driving distances to being prepared for rapidly changing weather and wildlife encounters on the road. By planning carefully and taking into account the unique conditions of Alaska's highways, you can ensure a safe and memorable journey through one of the world's most remarkable places.

Renting a car in Alaska is straightforward, with several major rental companies operating in key cities like Anchorage, Fairbanks, and Juneau. Anchorage, the largest city and a popular starting point for many travelers, offers numerous rental options at the Ted Stevens Anchorage International Airport, making it easy to pick up your vehicle as soon as you arrive. Companies like Hertz, Avis, and Budget have a presence at the airport, offering a range of vehicle types depending on your travel needs. For those planning to explore beyond the main highways or venture into more remote areas, renting an all-wheel-drive or four-wheel-drive vehicle is highly recommended, as it provides better traction and control on gravel roads or in rough weather conditions. Renting a car typically costs between $50 and $100 per day, depending on the size of the vehicle, the season, and the length of your rental period. Larger vehicles, such as SUVs, are more expensive but may be necessary if you're traveling with a group or if you plan to camp or carry a lot of gear.

If you are arriving in Fairbanks, car rentals are available at Fairbanks International Airport and from rental agencies in the city. The process is much the same as in Anchorage, and for those heading into Denali National Park, the Arctic Circle, or other northern destinations, renting a car gives you flexibility that scheduled tours or public transportation cannot offer. Fairbanks is about 120 miles from Denali's entrance, and many travelers use this route as part of their itinerary, stopping along the way to take in the dramatic scenery. When driving in this area, it's important to note that distances between services—such as gas stations and rest stops—can be long, so it's essential to plan your fuel stops and carry plenty of supplies, especially if you're venturing further into the wilderness.

Driving distances in Alaska are often longer than most visitors expect, due to the state's sheer size and the relative isolation of many towns and attractions. For instance, the drive from Anchorage to Fairbanks, two of Alaska's main cities, is approximately 360 miles and can take about 7 hours without any significant stops. While the highways are generally well-maintained, they can be narrower than what you might be used to in other states, with limited shoulders and frequent stretches that run through remote, mountainous areas. It's important to budget extra time for your road trips to account for stops, road conditions, and the slower pace required in some areas.

One of the most popular drives in Alaska is the journey along the Seward Highway, which stretches for about 125 miles from Anchorage to the small coastal town of Seward. This scenic route is known for its breathtaking views of mountains, fjords, and glaciers, with numerous pull-offs where you can stop to take photos or explore hiking trails. Along the way, you may also spot wildlife, such as eagles, moose, and even beluga whales in the waters of Turnagain Arm. The road is paved and generally easy to drive, but it can be winding in parts, so it's important to stay alert, especially if you're driving in poor weather. Driving this route can take anywhere from 2.5 to 4 hours, depending on how often you stop to take in the views.

For those planning to drive the Glenn Highway, which runs from Anchorage east to Glennallen and beyond, expect a similar mix of stunning scenery and long stretches of road between towns. This route offers access to Wrangell-St. Elias National Park, the largest national park in the United States, and is a gateway to some of Alaska's most rugged and remote terrain. When driving this highway, it's essential to be prepared for unpredictable weather, as conditions can change rapidly, especially in the mountains. Carrying extra water, food, and blankets in your vehicle is always a good idea, as help can be far away in case of a breakdown.

Highway safety is a critical consideration when driving in Alaska. The state's remote roads and variable conditions mean that drivers need to be more self-reliant than they might be in other parts of the country. One of the key things to be aware of is the presence of wildlife on or near the road. Moose, in particular, are a common sight in Alaska, and they can pose a significant hazard, especially at dawn or dusk when visibility is lower. Moose are large and can be difficult to see, so always drive cautiously, especially in areas where wildlife crossing signs are posted. If you do see a moose on or near the road, slow down and give the animal plenty of space, as they may be unpredictable in their movements.

Another safety tip is to be aware of Alaska's unique weather conditions. In the summer, driving is generally easier, with long daylight hours and clear roads. However, in the shoulder seasons (spring and fall), and especially in winter, road conditions can become treacherous due to snow, ice, and limited daylight. If you're planning to drive in the winter, make sure your vehicle is equipped with winter tires, and carry chains if you're heading into mountainous regions. Check the weather forecast before setting out, and always inform someone of your travel plans, especially if you're driving into more remote areas where cell phone reception may be limited.

Road maintenance in Alaska can also impact your travel plans. The state's extreme weather and rugged terrain mean that construction or repairs are common, particularly during the summer months when the roads are most accessible. Be prepared for potential delays, especially on longer routes, and always follow the posted speed limits in construction zones. Additionally, some of Alaska's highways, such as the Dalton Highway, are not fully paved and can be rough in parts, so driving at a slower speed and using a high-clearance vehicle is often necessary.

For those planning to drive an RV, Alaska is particularly accommodating. There are numerous RV parks and campgrounds along the state's highways, many of which offer full hookups, scenic views, and easy access to nearby attractions. Renting an RV is a popular option for families or groups who want to combine transportation and lodging in one, and there are several companies in Anchorage, Fairbanks, and other cities that specialize in RV rentals. Prices vary depending on the size of the RV and the rental period, but you can expect to pay between $150 and $300 per day. Driving an RV in Alaska requires extra caution due to the narrow roads and sharp turns, particularly on scenic routes like the Seward Highway or the Richardson Highway. Always make sure your RV is properly equipped with safety features and that you are comfortable handling a larger vehicle in varying conditions.

Booking a rental car or RV for your Alaskan road trip is typically done online through major rental agencies, but it's important to book well in advance, particularly during the summer months when demand is high. Many agencies also offer optional insurance coverage, which is highly recommended, especially if you plan to drive in more remote or rugged areas where road conditions can be unpredictable.

By Air: Regional flights and bush planes for accessing remote areas

Traveling by air in Alaska is one of the most efficient and sometimes the only way to access the state's remote regions. With Alaska's immense size and challenging geography, regional flights and bush planes are essential for reaching small communities, wilderness areas, and national parks that are otherwise unreachable by road. Alaska is home to thousands of isolated villages and outposts, many of which are spread across rugged mountains, vast forests, and pristine coastlines. These areas rely heavily on air travel for supplies, mail, and transportation, making small aircraft a lifeline for local residents as well as adventurous travelers. For those looking to explore the more untouched corners of Alaska, flying in a small regional plane or bush plane is not just a convenience, but often an unforgettable experience in itself, offering unparalleled views of the state's vast wilderness and wildlife.

Alaska's regional airlines, such as Ravn Alaska, Alaska Seaplanes, and Grant Aviation, operate regular flights between major cities and smaller communities. These airlines provide an essential service by connecting isolated villages and towns with regional hubs like Anchorage, Fairbanks, and Juneau. For travelers, these regional flights offer the ability to quickly reach areas that would otherwise take days to get to by boat or overland routes, if they can be reached at all. In many cases, flying is the only viable way to access remote national parks, coastal communities, and wilderness lodges.

One of the busiest air hubs in Alaska is Ted Stevens Anchorage International Airport, which not only serves as the main entry point for visitors from the lower 48 states and beyond, but also acts as a launching pad for smaller regional flights. From Anchorage, you can catch flights to places like Kodiak Island, Nome, Kotzebue, and even the Arctic communities of Barrow and Prudhoe Bay. These flights are typically on smaller regional aircraft that can land on short runways or gravel airstrips. For example, Ravn Alaska offers daily flights from Anchorage to Bethel, Dillingham, and Homer, with flight times ranging from one to two hours depending on the destination. Prices for these regional flights can vary greatly depending on the distance, season, and demand, but you can generally expect to pay anywhere from $150 to $400 for a one-way ticket on a regional carrier.

For travelers heading into Alaska's interior or northern regions, Fairbanks International Airport is another key hub. From here, regional flights can take you into the heart of the Arctic, as well as to smaller towns along the Yukon River and into the wilderness areas of Gates of the Arctic National Park. One of the highlights of flying into these remote areas is the chance to see Alaska's wilderness from above, whether it's spotting caribou herds on the tundra or catching a glimpse of the northern lights during a night flight. Regional airlines based in Fairbanks, such as Wright Air Service and Frontier Flying Service, specialize in providing access to places like Bettles, Coldfoot, and Fort Yukon, where road access is either limited or non-existent. These flights are an important way for adventurers to reach remote hiking trails, fishing spots, or backcountry lodges. Costs for flights to these areas can range from $200 to $500 or more, depending on the distance and seasonality.

One of the most iconic experiences in Alaska is flying in a bush plane. Bush planes are small, sturdy aircraft that are designed to land on rough terrain, gravel bars, frozen lakes, or even open water in the case of floatplanes. These planes are often the only way to reach certain parts of Alaska, such as the Brooks Range, isolated islands, or small, off-grid lodges deep in the wilderness. For travelers who want to explore Alaska's more remote national parks, hiring a bush plane is often the only way to get there, and the journey is as much a part of the adventure as the destination itself.

For example, Wrangell-St. Elias National Park, the largest national park in the United States, has few roads that penetrate its vast wilderness. To truly explore this park, many visitors opt to fly in with a bush pilot from the town of McCarthy or Chitina. These flights allow visitors to reach remote parts of the park where they can camp, hike, or fish in complete solitude. Bush planes are typically chartered by the hour, and prices vary depending on the size of the plane, the distance flown, and the number of passengers. Chartering a bush plane can cost anywhere from $250 to $800 per hour, but the experience of flying over glaciers, mountain peaks, and untouched wilderness is often considered priceless by those who take the journey.

In Southeast Alaska, seaplanes are a common mode of transportation, especially for reaching small communities scattered across the islands and coastal fjords. From Juneau, the state capital, Alaska Seaplanes operates daily flights to nearby towns like Haines, Skagway, and Gustavus, the gateway to Glacier Bay National Park. These seaplane flights offer a scenic and efficient way to travel between the islands, providing breathtaking views of the Tongass National Forest, tidewater glaciers, and the marine wildlife that inhabits the coastal waters. Seaplanes are also used for more adventurous outings, such as guided bear viewing tours or fishing trips in remote areas. A typical seaplane flight from Juneau to Gustavus takes about 30 minutes, and prices generally range from $150 to $300, depending on the route and time of year.

Flying in Alaska, whether on a regional airline or in a bush plane, is often more than just a means of transportation. The experience of flying over the vast Alaskan wilderness is a highlight for many travelers, providing a bird's-eye view of the dramatic landscapes that make the state so unique. Pilots in Alaska are known for their skill and expertise, particularly those who fly bush planes into remote areas. These pilots often act as guides as well as pilots, sharing their knowledge of the land and pointing out interesting features from the air. Whether you're flying over the rugged mountains of the Alaska Range, the sweeping tundra of the Arctic, or the icy expanse of a glacier, the views from the air are nothing short of spectacular.

When planning to fly to remote areas of Alaska, it's important to be prepared for the unique conditions that come with traveling in such an isolated region. Weather can be unpredictable, and flights may be delayed or canceled due to poor visibility, high winds, or other conditions. It's always a good idea to build some flexibility into your travel plans, especially if you are flying into a remote area for activities like hiking, fishing, or camping. Additionally, because many small airstrips or landing areas in Alaska lack the infrastructure of larger airports, you may need to pack accordingly, bringing your own supplies, including food, water, and camping gear if necessary. Communication in remote areas can also be limited, so it's important to check whether your destination has cell phone reception or whether you'll need to bring a satellite phone or other form of emergency communication.

Booking regional flights or bush plane charters in Alaska can typically be done online or by contacting the airlines directly. For more specialized bush plane services, such as flights into national parks or remote lodges, many tour operators work in partnership with local bush pilots, and they can help arrange the logistics of your flight. When booking these flights, it's important to check weight limits for luggage, as smaller planes often have strict weight restrictions due to their size and fuel requirements. Be sure to confirm all details well in advance, especially during the peak summer tourist season, when demand for flights is high and availability can be limited.

By Train: The Alaska Railroad and scenic train routes

Traveling by train in Alaska offers a unique and unforgettable way to experience the state's vast and rugged landscapes. The Alaska Railroad, which stretches from the southern coastal city of Seward to the northern hub of Fairbanks, is one of the most scenic and iconic train routes in the world. As the train winds its way through mountains, forests, and along glacial rivers, passengers are treated to panoramic views of some of Alaska's most stunning scenery, all from the comfort of the train's observation cars. For those who want to explore Alaska without the stress of driving long distances or navigating remote roads, traveling by train is an excellent option. It allows you to sit back, relax, and fully appreciate the beauty of Alaska's wilderness, while also providing convenient access to many of the state's key attractions.

The Alaska Railroad is more than just a means of transportation; it is a historic journey that has been a part of Alaska's development since the early 20th century. Built to connect remote communities and open up the state's interior for economic development, the railroad played a crucial role in Alaska's history, and today it serves as both a passenger service and a freight line. For travelers, the Alaska Railroad provides a comfortable and scenic way to reach some of the state's most popular destinations, including Denali National Park, Anchorage, Fairbanks, and Seward. The train operates year-round, with expanded services during the summer months when tourism is at its peak. Whether you're taking the train to explore Alaska's backcountry, visit national parks, or simply enjoy the ride, the experience of traveling by rail is one of the highlights of any trip to the state.

One of the most popular and scenic routes on the Alaska Railroad is the Denali Star, which runs from Anchorage to Fairbanks with a stop at Denali National Park. This 12-hour journey covers over 350 miles and offers passengers breathtaking views of mountains, rivers, and valleys along the way. The train passes through the heart of Alaska's wilderness, and on clear days, passengers can catch glimpses of Denali, the tallest mountain in North America, as it towers over the landscape. One of the key advantages of traveling by train on this route is the ability to see wildlife, including moose, bears, and eagles, from the large windows of the train. For many passengers, the chance to see animals in their natural habitat is a highlight of the journey.

The Denali Star offers two classes of service: Adventure Class and GoldStar Service. Adventure Class provides comfortable seating with access to the open-air viewing deck, where passengers can step outside to take in the fresh air and enjoy unobstructed views of the landscape. GoldStar Service, which is the premium option, includes glass-domed ceilings that provide panoramic views, as well as an upper-level observation deck and gourmet meals served in the dining car. Prices for Adventure Class typically range from $150 to $250 per person, depending on the season and length of the journey, while GoldStar Service costs more, usually between $300 and $450 per person. The higher cost of GoldStar Service is offset by the enhanced viewing experience and additional amenities, making it a popular choice for those who want to make the most of their time on the train.

Another scenic route on the Alaska Railroad is the Coastal Classic, which runs from Anchorage to Seward along the shores of Turnagain Arm and through the Chugach Mountains. This route is widely regarded as one of the most beautiful train journeys in the world, thanks to its dramatic coastal scenery and the chance to see wildlife such as beluga whales, Dall sheep, and bald eagles. The journey takes about four hours one way and covers approximately 120 miles. Along the way, the train passes through lush forests, crosses rushing rivers, and skirts the edges of glaciers, providing a stunning backdrop for the entire trip. Seward, the endpoint of the Coastal Classic route, is the gateway to Kenai Fjords National Park, making this train ride an excellent option for travelers looking to explore the park's glaciers and marine wildlife.

The Coastal Classic operates from mid-May to mid-September, with daily departures during the summer months. As with the Denali Star, passengers can choose between Adventure Class and GoldStar Service, with prices ranging from $100 to $200 for Adventure Class and $250 to $350 for GoldStar Service. For those continuing on to explore Kenai Fjords National Park, there are several tour operators in Seward that offer boat tours and guided hikes, making it easy to combine a train journey with a day of adventure in the park. Many travelers opt to take the Coastal Classic as part of a round-trip journey, allowing them to experience both the train ride and a visit to the national park in one or two days.

For travelers looking to explore Alaska's interior, the Aurora Winter Train offers a unique experience during the winter months. Running from Anchorage to Fairbanks, this train operates from September to May and is known for its serene winter landscapes, where snow-covered forests and frozen rivers create a tranquil atmosphere. The Aurora Winter Train is a slower journey than its summer counterpart, as the train operates on a less frequent schedule, making it ideal for those looking to enjoy a leisurely trip through the Alaskan wilderness. This route is also a popular choice for travelers hoping to catch a glimpse of the northern lights, which can often be seen from the train during the darker winter months. While the winter service does not offer GoldStar Service, Adventure Class passengers still have access to the viewing deck and can enjoy the cozy atmosphere of the train as it makes its way through the snow-covered landscape.

Another noteworthy route is the Hurricane Turn Train, one of the last flag-stop services in the United States. Operating from Talkeetna to Hurricane, this train allows passengers to get on or off at any point along the route, making it a lifeline for residents in remote areas who rely on the train for transportation and supplies. The Hurricane Turn Train travels through some of the most rugged and isolated parts of Alaska, providing passengers with a glimpse into the lifestyle of those living off the grid. The train crosses over the Susitna River and offers stunning views of Denali, as well as the chance to see wildlife such as moose and bears. For travelers looking for a more intimate and off-the-beaten-path experience, the Hurricane Turn Train is a fascinating journey that showcases the role of the railroad in Alaska's remote communities. Tickets for this service are more affordable, typically costing around $50 to $100, and the experience is truly one of a kind.

When planning a journey on the Alaska Railroad, it's important to book tickets in advance, especially during the busy summer months when seats on popular routes can sell out quickly. Tickets can be purchased online through the Alaska Railroad website, by phone, or in person at the train stations in Anchorage, Fairbanks, and other major stops. Many travelers choose to combine train travel with other forms of transportation, such as renting a car or taking a cruise, to create a well-rounded Alaskan adventure. The Alaska Railroad also offers multi-day packages that include accommodations, guided tours, and activities, making it easy to plan a complete trip without the hassle of arranging each element separately.

For those interested in the history and heritage of the Alaska Railroad, several train routes offer commentary from knowledgeable guides who provide insights into the railroad's role in Alaska's development, the wildlife and geology of the regions you pass through, and the stories of the people who live along the tracks. This adds an educational component to the journey, enriching the experience and giving passengers a deeper understanding of the state's culture and history.

By Boat: Ferries, cruise lines, and sailing between towns and islands

Traveling by boat in Alaska offers a distinct and immersive way to experience the state's coastal landscapes, vast waterways, and the numerous islands that dot its coastline. With over 6,000 miles of coastline, Alaska's geography is uniquely suited to maritime travel, and many of its towns and villages can only be accessed by water or air. Whether you are exploring the Southeast Alaska archipelago, sailing through the Inside Passage, or journeying along the remote coastlines of the Aleutian Islands, boats provide not only essential transportation between towns but also an unforgettable way to connect with Alaska's natural beauty. From large cruise liners to the state-operated ferry system, and even personal sailboats, the options for maritime travel in Alaska are as varied as the landscapes they traverse. This method of travel provides a leisurely pace, allowing passengers to soak in the sights, encounter wildlife, and visit communities that remain largely untouched by the road system.

One of the most significant and accessible ways to travel by boat in Alaska is through the Alaska Marine Highway System (AMHS). The AMHS operates a fleet of ferries that connect over 30 communities across the southeastern, southcentral, and southwestern regions of the state. This ferry system serves as a lifeline for many of Alaska's coastal towns and islands, providing vital transportation for both residents and visitors. The ferry routes cover vast distances, stretching from Bellingham, Washington, in the continental U.S., up through Southeast Alaska, and all the way west to the Aleutian Islands. For travelers who want a more flexible and local experience than a cruise ship offers, the AMHS ferries provide a fantastic option. Passengers can bring their cars, bicycles, or RVs on board, allowing them to explore the towns they stop in with ease.

The Inside Passage, a famed waterway in Southeast Alaska, is one of the most popular routes on the AMHS. This route takes passengers through a series of islands and fjords, offering incredible views of rainforests, glaciers, and coastal wildlife, including humpback whales, sea lions, and orcas. The ferry system makes stops in key towns such as Ketchikan, Juneau, Sitka, Wrangell, and Petersburg, giving travelers the chance to disembark and explore these communities at their own pace. Tickets for the Alaska Marine Highway System vary depending on the route and the class of service, but prices are generally affordable, especially for those who prefer to travel more independently. For example, a one-way ticket from Juneau to Ketchikan typically costs between $100 and $150, depending on the season and whether you bring a vehicle.

Traveling by ferry also allows for the opportunity to camp on board, as some of the larger ferries offer solariums with reclining lounge chairs or deck space where passengers can pitch tents for the journey. This is a budget-friendly option for travelers who want to save on accommodation costs while enjoying a memorable maritime experience. Alternatively, there are cabins available for rent on longer routes, which provide a private space to sleep and store your belongings. The Alaska Marine Highway System is popular with both locals and tourists, so it's recommended to book tickets in advance, especially during the summer months when demand is highest. Reservations can be made through the AMHS website or by contacting their customer service directly.

For travelers seeking a more luxurious and all-inclusive maritime experience, Alaska's cruise industry offers a wide array of options. Cruise lines such as Holland America, Princess Cruises, and Norwegian Cruise Line operate large ships that sail along Alaska's coastlines, offering passengers a full-service vacation while exploring the state's wilderness. These cruises typically depart from Seattle or Vancouver and travel through the Inside Passage, making stops in Southeast Alaska's most popular destinations, such as Juneau, Skagway, and Glacier Bay. Cruises offer a unique blend of adventure and comfort, with onboard amenities that include fine dining, entertainment, spas, and guided shore excursions. While cruises are more expensive than ferry travel, they provide a hassle-free way to see many of Alaska's key sights in a relatively short amount of time.

Prices for Alaska cruises vary widely depending on the cruise line, the length of the voyage, and the type of accommodations selected. A typical seven-day cruise through the Inside Passage can range from $800 to $3,000 per person, depending on the stateroom category and the time of year. Most cruises include all meals, onboard entertainment, and access to amenities, with additional costs for shore excursions such as whale watching, glacier tours, or cultural visits to indigenous villages. For travelers who want to experience Alaska's coastal beauty in comfort and style, an Alaskan cruise provides an all-in-one vacation that combines luxury with the awe of the wilderness.

In addition to large cruise ships and ferries, smaller expedition-style vessels offer an intimate way to explore Alaska's remote and lesser-visited regions. Companies like UnCruise Adventures and Alaskan Dream Cruises operate smaller ships that cater to travelers looking for a more immersive and active experience. These ships typically carry fewer passengers, often fewer than 100, which allows for personalized service and the ability to navigate into smaller bays and coves that larger ships cannot access. These smaller vessels offer a more hands-on experience, with a focus on wildlife viewing, kayaking, and guided hikes into the wilderness.

Expedition cruises often include stops in less-visited areas such as the remote fjords of Prince William Sound, the glaciers of College Fjord, or the secluded inlets of Southeast Alaska's Tongass National Forest. These ships offer comfortable accommodations but are designed for adventure, with daily excursions that bring passengers up close to Alaska's natural wonders. Prices for these types of cruises are higher than for larger cruise ships, often ranging from $4,000 to $10,000 for a weeklong expedition. However, for travelers looking to experience Alaska in a more intimate and adventurous way, these cruises are well worth the investment.

For those who prefer more independence and flexibility, chartering a sailboat or private yacht is another way to explore Alaska's coastline. Charter companies based in towns like Juneau, Homer, and Seward offer a range of vessels for hire, from smaller sailboats to fully-crewed yachts. Sailing in Alaska is an adventure that offers both solitude and access to some of the state's most pristine and untouched areas. Chartering a boat allows travelers to set their own itinerary, exploring remote coves, fishing in quiet bays, or anchoring near glaciers for a truly up-close experience. While chartering a private boat is one of the more expensive options, it offers unmatched freedom and the chance to experience Alaska's waters in a truly personal way.

Prices for sailboat charters vary depending on the size of the boat, whether it is crewed or bareboat (where you captain the boat yourself), and the duration of the charter. A weeklong bareboat charter for a 30- to 40-foot sailboat can cost anywhere from $3,000 to $6,000, while a fully-crewed yacht charter with meals and amenities included can easily exceed $10,000. For experienced sailors, bareboat charters provide the ultimate adventure, but for those who prefer to leave the navigation to someone else, hiring a crewed yacht offers the same sense of freedom with the added comfort of a professional crew to handle the logistics.

Whether you are traveling by ferry, cruise ship, or private sailboat, Alaska's waters offer an unparalleled way to explore the state. The experience of sailing between towns and islands provides an intimate connection to the land and sea, allowing travelers to see parts of Alaska that are inaccessible by road. In addition to the stunning landscapes, maritime travel also offers incredible wildlife viewing opportunities. Humpback whales breaching near your boat, sea otters floating in kelp beds, and eagles soaring overhead are common sights on Alaska's coastal routes. For those who appreciate the slower pace and the peacefulness of the sea, traveling by boat is one of the most rewarding ways to experience Alaska.

Public Transport: Buses, shuttles, and other options for navigating cities and towns

Navigating Alaska by public transport offers an interesting and sometimes essential way to explore the state's cities, towns, and even some of its more remote areas. Alaska is known for its vast landscapes and low population density, and unlike many other places, the road system is limited, particularly in rural and isolated regions. Despite this, public transportation plays an important role in connecting people and providing an affordable way to get around, especially in more populated areas like Anchorage, Fairbanks, and Juneau. For travelers without access to a rental car or those looking to avoid the expense and logistics of driving in remote regions, Alaska's network of buses, shuttles, and other transportation options can provide a practical solution for exploring both urban and rural destinations.

In Anchorage, Alaska's largest city, public transportation is well-developed compared to other parts of the state. The Anchorage People Mover is the city's primary bus system, operating several routes that cover a large portion of the city and its surrounding neighborhoods. The People Mover is a convenient and affordable way to navigate Anchorage, particularly for travelers who are staying in the downtown area and want to explore places such as the Anchorage Museum, the Alaska Native Heritage Center, or popular parks like Kincaid Park and Earthquake Park. With routes running from early morning to late evening, the People Mover is especially useful for those who want to avoid the hassle of driving and parking in the city.

Bus fares for the Anchorage People Mover are relatively inexpensive, with a standard adult fare costing around $2 per ride. There are also discounted rates for seniors, students, and people with disabilities. In addition to single-ride fares, travelers can purchase day passes for unlimited travel, making it a cost-effective option for visitors who plan to use the bus system frequently during their stay. While Anchorage's bus system is generally reliable, it's important to note that buses run less frequently on weekends and holidays, so planning ahead is recommended. Bus schedules and route maps can be easily accessed online or at the downtown transit center, and there are mobile apps available to track bus arrivals in real-time.

For travelers looking to venture outside of Anchorage or explore destinations beyond the reach of the People Mover, shuttle services are a popular option. Many of Alaska's key tourist attractions, national parks, and popular hiking areas are accessible via shuttle buses, which are often operated by local tour companies or state park services. For example, if you're planning to visit Denali National Park, there are several shuttle services that run from Anchorage, Fairbanks, and other nearby towns directly to the park's entrance. The Denali Park Road itself is only accessible by shuttle buses during the summer months, as private vehicles are not allowed to travel beyond the first 15 miles of the road.

The Denali National Park shuttle system offers several types of buses, including narrated tours and non-narrated transit buses, which allow passengers to hop on and off at various points along the road. The transit buses are an excellent option for budget-conscious travelers or those who want the freedom to explore the park at their own pace, as these buses stop at different locations for hiking, wildlife viewing, or photography. Tickets for the Denali shuttle buses vary depending on the distance traveled, but fares generally range from $30 to $60 per person, making it a relatively affordable way to explore one of Alaska's most iconic national parks. Booking in advance is recommended, especially during the peak summer months, as the shuttles can fill up quickly.

In addition to the larger bus systems, smaller shuttle services play a vital role in connecting remote areas of Alaska. In towns like Seward, Homer, and Talkeetna, shuttle buses are a common way for tourists and residents to travel between key points of interest, particularly during the busy summer months when tourism peaks. These shuttle services often operate on flexible schedules, providing transportation between hotels, campgrounds, and popular attractions such as boat docks, hiking trails, and visitor centers. For example, in Seward, a popular destination for visitors exploring Kenai Fjords National Park, shuttles connect travelers with the harbor, the Alaska SeaLife Center, and nearby hiking trails like the Exit Glacier trail. Shuttles in these smaller towns are generally affordable, with one-way fares typically ranging from $5 to $10, depending on the route.

For those traveling between cities and towns, long-distance bus services are available as well. Companies like the Alaska Park Connection offer bus routes that link Anchorage with other major destinations, including Seward, Talkeetna, and Denali. These buses provide an alternative to driving or flying, especially for travelers who want to enjoy the scenic landscapes without the responsibility of navigating the roads themselves. The Alaska Park Connection buses are equipped with comfortable seating and large windows, making them a great option for sightseeing as you travel. Fares for long-distance bus routes typically range from $50 to $150, depending on the distance and season, and reservations can be made online in advance.

In Southeast Alaska, where many of the towns are located on islands or along the coast and are not connected to the road system, public transportation options are more limited, but shuttles and ferries fill the gap. In Juneau, the state's capital, Capital Transit operates a public bus system that provides transportation around the city, including routes to popular sites like

Mendenhall Glacier, downtown Juneau, and the ferry terminal. The bus system in Juneau is an inexpensive way to get around, with fares typically costing about $2 per ride. The buses are frequent and reliable, especially during the summer tourist season, when many visitors arrive by cruise ship or ferry.

In addition to local buses, Juneau and other towns in Southeast Alaska rely heavily on the Alaska Marine Highway System (AMHS), the state-operated ferry network. These ferries provide transportation between the coastal towns and islands of Southeast Alaska, including Ketchikan, Sitka, Haines, and Skagway. For travelers without a car, the ferries are an essential way to travel between communities and explore Southeast Alaska's remote beauty. While the AMHS ferries are primarily designed for longer-distance travel, they often serve as a convenient form of public transportation for residents and tourists alike. Fares for the ferries vary based on the route and whether or not you bring a vehicle on board, but tickets for walk-on passengers are typically affordable, with one-way fares ranging from $40 to $100, depending on the distance traveled.

In some of Alaska's smaller towns and villages, particularly those located off the road system, public transportation options may be more limited, but many places offer seasonal shuttle services that cater to tourists during the summer months. These shuttle buses often connect local airports, ferry terminals, and hotels with popular attractions, such as hiking trails, wildlife viewing areas, or boat docks. While these shuttles may not operate year-round, they provide a convenient way to get around during the peak travel season, especially for visitors who prefer not to rent a car.

In remote communities where public transportation is scarce, many travelers opt to use taxis or rideshare services, particularly in larger towns like Anchorage and Fairbanks. While rideshare options like Uber and Lyft are available in Anchorage, they may not be as widely used in smaller towns, so it's always a good idea to check in advance and plan accordingly. Taxis are generally available at airports and in downtown areas, but fares can be expensive for longer trips, especially in areas where distances between locations are significant.

For travelers who want to explore Alaska's wilderness without the hassle of driving, many private shuttle services and tour operators offer transportation to key outdoor destinations, such as hiking trails, fishing spots, and remote lodges. These shuttle services often run on a flexible schedule, allowing travelers to be dropped off at one location and picked up at another, making them ideal for multi-day hikes or outdoor adventures. For example, in the Kenai Peninsula, several shuttle companies provide transportation between towns like Seward, Homer, and Cooper Landing, as well as access to popular hiking trails like the Resurrection Pass Trail. Prices for these shuttles vary, but they generally range from $30 to $100, depending on the distance and the specific service.

Chapter 10

Top Destinations and Attractions

Anchorage

Anchorage, the largest city in Alaska, is a vibrant and dynamic destination that offers a perfect blend of modern amenities and access to breathtaking natural landscapes. Located on the southern coast of Alaska, at the edge of Cook Inlet and nestled between the Chugach Mountains and the Pacific Ocean, Anchorage is both a gateway to the Alaskan wilderness and a bustling urban center with rich cultural, historical, and recreational offerings. With a population of nearly 300,000 people, Anchorage serves as the primary hub for business, transportation, and tourism in the state, while also being home to some of the most beautiful and accessible wilderness areas in Alaska. Whether you're interested in exploring the great outdoors, learning about Alaska's history and indigenous cultures, or enjoying world-class dining, Anchorage has something to offer for every type of traveler.

Getting to Anchorage is relatively straightforward, as the city is well connected by air, road, and sea. Ted Stevens Anchorage International Airport is the main point of entry for most visitors to the city, with direct flights from many major cities in the lower 48 states, as well as international flights from destinations like Canada and

Europe. The airport is located just a few miles from downtown Anchorage, making it easy to reach the city center by taxi, rideshare, or the local bus system. For those traveling by road, Anchorage is accessible via the Alaska Highway, which connects the state to Canada and the rest of the United States. Many visitors choose to drive the scenic Seward Highway if coming from towns like Seward or Homer, or the Glenn Highway if traveling from places like Palmer or Glennallen. Additionally, Anchorage is a key stop on the Alaska Railroad, which provides scenic train travel to and from other destinations such as Denali National Park, Fairbanks, and Seward.

Once you've arrived in Anchorage, there is no shortage of things to do, see, and experience. The city offers a wide array of must-see attractions, many of which highlight the unique blend of urban life and wilderness that defines Anchorage. One of the first places that visitors should explore is the Anchorage Museum, located in the heart of downtown. This world-class museum provides a comprehensive look at the history, art, and culture of Alaska, with exhibits ranging from indigenous artifacts to contemporary art installations. The museum also features a planetarium, where visitors can learn about the northern lights and the night sky in Alaska, and the Smithsonian Arctic Studies Center, which showcases a remarkable collection of Native Alaskan cultural items. A visit to the Anchorage Museum offers a deep dive into the history and identity of Alaska, making it a must-see for anyone interested in understanding the region.

Another essential stop in Anchorage is the Alaska Native Heritage Center, a cultural institution dedicated to preserving and sharing the traditions and stories of Alaska's indigenous peoples. Located just a short drive from downtown, the Heritage Center features exhibits, demonstrations, and performances that highlight the rich cultural heritage of Alaska's Native groups, including the Tlingit, Yupik, and Inupiaq peoples. Visitors can tour life-sized replicas of traditional indigenous dwellings, watch Native dance performances, and participate in hands-on activities such as beadwork or tool-making. The center provides an invaluable opportunity to learn about the diverse cultures that have shaped Alaska's history for thousands of years.

For outdoor enthusiasts, Anchorage is an absolute paradise, offering a wide range of activities that make the most of the city's stunning natural surroundings. One of the most popular activities in Anchorage is hiking, with trails that cater to all levels of experience and fitness. The Tony Knowles Coastal Trail is a favorite among locals and visitors alike, offering 11 miles of scenic, paved pathways along the coastline of Cook Inlet. The trail begins near downtown Anchorage and winds its way through parks, forests, and wetlands, providing breathtaking views of the water and, on clear days, distant mountains like Denali. The trail is also an excellent spot for wildlife viewing, with the chance to see moose, eagles, and even beluga whales in the inlet.

For those seeking a more challenging hike, Flattop Mountain in Chugach State Park is one of the most popular day hikes in the area. The trail to the summit of Flattop offers panoramic views of Anchorage, the Alaska Range, and the surrounding wilderness. It's a steep climb, but the rewards are well worth the effort, and on a clear day, the views from the top are truly spectacular. For those not keen on hiking all the way to the summit, there are several lookout points along the trail that still offer fantastic vistas.

In addition to hiking, Anchorage is a gateway for wildlife and glacier tours. A short drive south of the city along the scenic Seward Highway will take you to the Alaska Wildlife Conservation Center, where you can see animals such as bears, moose, bison, and musk ox in a natural setting. The conservation center is dedicated to the protection and rehabilitation of Alaska's wildlife and provides visitors with an up-close look at some of the state's most iconic animals. Further along the highway is Portage Glacier, where you can take a boat tour on Portage Lake to see the glacier up close and watch for calving icebergs.

Anchorage is also known for its thriving culinary scene, with a diverse array of restaurants that cater to a wide range of tastes. Seafood is a major highlight of dining in Anchorage, given Alaska's proximity to some of the richest fishing waters in the world. Many local restaurants serve fresh-caught salmon, halibut, and crab, often prepared in inventive ways that highlight the flavors of the region. One standout is Simon & Seafort's, a classic Anchorage seafood restaurant that has been a favorite for decades. Located downtown with views of

Cook Inlet, Simon & Seafort's offers dishes like Alaskan king crab legs, seared scallops, and cedar plank salmon, all served in a warm and welcoming atmosphere.

For those looking to try something a bit different, Moose's Tooth Pub and Pizzeria is an Anchorage institution, serving up some of the best pizza in the state. With a creative menu that includes everything from traditional pepperoni to inventive combinations like smoked salmon with dill cream cheese, Moose's Tooth has earned a reputation for quality and flavor. The pub also features a rotating selection of craft beers, many of which are brewed locally, making it a great place to relax and enjoy a casual meal after a day of exploring.

For a true taste of Alaska's wilderness, The Crow's Nest is a must-visit. Located atop the Hotel Captain Cook, this fine dining restaurant offers an elegant menu featuring Alaskan seafood and game, paired with an extensive wine list. The Crow's Nest is known not only for its exceptional cuisine but also for its stunning views of the surrounding mountains and water, making it a perfect choice for a special night out in Anchorage.

For those interested in the local arts scene, Anchorage offers a variety of galleries and performance venues that showcase both local and international talent. The Anchorage Concert Association hosts a wide range of performances throughout the year, including theater, music, and dance, while the Alaska Center for the Performing Arts is home to the Anchorage Symphony Orchestra, Anchorage Opera, and other performing arts organizations. In the summer, the city's downtown area comes alive with events like the Anchorage Market & Festival, an open-air market where you can find everything from local crafts to fresh produce and live music.

Anchorage is also the perfect base for winter activities. When the snow falls, the city becomes a hub for skiing, snowshoeing, and dog sledding. Hilltop Ski Area, located just outside of downtown, offers a convenient place for skiing and snowboarding, while nearby Alyeska Resort in Girdwood provides more challenging slopes for avid skiers. For those looking to experience the thrill of dog sledding, several operators offer tours that allow you to ride through the snow-covered wilderness behind a team of Alaskan huskies. Winter also brings the chance to witness the northern lights, and many visitors choose to head just outside the city to get away from the light pollution and take in the spectacular natural light show.

Juneau: Exploring the capital city – historic sites, whale watching, and more

Juneau, Alaska's capital city, is a destination unlike any other in the United States. Nestled between towering mountains and the waters of the Inside Passage, Juneau offers a unique blend of natural beauty, rich history, and cultural experiences that make it a must-visit for anyone exploring Alaska. As the second-largest city in Alaska by area, Juneau encompasses a vast expanse of wilderness, but its urban heart is compact and easy to explore, filled with historic sites, museums, and vibrant local culture. Located in Southeast Alaska, Juneau is part of the Tongass National Forest, the largest temperate rainforest in the world, which adds to the city's lush, green surroundings. While the city itself is modern and welcoming, it is also remote in its own way: Juneau is only accessible by boat or plane, as no roads connect the city to the rest of the state or mainland North America. This sense of isolation, combined with the city's spectacular setting, creates a truly special atmosphere for visitors.

Getting to Juneau may seem a bit daunting, but it's actually quite straightforward. Most travelers arrive by air, with regular flights to Juneau International Airport from major cities such as Seattle, Anchorage, and smaller Southeast Alaskan towns. Alaska Airlines is the primary carrier serving the region, offering several daily flights to and from Juneau. The airport is located just 8 miles from downtown, and getting to the city center is easy via taxi, shuttle, or rental car. For those who prefer to travel by sea, the Alaska Marine Highway System operates ferries that connect Juneau to other Southeast Alaska communities as well as Bellingham, Washington. Ferries offer a scenic, if slower, way to reach the capital, and are particularly popular with travelers looking for a more leisurely journey or those bringing vehicles to the city. Additionally, many visitors arrive in Juneau aboard cruise ships, as the city is a key stop on many Alaska cruise itineraries.

Once you've arrived, Juneau is a city that offers an incredible variety of activities and experiences, from outdoor adventures to cultural attractions. One of the most iconic landmarks near Juneau is the Mendenhall Glacier, a 13-mile-long river of ice that is easily accessible from downtown. Located just 12 miles from the city center, the glacier is part of the Tongass National Forest and is a must-see for any visitor. The Mendenhall Glacier Visitor Center offers exhibits on the glacier's formation and the surrounding ecosystem, as well as stunning views of the glacier itself. Several hiking trails start at the visitor center, ranging from short, easy walks to more challenging routes that take you closer to the glacier. The Nugget Falls Trail, a relatively easy 2-mile round trip, brings hikers to the base of Nugget Falls, a beautiful waterfall with a perfect view of the glacier in the background.

For a closer look at the glacier, visitors can take guided tours that include kayaking, canoeing, or even trekking on the glacier itself. Glacier trekking and ice-climbing tours allow adventurous travelers to strap on crampons and explore the crevasses and ice formations of Mendenhall Glacier with a knowledgeable guide. These experiences offer a unique and up-close perspective on the ever-changing landscape of the glacier. Prices for guided glacier tours vary depending on the activity and duration, but they typically range from $100 to $300 per person.

Another highlight of Juneau is the opportunity to go whale watching, as the waters surrounding the city are home to some of the most spectacular marine wildlife in Alaska. Humpback whales, orcas, sea lions, and porpoises can all be spotted in the waters of the Inside Passage, making Juneau one of the best places in the world for whale watching. Several tour operators in the city offer boat trips that take visitors out into the waters of Auke Bay or Stephens Passage, where humpback whales are known to feed during the summer months. These tours are not only a chance to see whales breaching and tail-slapping up close but also offer incredible views of the surrounding islands and mountains. Whale-watching tours in Juneau typically last around three to four hours and cost between $120 and $200 per person. Many tours guarantee whale sightings, making it a safe bet for wildlife enthusiasts.

Juneau's historical and cultural attractions provide a fascinating glimpse into Alaska's past, from its indigenous roots to its Gold Rush boom. One of the best places to start exploring Juneau's history is the Alaska State Museum, located in the heart of downtown. The museum features exhibits on Alaska's Native cultures, the Russian period of colonization, the Gold Rush, and Alaska's path to statehood. Visitors can view artifacts ranging from traditional indigenous clothing and tools to Gold Rush-era mining equipment. The museum also hosts rotating exhibits of contemporary Alaskan art, giving visitors a chance to see how modern artists interpret the state's culture and environment.

For those interested in the history of Alaska's statehood and government, a visit to the Alaska State Capitol is a must. The Capitol, located just a short walk from downtown, is a working government building where the state legislature meets. Guided tours of the Capitol offer insights into the state's political history, architecture, and the process of Alaska's admission to the Union in 1959. The building is modest compared to many other state capitols, reflecting Alaska's frontier spirit, but it is steeped in history and provides an important perspective on how the state is governed today.

Another historic site worth visiting is the St. Nicholas Russian Orthodox Church, one of the oldest buildings in Juneau. Built in 1894, this small, charming church is a reminder of Alaska's Russian heritage, which predates the state's purchase by the United States. The church is still in use today and is open to visitors who want to learn about its history and see its beautiful icons and religious art.

In addition to its historic sites, Juneau is home to a vibrant arts and culture scene. The Juneau Arts & Humanities Council hosts a variety of events throughout the year, including art exhibits, live music, theater performances, and film screenings. During the summer months, downtown Juneau comes alive with public art displays, outdoor concerts, and festivals celebrating everything from Alaskan seafood to Native heritage. One of the most popular annual events is Celebration, a biennial festival held by the Tlingit, Haida, and Tsimshian peoples to celebrate their cultures through dance, song, and storytelling. This festival draws indigenous people from all over Southeast Alaska and beyond, making it one of the largest gatherings of its kind in the state.

For those who love the outdoors, there's no shortage of activities in and around Juneau. In addition to the Mendenhall Glacier, visitors can explore the surrounding wilderness through hiking, fishing, and kayaking. One of the best places for hiking is Mount Roberts, which towers over downtown Juneau and offers some of the best views in the area. The Mount Roberts Trail begins near the base of the Mount Roberts Tramway, and hikers can either take the tram up to the trailhead or hike the entire way from the bottom. The hike is challenging but rewarding, with panoramic views of the city, Gastineau Channel, and the surrounding mountains.

For a more relaxing way to experience the beauty of Mount Roberts, visitors can take the Mount Roberts Tramway, a gondola that lifts passengers 1,800 feet up the mountain. At the top, there's a visitor center with exhibits on the local environment and Tlingit culture, as well as a gift shop and a restaurant. From the tram's upper station, visitors can explore short hiking trails or simply enjoy the views from the observation deck. The tram operates during the summer months, and tickets cost around $35 per person for a round trip.

Juneau is also known for its outstanding seafood, and visitors should make a point of sampling the local cuisine while in town. Many restaurants in Juneau serve fresh-caught salmon, halibut, and crab, often prepared in ways that highlight the flavors of the region. Tracy's

King Crab Shack, located on the downtown waterfront, is one of the most popular spots in Juneau for seafood. Specializing in Alaskan king crab, this casual eatery serves up heaping portions of crab legs, crab bisque, and crab cakes, all with incredible views of the harbor. Another excellent option is Salt, a contemporary restaurant offering a mix of Alaskan seafood and international flavors in a chic, modern setting. For those looking for a more casual experience, The Rookery Café offers gourmet sandwiches, fresh salads, and espresso drinks in a cozy atmosphere.

After a day of exploring, Juneau's nightlife scene offers a variety of options for relaxing and enjoying local culture. The Alaskan Hotel & Bar, the oldest operating hotel in Alaska, features live music and a historic atmosphere that recalls the Gold Rush era. For craft beer lovers, the Alaskan Brewing Company offers tours and tastings of its award-winning beers, many of which are brewed using local ingredients like glacier water. The brewery is located just a few miles from downtown, and it's a popular stop for visitors looking to sample some of Alaska's best brews.

Fairbanks: Northern lights viewing, outdoor adventures, and cultural experiences

Fairbanks, located in the heart of Alaska's interior, is a city known for its spectacular northern lights, rich cultural experiences, and access to some of the state's most stunning wilderness areas. Situated on the banks of the Chena River, approximately 150 miles south of the Arctic Circle, Fairbanks is the largest city in the interior region of Alaska and serves as a gateway to both the Arctic and Denali National Park. With its unique subarctic climate, Fairbanks offers distinct seasonal activities, ranging from incredible aurora borealis viewing in the winter to endless daylight during the summer months, providing visitors with a wide variety of outdoor adventures. Whether you're visiting Fairbanks to witness the northern lights, explore its cultural heritage, or embark on an unforgettable wilderness excursion, the city has something to offer for every type of traveler.

Reaching Fairbanks is relatively easy, despite its remote location. Most travelers arrive by air via Fairbanks International Airport, which offers regular flights from Anchorage, Seattle, and other major U.S. cities. The airport is conveniently located just a few miles from downtown Fairbanks, making it easy to get into the city by taxi, shuttle, or rental car. For those traveling by road, Fairbanks is connected to Anchorage and other parts of Alaska via the George Parks Highway, a scenic 360-mile drive that takes you through some of the state's most breathtaking landscapes. Additionally, Fairbanks is a key stop on the Alaska Railroad, which offers daily train service from Anchorage during the summer months. The railroad journey from Anchorage to Fairbanks is considered one of the most scenic train rides in the world, providing travelers with views of mountains, rivers, and wildlife along the way.

Once you arrive in Fairbanks, there are countless activities to make your visit memorable, starting with the city's most famous attraction: the northern lights. Fairbanks is one of the best places in the world to see the aurora borealis, thanks to its location directly under the auroral oval, a ring-shaped zone that circles the Earth's magnetic poles where the northern lights are most active. The best time to view the aurora in Fairbanks is from late August to mid-April, when the skies are dark and the chances of a clear night are high. Visitors can view the northern lights from a variety of locations in and around Fairbanks, but for the best experience, many opt to stay at lodges or resorts specifically designed for aurora viewing.

One popular option is the Chena Hot Springs Resort, located about an hour's drive from Fairbanks. This remote resort not only offers prime northern lights viewing but also provides the opportunity to relax in natural hot springs under the glow of the aurora. The combination of the warm waters and the dancing lights above creates a magical and unforgettable experience. Chena Hot Springs also offers a range of other activities, including dog sledding, snowmobiling, and guided aurora tours, making it a great base for a winter adventure.

For those who prefer to stay in town, the University of Alaska Fairbanks' Geophysical Institute operates the Aurora Forecast, which provides real-time updates on aurora activity and viewing conditions. This allows visitors to plan their northern lights outings with a higher chance of success. Additionally, several tour companies in Fairbanks offer northern lights viewing excursions that take you out of the city and into the surrounding wilderness for the best possible chance of seeing the aurora. These tours often include transportation, heated viewing cabins, and knowledgeable guides who can explain the science behind the lights.

Beyond the northern lights, Fairbanks is also a hub for outdoor adventures year-round. In the winter, the city is transformed into a winter wonderland, offering activities like dog sledding, snowshoeing, ice fishing, and snowmobiling. Dog sledding, in particular, is a quintessential Alaskan experience, and Fairbanks is one of the best places to try it. Several local tour operators offer dog sledding tours, where you can learn about the history of mushing, meet the sled dogs, and even take a turn driving the sled yourself. These tours range from short introductory rides to multi-day mushing expeditions, allowing visitors to experience the thrill of racing across the snowy wilderness behind a team of enthusiastic Alaskan huskies.

Ice fishing is another popular winter activity in Fairbanks, offering visitors a chance to try their hand at catching fish in the frozen lakes and rivers surrounding the city. Guided ice fishing tours typically provide all the necessary equipment, including heated fishing huts, and are a great way to experience the quiet beauty of Alaska's winter landscape while learning a new skill.

When the snow melts and the long days of summer arrive, Fairbanks becomes a haven for hiking, boating, and wildlife viewing. The Midnight Sun, a natural phenomenon where the sun never fully sets during the summer months, creates nearly 24 hours of daylight in Fairbanks, giving visitors endless opportunities for outdoor exploration. One of the best places to experience the Midnight Sun is at the top of Ester Dome, a popular hiking spot located just outside of town. The trail to the summit of Ester Dome offers stunning views of the surrounding mountains and valleys, and on clear days, you can even see Denali in the distance. The hike is relatively short but steep, and the panoramic views from the top make it well worth the effort.

Fairbanks also offers access to several rivers, including the Chena and Tanana Rivers, which are perfect for canoeing, kayaking, or paddleboarding during the summer months. For a more leisurely way to enjoy the water, many visitors opt to take a riverboat tour on the Chena River, which offers a relaxing and informative way to see the city and its surrounding landscapes. The Riverboat Discovery, a popular attraction in Fairbanks, takes passengers on a guided cruise down the Chena River, where they can learn about the history of the area, visit a traditional Athabascan village, and watch a dog mushing demonstration.

Fairbanks is also home to a number of cultural experiences that highlight the rich history and heritage of the region. The Morris Thompson Cultural and Visitors Center is an excellent place to start, offering exhibits on the history, culture, and natural environment of Interior Alaska. The center provides a comprehensive introduction to Fairbanks and the surrounding area, with displays on the indigenous peoples of Alaska, the Gold Rush, and the wildlife of the region. The center also serves as a hub for local tour operators, making it a convenient place to plan excursions and activities during your stay.

Another cultural gem in Fairbanks is the University of Alaska Museum of the North, located on the University of Alaska Fairbanks campus. This museum features an impressive collection of artifacts, art, and exhibits that showcase the history, culture, and natural wonders of Alaska. Highlights of the museum include its extensive collection of Native Alaskan art and artifacts, as well as exhibits on Alaska's wildlife, geology, and archaeology. One of the museum's most popular attractions is the "Place Where You Go to Listen," an immersive sound and light installation that reflects real-time changes in the natural environment of Alaska, such as the aurora, earthquakes, and daylight. The Museum of the North offers a fascinating and educational experience that is perfect for visitors of all ages.

Fairbanks also offers a number of historic sites that provide a glimpse into the city's past. The Pioneer Park, located just a few minutes from downtown, is a living history museum that celebrates Alaska's frontier history. The park features several historic buildings, including Gold Rush-era cabins, a sternwheeler riverboat, and a railroad museum. Visitors can explore the park's exhibits, watch live demonstrations, and even try their hand at gold panning. Pioneer Park is a fun and family-friendly destination that offers a unique look at Fairbanks' history.

For those interested in exploring the wilderness beyond Fairbanks, the city serves as a gateway to several incredible outdoor destinations. One of the most popular is Denali National Park, which is located about a two-hour drive south of Fairbanks. Denali, home to North America's tallest peak, offers world-class hiking, wildlife viewing, and camping opportunities. Visitors to Denali can take guided bus tours into the park, where they can spot wildlife such as bears, moose, wolves, and caribou, or explore the park's extensive trail system on foot.

Fairbanks is also a starting point for journeys into the Arctic. Several tour operators in the city offer guided trips to the Arctic Circle, where visitors can experience the remote beauty of Alaska's far north. These tours typically include stops at key landmarks, such as the Yukon River and the Arctic Circle sign, and often offer opportunities for wildlife viewing and photography. For those interested in a more adventurous experience, multi-day expeditions into the Arctic National Wildlife Refuge or Gates of the Arctic National Park are also available.

No visit to Fairbanks would be complete without sampling some of the local cuisine. The city offers a variety of dining options, from casual cafes to fine dining restaurants, many of which highlight the flavors of Alaska. Fresh seafood is a staple of the local diet, and many restaurants in Fairbanks serve dishes featuring Alaskan salmon, halibut, and crab. The Pump House Restaurant, located along the Chena River, is a popular spot for both locals and visitors, offering a menu that includes fresh seafood, game meats, and local produce. For a more casual dining experience, The Cookie Jar Restaurant is a local favorite, known for its hearty breakfasts and homemade baked goods.

Seward: Gateway to Kenai Fjords National Park

Seward, located on the southern coast of Alaska's Kenai Peninsula, is a picturesque town known as the gateway to Kenai Fjords National Park, one of Alaska's most stunning and ecologically significant areas. With its dramatic fjords, towering glaciers, abundant wildlife, and pristine waters, Seward offers a perfect combination of breathtaking natural beauty and outdoor adventure. Nestled between Resurrection Bay and the rugged Kenai Mountains, Seward is surrounded by wilderness yet easily accessible, making it an ideal destination for travelers seeking to experience Alaska's wild landscapes up close. In addition to its proximity to Kenai Fjords National Park, Seward itself is a charming and historic town with plenty to offer, from local restaurants and museums to scenic hikes and water-based activities.

Getting to Seward is relatively straightforward, whether you're coming from Anchorage or elsewhere in Alaska. One of the most popular ways to reach Seward is by car, as the town is connected to Anchorage by the scenic Seward Highway, a 125-mile route that takes you through some of the most stunning landscapes in Alaska. The drive from Anchorage to Seward typically takes about 2.5 to 3 hours, but many travelers choose to take their time along the way, stopping to admire the views, take photographs, and explore the surrounding areas. The highway runs along Turnagain Arm, a body of water known for its dramatic tides and wildlife, and continues through the Chugach Mountains, offering sweeping views of glaciers, forests, and alpine meadows. Along the way, there are plenty of opportunities to spot wildlife, such as moose, eagles, and even beluga whales in the waters of Turnagain Arm.

For those who prefer not to drive, another excellent option for getting to Seward is the Alaska Railroad's Coastal Classic route. This scenic train journey is considered one of the most beautiful in the state, taking passengers through the rugged wilderness of the Kenai Peninsula, with views of mountains, glaciers, and wildlife along the way. The train departs from Anchorage and takes approximately 4 hours to reach Seward, offering a relaxing and comfortable alternative to driving. The Alaska Railroad features large windows in its passenger cars, making it easy to enjoy the spectacular scenery, and there are options for both standard and premium seating, with GoldStar Service offering glass-dome ceilings for an even better view.

Many visitors find that the train journey itself is a highlight of their trip to Seward.

Once you've arrived in Seward, you'll quickly discover that the town is the perfect base for exploring the incredible natural wonders of Kenai Fjords National Park. This 669,000-acre park is famous for its fjords, glaciers, and diverse marine life, and it's one of the best places in Alaska to experience the power and beauty of the state's glaciers. The most accessible and popular glacier in the park is Exit Glacier, located just a short drive from downtown Seward. Exit Glacier is one of the few glaciers in Alaska that is easily reachable by road, and visitors can hike right up to the face of the glacier, where they can observe the massive river of ice up close. The Exit Glacier Nature Center offers educational exhibits about the glacier's formation and the impact of climate change, as well as information about the park's wildlife and geology.

Several hiking trails begin at the Exit Glacier area, with the most popular being the Glacier View Loop, a short and easy trail that provides excellent views of the glacier from multiple vantage points. For more adventurous hikers, the Harding Icefield Trail is a challenging 8.2-mile round trip that climbs over 3,000 feet in elevation and offers stunning panoramic views of the massive Harding Icefield, which stretches for miles in all directions. This trail is strenuous and takes several hours to complete, but for those who make the trek, the reward is a breathtaking view of one of the largest icefields in North America.

In addition to Exit Glacier, one of the main attractions of Kenai Fjords National Park is its coastal fjords, which are best explored by boat. Several tour companies in Seward offer boat tours of Resurrection Bay and the park's outer coast, where visitors can see glaciers calving into the sea, spot marine wildlife, and experience the grandeur of the park's rugged coastline. These boat tours range from half-day to full-day excursions, and many of them include visits to tidewater glaciers such as Aialik Glacier or Holgate Glacier. The sight of a massive glacier calving, or breaking off chunks of ice into the ocean, is a truly awe-inspiring experience, as the sound of the ice cracking and crashing into the water reverberates across the bay.

Wildlife viewing is another major highlight of these boat tours. Resurrection Bay and the waters of Kenai Fjords National Park are home to a rich variety of marine life, including sea otters, harbor seals, Steller sea lions, and a variety of seabirds such as puffins and kittiwakes. During the summer months, it's also common to see humpback whales and orcas in the bay, making these boat tours a fantastic opportunity for whale watching. Some tours also offer kayaking opportunities, allowing visitors to paddle through the calm waters of the fjords and get an even closer look at the park's glaciers and wildlife.

For those who prefer to stay on land, Seward offers plenty of outdoor activities and attractions. One of the most popular hikes in the area is the Mount Marathon Trail, which climbs from sea level to the summit of

Mount Marathon, offering spectacular views of Seward, Resurrection Bay, and the surrounding mountains. The trail is steep and challenging, but the views from the top are worth the effort. Mount Marathon is famous for the annual Mount Marathon Race, held every Fourth of July, in which participants race up and down the mountain in one of the most grueling footraces in the world.

In addition to hiking, Seward is a great place for fishing, and many visitors come to the town specifically for the opportunity to catch salmon, halibut, and other fish in the rich waters of Resurrection Bay. Several local charter companies offer fishing trips, ranging from half-day excursions to multi-day fishing adventures. Whether you're an experienced angler or a first-time fisherman, these charters provide all the necessary gear and guidance to help you land a big catch. Fishing in Seward is not only a popular activity but also a way to experience the rich maritime culture of the town, which has long been associated with commercial and sport fishing.

Another must-visit attraction in Seward is the Alaska SeaLife Center, the state's premier public aquarium and marine research facility. Located on the waterfront in downtown Seward, the SeaLife Center is home to a variety of marine animals, including sea lions, seals, puffins, and octopuses. The center's exhibits focus on the marine ecosystems of Alaska and the challenges they face due to climate change, pollution, and human activity. Visitors can observe marine mammals up close, learn about the center's conservation efforts, and even participate in interactive programs such as feeding the sea lions or taking a behind-the-scenes tour. The Alaska SeaLife Center is not only an educational experience but also a great way to support marine conservation in Alaska.

Seward's rich history is also worth exploring. The town was founded in 1903 as the southern terminus of the Alaska Railroad, and it played a key role in the development of the state's transportation infrastructure. Today, visitors can learn about the town's history at the Seward Museum, which features exhibits on the Alaska Railroad, the 1964 earthquake and tsunami that devastated the town, and the area's Native heritage. The town itself has a charming, walkable downtown area, with a mix of historic buildings, shops, galleries, and restaurants.

For dining, Seward offers a variety of options that showcase the flavors of Alaska, particularly its fresh seafood. Many local restaurants serve dishes featuring salmon, halibut, and crab, often sourced directly from the waters of Resurrection Bay. One of the most popular spots in town is The Cookery, a cozy bistro that offers a farm-to-table dining experience with a focus on fresh, local ingredients. Another favorite is Chinooks, located on the harbor, where diners can enjoy fresh seafood while watching the boats come and go. For a more casual experience, visitors can stop by Woody's Thai Kitchen, a local favorite known for its delicious Thai food and laid-back atmosphere.

Seward is also a gateway for scenic drives and road trips on the Kenai Peninsula. The Seward Highway, which connects the town to Anchorage, is itself a destination, offering incredible views of mountains, glaciers, and the coastline. Along the way, travelers can stop at scenic viewpoints, hiking trails, and picnic spots to take in the beauty of the Kenai Peninsula. Another popular drive is the route to Homer, located on the southwestern tip of the peninsula, which passes through the charming towns of Soldotna and Kenai, as well as the pristine wilderness of the Kenai National Wildlife Refuge.

Denali National Park: A guide to experiencing the highest peak in North America

Denali National Park, located in the heart of Alaska, is home to the highest peak in North America: Denali, which rises 20,310 feet above sea level. The park itself spans over six million acres of pristine wilderness, encompassing forests, tundra, glaciers, and vast open valleys, making it one of the most breathtaking and diverse landscapes in the world. A visit to Denali is a once-in-a-lifetime experience for many travelers, offering the opportunity to witness not only the iconic mountain itself but also the extraordinary wildlife and natural beauty that define the Alaskan wilderness. From scenic drives and hiking trails to wildlife viewing and mountaineering, Denali National Park offers a wide range of activities for visitors, whether you're seeking adventure, tranquility, or a deep connection with nature.

Denali National Park is located about 240 miles north of Anchorage and approximately 125 miles south of Fairbanks, making it relatively easy to access from either city. There are several ways to get to the park, with driving being one of the most popular options. If you're coming from Anchorage, you can take the George Parks Highway, a scenic route that runs directly from the city to the park entrance. The drive typically takes about five hours and offers stunning views of the Alaskan landscape, including rivers, mountains, and valleys. Along the way, you can stop at several points of interest, such as Talkeetna, a charming town known for its connection to Denali climbing expeditions, or the town of Cantwell, which is just south of the park entrance. The drive from Fairbanks is shorter, taking about two and a half hours, and also follows the George Parks Highway.

For those who prefer not to drive, the Alaska Railroad provides an unforgettable alternative. The Denali Star Train, which runs between Anchorage and Fairbanks, offers daily service to the park during the summer months. The train ride is widely considered one of the most scenic in North America, with large windows providing panoramic views of the rugged Alaskan wilderness. The journey includes views of rivers, forests, and—if the weather cooperates—Denali itself, towering above the surrounding landscape. Traveling by train is not only a comfortable way to reach the park but also a highlight of many visitors' trips, as it allows you to sit back and fully appreciate the beauty of Alaska's interior.

Once you arrive at Denali National Park, the first thing that strikes most visitors is the sheer vastness of the landscape. Denali, formerly known as Mount McKinley, dominates the skyline on clear days, its snow-capped peak gleaming in the distance. However, the park offers much more than just the mountain. With its diverse ecosystems, ranging from dense spruce forests in the lower elevations to open tundra and glaciers in the higher regions, Denali is a haven for wildlife and outdoor enthusiasts alike.

One of the best ways to experience the park is through a bus tour, as personal vehicles are only allowed to drive the first 15 miles of the Denali Park Road. Beyond this point, the road is open only to park-operated shuttle buses and guided tour buses, which help preserve the park's wilderness while allowing visitors to explore its deeper regions. These buses travel the full length of the 92-mile Denali Park Road, taking passengers through different ecological zones and offering incredible opportunities to see wildlife such as grizzly bears, moose, caribou, Dall sheep, and wolves. Some tours are narrated by knowledgeable guides who provide insights into the park's history, geology, and wildlife, while others are non-narrated shuttles that allow passengers to get on and off at different points along the road to hike or explore on their own.

The bus tours vary in length, with some trips lasting four to five hours and others taking up to 12 hours, depending on how far into the park you go. The full-length tour to Wonder Lake, located 85 miles into the park, is one of the most popular, as it offers spectacular views of Denali and the surrounding wilderness. On clear days, the reflection of the mountain in the calm waters of Wonder Lake is one of the most iconic sights in the park. However, even shorter tours, such as the trip to Eielson Visitor Center (located at mile 66), offer incredible scenery and wildlife viewing opportunities. The visitor center itself provides exhibits on the park's natural and cultural history, as well as trails that lead to stunning viewpoints of the mountain.

For visitors who prefer to explore the park on foot, Denali offers numerous hiking opportunities, ranging from short, easy walks to challenging backcountry adventures. Near the park entrance, there are several well-maintained trails that allow for easy exploration of the surrounding forests and rivers. The Horseshoe Lake Trail, for example, is a 3-mile loop that takes hikers through a scenic forested area to a peaceful lake, while the Mount Healy Overlook Trail is a more challenging 5-mile hike that rewards climbers with panoramic views of the park and the surrounding mountains.

For more experienced hikers and adventurers, Denali's backcountry offers unparalleled opportunities for wilderness exploration. The park does not have established backcountry trails, meaning that those who venture into the wild must rely on their navigation skills and knowledge of the terrain. However, for those who are prepared, the experience of trekking through Denali's unspoiled wilderness is unmatched. Backpackers can explore the open tundra, cross rivers, and camp in remote areas where they are likely to encounter no one else. Backcountry permits are required for overnight trips, and the park provides information and resources for those planning backcountry excursions.

Wildlife viewing is one of the major draws of Denali National Park, and the park's vast, undeveloped landscape provides a habitat for a wide range of animals. Visitors often spot large mammals such as grizzly bears, moose, caribou, and Dall sheep while traveling along the park road or hiking in the backcountry. Birdwatchers will also find plenty to enjoy, as the park is home to a variety of bird species, including golden eagles, ptarmigans, and several species of waterfowl. The park's wolves, while more elusive, are occasionally seen by lucky visitors, especially those venturing further into the park's more remote areas.

In addition to its wildlife and natural beauty, Denali National Park is also a premier destination for mountaineering. Climbing Denali is considered one of the most challenging feats in the world of mountaineering, and each year, hundreds of climbers attempt to summit the mountain. The climbing season typically runs from May to July, and only a small percentage of those who set out to conquer Denali's peak actually make it to the top due to the extreme weather and physical demands of the climb. For those who are not ready to take on the challenge of climbing Denali, the park offers other mountaineering experiences, such as glacier trekking and ice climbing, that allow visitors to explore the park's glaciers and rugged terrain in a more accessible way.

Another unique way to experience Denali is through a flightseeing tour. Several companies in the area offer scenic flights that take passengers over the park, providing unparalleled views of Denali's towering peak, glaciers, and valleys. Some tours even include the option to land on a glacier, allowing passengers to step out of the plane and experience the icy expanse firsthand. Flightseeing tours are particularly popular during the summer months when the weather is more stable and visibility is generally good. These tours offer a once-in-a-lifetime opportunity to see the scale and grandeur of Denali from a perspective that few people get to experience.

Winter in Denali National Park brings a different kind of adventure, as the park transforms into a snow-covered wonderland. While most of the park's facilities close during the winter months, visitors can still access the park entrance area for activities such as cross-country skiing, snowshoeing, and dog sledding. Denali is one of the few national parks in the United States where dog sledding is still an active and essential form of transportation, and visitors in the winter can take guided dog sledding tours that allow them to experience this traditional Alaskan mode of travel. In addition, winter visitors have the chance to see the northern lights, as the long, dark nights provide ideal conditions for aurora viewing.

Throughout the year, Denali National Park offers educational programs and ranger-led activities that allow visitors to learn more about the park's ecosystems, wildlife, and history. These programs include guided walks, evening presentations, and wildlife talks, and they are a great way to deepen your understanding of the park's unique environment. The Denali Visitor Center, located near the park entrance, serves as a hub for information, exhibits, and park services, and it's a good starting point for planning your visit.

For accommodations, there are several options both inside and near Denali National Park. Within the park, there are a number of campgrounds that offer the opportunity to stay in the wilderness and enjoy the peace and solitude of the park after the day visitors have left. The Riley Creek Campground, located near the park entrance, is the most accessible and offers amenities such as potable water and picnic tables. For those looking for a more remote camping experience, the Teklanika River Campground, located 29 miles into the park, provides a more rugged setting with fewer amenities but greater access to the park's interior. In addition to campgrounds, several lodges and hotels are located just outside the park, offering comfortable accommodations for visitors who prefer not to camp.

Glacier Bay National Park: Highlights and tips for visiting Alaska's famous glaciers

For those looking to arrive independently, the gateway to Glacier Bay National Park is the small town of Gustavus, located just outside the park's boundaries. Gustavus is accessible by daily flights from Juneau via small aircraft, with flights lasting about 30 minutes. Once in Gustavus, visitors can take a short 10-mile drive to Bartlett Cove, the main entrance to the park. In addition to flights, Gustavus can also be reached by the Alaska Marine Highway ferry system, with ferries running from Juneau during the summer months. The ferry journey is a scenic and leisurely way to travel, taking about four hours and providing beautiful views of the islands and waterways of Southeast Alaska. Once you arrive in Gustavus, transportation options to Bartlett Cove include rental cars, shuttles, or even bicycles, for those who prefer a more active approach.

One of the most iconic experiences in Glacier Bay National Park is witnessing the glaciers themselves. The park's tidewater glaciers, which descend from the St. Elias Mountains and flow directly into the sea, are among the most accessible glaciers in the world. Visitors can see these massive rivers of ice up close by taking a boat tour from Bartlett Cove, which brings travelers deep into the park's fjords, providing stunning views of the glaciers and the surrounding landscape. The most popular destination on these boat tours is Margerie Glacier, one of the park's most active and photogenic glaciers. Margerie Glacier stretches for over a mile and towers 250 feet above the water, with ice that glows an otherworldly blue in the sunlight. Visitors on these tours often have the chance to see the glacier calving, a process in which massive chunks of ice break off from the glacier's face and crash into the sea, creating thunderous booms and sending waves rippling through the water.

Another highlight of these boat tours is Johns Hopkins Glacier, located in the farthest reaches of the bay. This glacier is particularly dramatic, as it is surrounded by some of the park's most rugged and remote scenery. The icebergs in front of Johns Hopkins Glacier are often filled with seals, which use the ice as a safe place to rest and give birth to their pups. The presence of seals and other wildlife, combined with the towering ice faces and snow-capped peaks, creates an unforgettable experience.

In addition to boat tours, there are numerous ways to explore Glacier Bay National Park, making it a destination that caters to adventurers and nature lovers alike. Kayaking is one of the most popular activities in the park, offering a serene and immersive way to explore the park's inlets, coves, and waterways. Kayakers have the unique opportunity to paddle among the icebergs, approach the glaciers from water level, and get close to wildlife without disturbing the natural environment. Kayaking in Glacier Bay requires careful planning, as tides and weather can change rapidly, but for those prepared, it is one of the most rewarding ways to experience the park's beauty. Kayak rentals and guided tours are available at Bartlett Cove, and for those seeking an extended adventure, multi-day kayaking trips with overnight camping are also possible.

For hikers, Glacier Bay National Park offers a variety of trails, ranging from short walks to more challenging backcountry routes. Near Bartlett Cove, the Forest Loop Trail is a pleasant 1-mile walk through the temperate rainforest, offering a chance to see the rich plant life and wildlife of the area. The Bartlett River Trail is a slightly longer hike, following the river through the forest to a tidal meadow, where visitors can see eagles, otters, and occasionally bears. The Bartlett Lake Trail, a more challenging hike, takes adventurers deeper into the wilderness and provides stunning views of the surrounding landscape. For those interested in more off-the-beaten-path adventures, backcountry hiking and camping in Glacier Bay's wilderness areas are permitted, though these require proper preparation and navigation skills, as there are no established trails in much of the park.

Wildlife viewing is another highlight of any visit to Glacier Bay National Park. The park's remote location and rich ecosystems make it a prime habitat for a wide variety of animals, both on land and in the sea. Marine wildlife is abundant, and visitors often spot humpback whales, orcas, porpoises, and sea otters in the waters of Glacier Bay. Birdwatchers will find a wealth of species in the park, from puffins and kittiwakes to bald eagles, which can often be seen soaring overhead. On land, black and brown bears, moose, mountain goats, and wolves roam the forests and tundra, and visitors on hikes or boat tours may have the chance to see these iconic Alaskan animals in their natural habitat. The diversity of wildlife in Glacier Bay is a testament to the park's rich and unspoiled ecosystems, and each season brings its own opportunities for wildlife encounters.

For visitors looking to learn more about the park's natural and cultural history, the Glacier Bay Visitor Center at Bartlett Cove is an excellent resource. The visitor center features exhibits on the park's geology, glaciers, and ecosystems, as well as the Tlingit people, who have lived in the area for thousands of years. The Tlingit's connection to the land and glaciers is an important part of the park's cultural heritage, and visitors can learn about their history, traditions, and the ways in which they have adapted to life in the coastal wilderness. The visitor center also offers ranger-led programs, including guided walks, talks, and evening presentations that provide deeper insights into the park's natural wonders.

For those staying overnight, there are several accommodation options both in and near Glacier Bay National Park. The Glacier Bay Lodge, located in Bartlett Cove, is the only hotel within the park boundaries and offers comfortable accommodations with stunning views of the bay. The lodge also serves as a departure point for many of the park's boat tours and activities, making it a convenient base for exploring the area. In addition to the lodge, there is a campground near Bartlett Cove that offers a more rustic experience for those who prefer to camp. The campground is located in a forested area and provides easy access to the park's hiking trails and the visitor center. For visitors staying in Gustavus, there are also a number of small inns, cabins, and bed-and-breakfasts that offer a cozy and welcoming place to rest after a day of exploring the park.

No matter how you choose to experience Glacier Bay National Park, there are a few tips that can help make your visit even more enjoyable. First, be prepared for unpredictable weather, as Southeast Alaska is known for its rapidly changing conditions. Even in the summer, rain and cooler temperatures are common, so it's important to pack layers and waterproof clothing. Binoculars and a camera with a good zoom lens are also recommended, as they can enhance your wildlife viewing and help capture the stunning scenery. If you're planning to hike or kayak, make sure to check the tide charts and talk to park rangers about the conditions, as the park's coastal environment can present challenges for those unfamiliar with the area.

Off-the-Beaten-Path Locations: Lesser-known gems and hidden treasures throughout the state

Alaska is known for its vast wilderness, towering mountains, and spectacular glaciers, but beyond the well-trodden paths of Denali, Anchorage, and Glacier Bay, there are countless hidden gems scattered throughout the state. These lesser-known locations offer an experience of Alaska that is raw, untouched, and authentic, far from the crowds and bustle of more popular tourist destinations. These off-the-beaten-path locations are the heart of Alaska's wild and untamed beauty, waiting for those adventurous enough to seek them out. Exploring these remote treasures not only allows visitors to connect deeply with Alaska's rugged landscapes but also provides a chance to encounter unique local cultures, wildlife, and ecosystems that remain largely unchanged by time. Reaching these places can be an adventure in itself, as many are accessible only by boat, plane, or rough gravel roads, adding to the thrill of discovering the lesser-seen corners of the Last Frontier.

One such hidden gem is the town of McCarthy and the nearby Kennicott Mine, located in the heart of Wrangell-St. Elias National Park, the largest national park in the United States. Wrangell-St. Elias is a staggering wilderness area, encompassing over 13 million acres of glaciers, mountains, and rivers, yet it remains one of the least-visited national parks in the country due to its remote location. McCarthy, a tiny town with a population of less than 50, serves as the gateway to this massive park and is known for its rugged, off-the-grid charm. Visitors to McCarthy often feel like they've stepped back in time, as the town has preserved much of its historic character, with dirt roads, old wooden buildings, and a peaceful, laid-back atmosphere. The nearby Kennicott Mine, once a thriving copper mining town, is now a ghost town with well-preserved buildings that provide a fascinating glimpse into Alaska's mining history. The Kennicott

Mill, perched high on a hillside overlooking the Root Glacier, is an iconic sight, and visitors can tour the old mill buildings to learn about the area's past.

To reach McCarthy and Kennicott, travelers must be prepared for a journey. The road to McCarthy, the McCarthy Road, is a 60-mile gravel road that begins in Chitina, a small town located about 120 miles east of Valdez. The road follows the route of an old railroad line and offers spectacular views of the Copper River and the surrounding wilderness, but it's not for the faint of heart. The road is rough, with potholes and narrow sections, and drivers should be cautious, particularly during wet weather. Despite the challenges, the drive to McCarthy is part of the adventure, and for those who prefer not to drive, shuttle services from Chitina are available. Once in McCarthy, visitors can explore the town on foot, take a guided tour of the Kennicott Mine, or hike to nearby glaciers, where they can walk on the ice and explore the crevasses and ice caves. For those seeking a true wilderness experience, Wrangell-St. Elias offers endless opportunities for backpacking, mountaineering, and flightseeing.

Another off-the-beaten-path destination worth exploring is the Pribilof Islands, located in the Bering Sea, about 300 miles off the coast of mainland Alaska. The Pribilof Islands, particularly the islands of St. Paul and St. George, are known for their incredible wildlife, especially their thriving populations of northern fur seals and seabirds. These islands are a paradise for birdwatchers, as they are home to millions of nesting seabirds, including puffins, auklets, and murres, many of which are rarely seen elsewhere. The islands are also an important site for marine research, and the Bering Sea's nutrient-rich waters support a diverse range of marine life, including whales, sea lions, and walruses.

Getting to the Pribilof Islands requires a bit of planning, as there are no roads connecting the islands to the mainland. The only way to reach St. Paul and St. George is by air, with flights available from Anchorage. Once on the islands, visitors can explore the rugged coastlines, hike to bird cliffs, and take guided wildlife tours. The islands' remote location and stark beauty make them a perfect destination for those seeking solitude and a closer connection with Alaska's wild side. In addition to its wildlife, the Pribilof Islands have a rich cultural history, as they are home to the Unangan people, also known as the Aleut. Visitors can learn about the Unangan's traditional way of life and the impact of the fur trade on the islands, which played a significant role in the history of the region.

If you're looking for an off-the-beaten-path adventure in Alaska's far north, the village of Kotzebue offers an authentic glimpse into life above the Arctic Circle. Located on the shores of Kotzebue Sound, about 30 miles north of the Arctic Circle, Kotzebue is a hub for the Inupiat people and serves as a gateway to the remote Kobuk Valley National Park and the Noatak National Preserve. These vast wilderness areas are some of the most untouched regions in the state, offering visitors the chance to experience the Arctic's stark beauty, from the shifting sands of the Great Kobuk Sand Dunes to the rolling tundra of the Noatak River Valley. Kotzebue itself is a fascinating blend of traditional Inupiat culture and modern life, and visitors can explore the town's heritage at the Northwest Arctic Heritage Center, which features exhibits on the region's history, culture, and wildlife.

Reaching Kotzebue is easiest by plane, with daily flights from Anchorage available year-round. Once in Kotzebue, visitors can take guided tours of the surrounding wilderness, including boat trips along the Noatak River, flightseeing tours of the Great Kobuk Sand Dunes, or cultural tours that provide insight into the Inupiat way of life. For those visiting in the winter, Kotzebue offers opportunities for dog sledding, snowmobiling, and northern lights viewing, making it an excellent destination for those seeking an authentic Arctic experience.

Another hidden treasure in Alaska is the town of Cordova, located in Prince William Sound. Cordova is often overlooked by travelers, as it is not on the road system and can only be reached by plane or ferry, but this charming fishing town is a hidden gem with much to offer. Surrounded by mountains, glaciers, and pristine waters, Cordova is a paradise for outdoor enthusiasts, offering world-class fishing, hiking, and wildlife viewing. The town is known for its strong connection to the fishing industry, particularly the salmon fisheries of the Copper River, and visitors can learn about the area's fishing heritage at the Cordova Historical Museum.

One of the highlights of visiting Cordova is exploring the nearby Childs Glacier, located about 30 miles from town. The glacier is accessible by a scenic drive along the Copper River Highway, and visitors can stand just a few hundred feet from the glacier's face as massive chunks of ice calve into the river below. The sight and sound of the ice crashing into the water is truly awe-inspiring, and the surrounding scenery, with its towering mountains and dense forests, adds to the experience. In addition to glacier viewing, Cordova offers excellent opportunities for kayaking in the calm waters of Prince William Sound, where paddlers can explore hidden coves, watch for sea otters and seals, and even spot the occasional humpback whale.

To get to Cordova, travelers can fly from Anchorage via small regional airlines, or take the Alaska Marine Highway ferry from Whittier or Valdez. The ferry ride through Prince William Sound is a scenic experience in itself, with views of glaciers, waterfalls, and wildlife along the way. Once in Cordova, visitors can explore the town's many hiking trails, take a boat tour to nearby glaciers, or simply relax and enjoy the peaceful surroundings.

For those seeking true isolation and adventure, the Aleutian Islands offer some of the most remote and untouched landscapes in Alaska. The Aleutian chain stretches over 1,200 miles from the Alaskan mainland into the Pacific Ocean, and its volcanic islands are home to rugged coastlines, dramatic peaks, and rich marine life. One of the most interesting islands to visit is

Unalaska, home to the town of Dutch Harbor, which gained fame as the setting for the television show "Deadliest Catch." Dutch Harbor is the largest fishing port in the United States by volume, and visitors can learn about the area's fishing industry and World War II history at the Museum of the Aleutians and the World War II National Historic Area.

The Aleutians are also home to numerous active volcanoes, and adventurous travelers can hike through the islands' wild landscapes, where few visitors ever tread. Wildlife is abundant in the Aleutians, with sea otters, puffins, and whales commonly spotted in the surrounding waters. The isolation of the islands adds to their allure, offering a sense of exploration and discovery that is hard to find elsewhere. To reach Unalaska and the Aleutians, travelers can fly from Anchorage, though flights are often dependent on weather conditions, making the journey itself an adventure.

Chapter 11

Wildlife and Nature Experiences

Wildlife Viewing

Alaska is often referred to as "The Last Frontier," and nowhere is this more evident than in the state's rich and diverse wildlife. From towering grizzly bears fishing for salmon in glacial rivers to pods of humpback whales breaching in the icy waters of the Inside Passage, Alaska's wildlife is one of its most captivating attractions. For those visiting the state, wildlife viewing is not just an activity—it's an essential part of the Alaskan experience, providing an opportunity to witness the raw, untamed beauty of nature at its finest. Whether you're seeking a glimpse of bears, moose, caribou, whales, or eagles, Alaska offers a wealth of places and times to see its most iconic species. For any visitor eager to encounter Alaska's wildlife in its natural habitat, understanding when and where to go is key to making the most of the experience.

One of the best-known wildlife species in Alaska is the bear, and the state is home to three types: grizzly bears, black bears, and the rarely seen polar bears. Grizzly bears, also known as brown bears, are perhaps the most iconic of Alaska's wildlife. These majestic animals are found throughout much of the state, but some of the best places to see them are in the coastal areas where they congregate to fish for salmon during the summer months. One of the most famous bear-viewing destinations in Alaska is Katmai National Park and Preserve, located on the Alaska Peninsula. Katmai is renowned for the large number of brown bears that gather along the Brooks River each summer to fish for salmon. The sight of these massive bears catching fish in the rushing waters is one of the most iconic wildlife experiences in the world, and Katmai is often considered the best place on Earth to see bears in the wild.

Getting to Katmai is an adventure in itself, as the park is accessible only by air. Visitors typically fly from Anchorage or King Salmon via small plane to Brooks Camp, the main visitor area in the park. Once at Brooks Camp, there are viewing platforms along the river that provide a safe and unobstructed view of the bears as they fish and interact with each other. The best time to visit Katmai for bear viewing is from late June to early September, when the salmon runs are at their peak and the bears are most active. For those interested in an extended stay, the park offers camping and lodging options, allowing visitors to fully immerse themselves in the wilderness.

Another excellent destination for bear viewing is Lake Clark National Park and Preserve, located just south of Anchorage. Like Katmai, Lake Clark is known for its abundant population of brown bears, which gather along the park's rivers and lakes to feed on salmon. The park's remote location ensures that it remains less crowded than some other bear-viewing spots, providing a more intimate experience with nature. Access to Lake Clark is also by small plane, with flights departing from Anchorage or Homer. Once in the park, visitors can take guided bear-viewing tours or explore on their own. The best time for bear viewing in Lake Clark is also during the summer months when the salmon are running.

For those looking to see polar bears, the best destination is the town of Kaktovik, located on the northern coast of Alaska in the Arctic. Kaktovik sits on the shores of the Beaufort Sea and is one of the few places in Alaska where visitors have the chance to see polar bears in the wild. The bears gather in the area in late summer and fall as they wait for the sea ice to form, which allows them to hunt for seals. Polar bear viewing tours are available from local guides in Kaktovik, and flights to the town are available from Fairbanks. Viewing polar bears is a once-in-a-lifetime experience for many travelers, as these magnificent creatures are increasingly threatened by climate change and habitat loss.

While bears are one of Alaska's most sought-after wildlife species, the state is also home to the moose, another iconic symbol of the Alaskan wilderness. Moose are the largest members of the deer family and can weigh up to 1,600 pounds, with impressive antlers that can span up to six feet. These massive animals are found throughout much of Alaska, particularly in forested areas near lakes, rivers, and wetlands. Some of the best places to see moose include Denali National Park, Anchorage, and the Kenai Peninsula.

In Denali National Park, moose are often seen in the open tundra and along the park road, especially during the fall mating season, known as the rut. During this time, bull moose can be seen displaying their antlers and engaging in battles with other males for dominance. The park's bus tours provide excellent opportunities for spotting moose, as well as other wildlife such as caribou, wolves, and Dall sheep.

Anchorage, Alaska's largest city, is surprisingly one of the best places to see moose. The city is surrounded by wilderness, and moose frequently wander into residential neighborhoods and parks. In winter, moose can often be spotted along the city's many trails, including the Tony Knowles Coastal Trail, where they come to forage for food. During the summer, moose are commonly seen in the nearby Chugach State Park, particularly in the areas around Flattop Mountain and the Eagle River Nature Center.

For those visiting the Kenai Peninsula, the Kenai National Wildlife Refuge is another excellent spot for moose viewing. The refuge, located near the town of Soldotna, is home to a large population of moose, as well as bears, wolves, and other wildlife. Visitors can explore the refuge by car, on foot, or by boat, and the best times for moose viewing are early morning or late evening when the animals are most active.

Alaska's waters are also teeming with wildlife, particularly whales, which are one of the biggest draws for visitors to the state's coastal regions. Several species of whales can be seen in Alaska, including humpback whales, orcas, gray whales, and beluga whales. The best places for whale watching are in Southeast Alaska, Prince William Sound, and the Kenai Peninsula, with tours departing from towns such as Juneau, Seward, and Valdez.

Humpback whales are the most commonly seen species in Alaska, and they migrate to the state's waters each summer to feed on the abundant supply of krill and small fish. One of the best places to see humpback whales is in the waters of the Inside Passage, particularly near Juneau. Whale-watching tours from Juneau take visitors into Auke Bay and the surrounding waters, where humpback whales are frequently seen breaching, tail-slapping, and feeding. These tours often guarantee whale sightings, as the waters around Juneau are some of the most reliable for seeing humpbacks.

Orcas, or killer whales, are another popular species for whale watchers in Alaska. Unlike humpback whales, which migrate seasonally, orcas are found in Alaska's waters year-round. One of the best places to see orcas is in the waters around Seward and Kenai Fjords National Park, where they can often be spotted hunting for fish or seals. Whale-watching tours from Seward provide a chance to see orcas, as well as humpback whales, sea otters, and other marine wildlife.

Beluga whales, known for their distinctive white color and bulbous heads, are another species that can be seen in Alaska. One of the best places to see belugas is in

Turnagain Arm, a narrow inlet near Anchorage. Belugas can often be seen from the Seward Highway as they swim along the shoreline, particularly during the fall when they come to feed on salmon. Beluga Point, a scenic pullout along the highway, is a popular spot for viewing these unique whales.

Alaska's coastal waters are also home to a variety of other marine wildlife, including sea lions, harbor seals, and sea otters. These animals can be seen in many of the same areas as whales, particularly in places like Kenai Fjords National Park, Prince William Sound, and Glacier Bay National Park. Sea otters, in particular, are a favorite among visitors for their playful behavior and habit of floating on their backs. They can often be seen in large groups, called rafts, near the shorelines of these coastal areas.

For those interested in birdwatching, Alaska is home to a diverse array of bird species, including bald eagles, puffins, and a variety of seabirds. Bald eagles are perhaps the most iconic bird species in Alaska, and they can be seen throughout much of the state, particularly near rivers and coastlines. One of the best places to see bald eagles is in the town of Haines, located in Southeast Alaska. Haines is home to the Chilkat Bald Eagle Preserve, which hosts the largest congregation of bald eagles in the world each fall. During the late fall, thousands of eagles gather along the Chilkat River to feed on salmon, creating a spectacular sight for birdwatchers and photographers.

Puffins, with their colorful beaks and distinctive appearance, are another favorite bird species in Alaska. Puffins can be seen nesting on the cliffs and islands along the coast, particularly in places like the Pribilof Islands, Kenai Fjords National Park, and St. Lazaria Island near Sitka. These small, charismatic birds are best seen during the summer months when they come ashore to breed.

Birdwatching: Top birdwatching locations and what species to look for

Birdwatching in Alaska offers a unique and unparalleled experience for enthusiasts and casual observers alike. As one of the last great wildernesses in the world, Alaska is home to an astonishing diversity of bird species, many of which can be seen nowhere else in the United States. Whether you're scanning the skies for bald eagles, watching colorful puffins nesting on cliffs, or marveling at vast migrations of shorebirds, Alaska provides countless opportunities for birdwatchers to witness these creatures in their natural habitat. The sheer variety of habitats, from coastal rainforests to tundra, rivers, and wetlands, creates an environment that attracts millions of birds throughout the year, making it a must-visit destination for birdwatchers from around the world. With over 500 bird species recorded across the state, Alaska is a birdwatcher's paradise, and each region offers its own unique array of species to discover.

One of the top birdwatching locations in Alaska is the Stikine River Delta, located near the town of Wrangell in Southeast Alaska. This expansive wetland area is an important stopover for migrating birds, particularly in the spring, when hundreds of thousands of shorebirds and waterfowl pass through on their way north. Among the most impressive sights at the Stikine River Delta is the annual migration of snow geese and greater white-fronted geese, which fill the sky as they stop to rest and feed in the marshes. This migration typically peaks in late April and early May, and it's a breathtaking spectacle for birdwatchers who are lucky enough to witness it. In addition to geese, the delta is also a prime location for spotting sandhill cranes, swans, and a variety of ducks.

Getting to the Stikine River Delta is relatively easy, especially if you're already visiting Southeast Alaska. Wrangell can be reached by air via Alaska Airlines flights from Juneau or Ketchikan, and once in Wrangell, local guides and outfitters offer boat trips to the delta, where birdwatchers can get close to the action. Kayaking through the delta is another popular option for those who prefer a quieter, more intimate birdwatching experience. For those visiting in spring, the annual Stikine River Birding Festival celebrates the migration season with guided tours, workshops, and birdwatching excursions, making it an excellent time to explore this bird-rich area.

Further to the north, the Copper River Delta is another world-renowned birdwatching destination. Located near the town of Cordova on the Gulf of Alaska, the Copper

River Delta is the largest wetland in North America, spanning nearly 700,000 acres of mudflats, marshes, and tidal estuaries. This remote and expansive delta serves as a critical stopover for millions of shorebirds during their spring migration, making it one of the best places in Alaska to see large flocks of western sandpipers, dunlins, and other shorebirds. The delta is particularly famous for hosting one of the largest gatherings of shorebirds in the world, with up to five million birds passing through each spring. The sheer number of birds, combined with the stunning backdrop of the Chugach Mountains, creates an unforgettable experience for birdwatchers.

The Copper River Delta can be reached from Cordova, which is accessible by small plane from Anchorage or by ferry from Whittier or Valdez via the Alaska Marine Highway. Once in Cordova, visitors can explore the delta by taking a boat or guided tour, or they can venture out on their own to explore the area's trails and viewing platforms. The best time to visit is in late April or early May, when the shorebird migration is at its peak. Like Wrangell, Cordova also hosts a birding festival in spring—the Copper River Delta Shorebird Festival—which offers guided birding trips, presentations, and opportunities to learn more about the unique ecology of the region.

For those interested in seabirds, the Pribilof Islands, located in the Bering Sea, are a must-visit destination. The islands, particularly St. Paul and St. George, are home to millions of nesting seabirds, including puffins, auklets, murres, and kittiwakes. These islands serve as a crucial breeding ground for seabirds that spend most of their lives at sea, and during the summer months, the cliffs of the Pribilofs come alive with the sound and sight of birds returning to nest. One of the highlights of visiting the Pribilofs is the opportunity to see tufted puffins and horned puffins, two species that are beloved by birdwatchers for their colorful plumage and distinctive appearance. In addition to puffins, the islands are also home to red-faced cormorants, northern fulmars, and the rare red-legged kittiwake, which breeds almost exclusively on the Pribilof Islands.

Reaching the Pribilof Islands is an adventure in itself, as the islands are located over 300 miles off the coast of mainland Alaska. Visitors can fly to St. Paul or St. George from Anchorage via small regional airlines, and once on the islands, guided birdwatching tours are available. The remote and isolated nature of the Pribilofs means that visitors often feel as though they have stepped into another world, surrounded by vast expanses of ocean and teeming birdlife. In addition to birdwatching, the islands also offer opportunities to see marine mammals such as northern fur seals and sea lions, adding to the allure of this far-flung destination.

In the far northern reaches of Alaska, the Arctic Coastal Plain provides a unique birdwatching experience, particularly for those interested in seeing Arctic species that are rarely found elsewhere. The town of Utqiaġvik (formerly known as Barrow), located on the shores of the Arctic Ocean, is one of the best places to see birds that inhabit the tundra and coastal areas of the Arctic.

One of the most sought-after species in Utqiaġvik is the snowy owl, which nests in the tundra around the town and can often be seen perched on the ground or flying low over the landscape. The snowy owl's striking white plumage makes it a favorite among birdwatchers, and Utqiaġvik offers one of the best chances to see this elusive bird in the wild.

In addition to snowy owls, the Arctic Coastal Plain is home to a variety of shorebirds, waterfowl, and seabirds, including king eiders, red phalaropes, and long-tailed ducks. During the summer, the long daylight hours and abundance of food make the Arctic a prime breeding ground for many bird species, and birdwatchers who visit the region during this time are often rewarded with sightings of birds that are difficult to find elsewhere. Getting to Utqiaġvik is easiest by plane, with regular flights available from Anchorage. Once in Utqiaġvik, visitors can explore the surrounding tundra on foot or by guided tour, and the nearby lagoons and ponds provide excellent opportunities for spotting waterfowl and shorebirds.

Moving down to Southcentral Alaska, the Kenai Peninsula offers a variety of birdwatching opportunities, from coastal species to woodland birds. The town of Homer, located on the southern tip of the peninsula, is a particularly good spot for birdwatching, thanks to its location along the shores of Kachemak Bay. Homer is known as the "halibut fishing capital of the world," but it's also a birdwatching hotspot, especially during the spring migration. Each May, Homer hosts the Kachemak

Bay Shorebird Festival, which celebrates the arrival of thousands of migrating shorebirds, including western sandpipers, dunlins, and plovers. During the festival, birdwatchers can participate in guided walks, boat tours, and educational programs that highlight the diversity of birdlife in the area.

In addition to shorebirds, Homer is a great place to see bald eagles, which are commonly spotted along the shoreline and in the surrounding forests. Bald eagles are abundant in this region, and visitors are likely to see these majestic birds perched in trees, soaring overhead, or swooping down to catch fish. Homer's coastal environment also attracts a variety of seabirds, and boat tours into Kachemak Bay offer the chance to see puffins, murres, and cormorants.

For those exploring the Kenai Peninsula further north, the Kenai National Wildlife Refuge near Soldotna is another excellent birdwatching destination. The refuge encompasses over 1.9 million acres of diverse habitats, including forests, wetlands, and lakes, making it home to a wide range of bird species. Visitors to the refuge can spot birds such as trumpeter swans, northern goshawks, and spruce grouse, as well as a variety of songbirds that inhabit the forests. The refuge's trails and viewing platforms provide easy access to some of the best birdwatching areas, and guided tours are available for those looking to learn more about the local birdlife.

Another highlight of birdwatching in Alaska is the chance to see the rare and endangered Steller's eider, a small sea duck that breeds in the tundra of western Alaska. The best place to see Steller's eiders is along the western coast of Alaska, particularly in the region around Bethel and the Yukon-Kuskokwim Delta. This area is a rich wetland environment that supports a wide variety of waterfowl, shorebirds, and other bird species, making it a prime birdwatching destination. During the summer breeding season, birdwatchers can spot not only Steller's eiders but also spectacled eiders, another rare species that is found in the region.

To reach the Yukon-Kuskokwim Delta, visitors can fly to Bethel from Anchorage, and from there, local outfitters and guides offer birdwatching tours into the surrounding wetlands. The area is remote and relatively undeveloped, providing a true wilderness experience for those looking to see some of Alaska's most elusive bird species.

Fishing in Alaska: The best spots for fishing and what you need to know about licenses

Fishing in Alaska is one of the most iconic and sought-after experiences for both seasoned anglers and newcomers to the sport. The state's vast network of rivers, lakes, and coastal waters makes it an angler's paradise, offering some of the best fishing in the world. Whether you're fishing for the prized wild salmon, battling halibut in the deep waters of the Gulf of Alaska, or casting for rainbow trout in pristine mountain streams, Alaska's fishing opportunities are as diverse as its landscapes. Fishing in Alaska isn't just about catching fish—it's about the entire experience: the breathtaking scenery, the abundant wildlife, and the feeling of being in a place that is still wild and untamed. However, before embarking on your fishing adventure, there are a few things to know about the best fishing spots, licenses, and what makes each location special. This guide provides a deep dive into what you need to make your Alaska fishing trip unforgettable.

One of the most famous destinations for fishing in Alaska is the Kenai River, located on the Kenai Peninsula in Southcentral Alaska. The Kenai River is world-renowned for its king salmon runs, which draw anglers from all over the globe. King salmon, also known as Chinook salmon, are the largest species of Pacific salmon, with some weighing over 70 pounds. The Kenai River holds the record for the largest king salmon ever caught, a whopping 97.4-pound fish, making it a bucket-list destination for serious anglers. In addition to king salmon, the Kenai River is home to sockeye salmon, coho salmon, rainbow trout, and Dolly Varden, providing a diverse range of fishing opportunities throughout the season. The best time to fish for king salmon on the Kenai is from mid-May to late July, while sockeye salmon runs peak in late June and July. Coho salmon can be caught from August through September.

Getting to the Kenai River is relatively easy. The town of Soldotna, located near the river's prime fishing spots, is a two-and-a-half-hour drive from Anchorage along the scenic Seward Highway. For those without a car, there are shuttle services and guided fishing tours that depart from Anchorage. Once in Soldotna, anglers can hire local guides to take them to the best fishing spots along the river, or they can fish from the bank at designated areas. Many visitors choose to book guided fishing trips, as local guides are knowledgeable about the river's currents, fishing regulations, and the best techniques for landing a big catch. For those interested in a more rustic experience, there are several campgrounds and lodges along the river where anglers can stay, waking up each morning to fish in some of the most beautiful surroundings in Alaska.

Another must-visit fishing destination in Alaska is Bristol Bay, located in the southwestern part of the state. Bristol Bay is famous for its massive sockeye salmon runs, which are the largest in the world. Each summer, millions of sockeye salmon return to the rivers and streams that flow into Bristol Bay, creating one of the most spectacular natural phenomena in Alaska. The abundance of salmon in the bay's rivers not only provides excellent fishing but also supports a thriving ecosystem, with bears, eagles, and other wildlife all relying on the salmon as a food source. The Naknek and Kvichak Rivers are two of the most popular spots for fishing in Bristol Bay, known for their large sockeye runs as well as their trophy-sized rainbow trout.

Getting to Bristol Bay requires a bit more planning, as the region is remote and accessible only by plane. Most visitors fly into King Salmon or Dillingham from

Anchorage, and from there, they can take a small plane or boat to their chosen fishing lodge or river. Many fishing lodges in the area offer all-inclusive packages that include transportation, lodging, meals, and guided fishing trips, making it easy for anglers to focus on the fishing and leave the logistics to the experts. The best time to fish for sockeye salmon in Bristol Bay is from late June to early August, while rainbow trout fishing is excellent throughout the summer and into the fall. For those seeking a true wilderness fishing experience, Bristol Bay is hard to beat.

In addition to salmon fishing, Alaska is known for its incredible halibut fishing, particularly in the waters of the Gulf of Alaska. Halibut are massive flatfish that can grow to over 400 pounds, and they are prized for their firm, white flesh. One of the best places to fish for halibut in Alaska is the town of Homer, located on the southern tip of the Kenai Peninsula. Homer is known as the "Halibut Fishing Capital of the World," and anglers flock here each summer to try their luck at catching these giant fish. Halibut fishing in Homer is typically done from charter boats, which take anglers out into the deep waters of Kachemak Bay and beyond. The fishing season for halibut runs from May through September, with the peak season occurring in June and July.

To get to Homer, visitors can drive from Anchorage along the Seward Highway and the Sterling Highway, a journey that takes about five hours. Once in Homer, there are numerous charter companies that offer half-day or full-day halibut fishing trips. These charters provide all the necessary equipment, including rods, reels, bait, and tackle, and the experienced crews help guide anglers through the process of landing these powerful fish. For those looking for a complete fishing experience, many charters also offer combination trips, where anglers can fish for both halibut and salmon in the same day. After a successful day on the water, visitors can have their catch processed and shipped home, allowing them to enjoy fresh Alaskan halibut long after their trip is over.

For those interested in fly fishing, Alaska offers some of the best opportunities in the world, particularly for rainbow trout, Arctic grayling, and salmon. The Alaska Peninsula, stretching between the mainland and the Aleutian Islands, is a premier destination for fly fishing, with its remote rivers and streams providing excellent habitat for these species. One of the most famous fly fishing rivers in Alaska is the Alagnak River, located near the town of King Salmon in Bristol Bay. The Alagnak is known for its large runs of sockeye salmon, as well as its trophy-sized rainbow trout, which can reach lengths of over 30 inches. The river's clear waters and varied terrain make it an ideal spot for both novice and experienced fly fishers.

Getting to the Alagnak River typically involves flying into King Salmon and then taking a boat or small plane to one of the fishing lodges located along the river. Many of these lodges offer guided fly fishing trips, where expert guides take anglers to the best fishing spots and provide tips on technique. The best time for fly fishing on the Alagnak River is from late June to early

September, with the peak season for sockeye salmon in July. In addition to salmon and trout, the river is also home to Arctic grayling, which are a favorite among fly fishers for their beauty and feisty nature.

In addition to the logistics of getting to Alaska's top fishing spots, it's important for anglers to understand the state's fishing regulations and licensing requirements. All non-resident anglers over the age of 16 are required to have a fishing license to fish in Alaska, and additional permits may be needed for certain species, such as king salmon. Fishing licenses can be purchased online through the Alaska Department of Fish and Game website, or at many sporting goods stores and fishing lodges throughout the state. The cost of a non-resident fishing license varies depending on the length of time, with options ranging from one day to a full year. For those planning to fish for king salmon, a separate king salmon stamp is required, which can also be purchased online or in person.

Fishing regulations in Alaska are strictly enforced to ensure the sustainability of fish populations and the health of the state's ecosystems. Anglers should familiarize themselves with the specific rules for the area they plan to fish in, as regulations can vary depending on the region, species, and time of year. For example, catch limits for salmon and halibut are typically set each season by the Alaska Department of Fish and Game, and these limits can fluctuate based on the health of the fishery. In addition to catch limits, some rivers and lakes may have restrictions on fishing methods, such as the use of barbless hooks or catch-and-release requirements for certain species.

For those new to fishing or unfamiliar with Alaska's waters, hiring a local guide is one of the best ways to ensure a successful and enjoyable trip. Guides are not only knowledgeable about the best fishing spots and techniques, but they are also familiar with local regulations and can help ensure that anglers are fishing legally and responsibly. Many guided trips include all the necessary equipment, making it easy for visitors to enjoy a hassle-free fishing experience.

Beyond the fishing itself, Alaska offers countless ways to enhance your trip and make the experience truly memorable. Whether it's watching bald eagles soar overhead as you fish for salmon, seeing bears catch fish in the rivers, or simply soaking in the tranquility of Alaska's wilderness, fishing in Alaska is about more than just catching fish—it's about immersing yourself in one of the most beautiful and wild places on Earth. After a day on the water, visitors can explore the local culture, dine on fresh seafood, and share stories of their adventures with fellow anglers. Alaska's fishing lodges, often located in remote and scenic areas, offer a chance to disconnect from the modern world and reconnect with nature, making for a truly unforgettable experience.

Hiking and Backpacking: Famous trails, safety tips, and gear recommendations

Hiking and backpacking in Alaska is an experience like no other. Alaska, with its rugged mountains, vast wilderness, and diverse landscapes, offers some of the most spectacular hiking and backpacking trails in the world. From the majestic peaks of Denali National Park to the coastal beauty of the Kenai Peninsula, Alaska's hiking opportunities are vast and varied, attracting outdoor enthusiasts from across the globe. Whether you're looking for a challenging multi-day trek through remote wilderness or a scenic day hike to take in the breathtaking views, Alaska has something for everyone. However, venturing into the wilds of Alaska requires careful preparation, respect for the natural environment, and a solid understanding of the terrain. Knowing where to hike, how to stay safe, and what gear to bring are essential components of a successful hiking and backpacking trip in Alaska.

One of the most famous hiking destinations in Alaska is Denali National Park and Preserve, home to North America's tallest peak, Denali, standing at 20,310 feet. The park itself spans over six million acres of wilderness, offering endless hiking and backpacking opportunities for adventurers. One of the unique aspects of hiking in Denali is that, unlike many national parks, there are very few established trails. This allows hikers the freedom to explore the vast tundra and alpine landscapes at their own pace, often without seeing another person for miles. For those new to backcountry navigation, this lack of trails can be daunting, but it also provides a true sense of wilderness and solitude that is hard to find anywhere else.

For those looking for a more structured hiking experience in Denali, there are a few established trails near the park entrance. The Mount Healy Overlook Trail is one of the most popular, offering a challenging 5-mile round-trip hike with an elevation gain of over 1,700 feet. The trail takes hikers through spruce forests and up into the alpine zone, where panoramic views of the park and surrounding mountains await. Another popular hike is the Horseshoe Lake Trail, a relatively easy 3-mile loop that winds through forested areas and along a picturesque lake. For more experienced hikers, backcountry permits are available for those who wish to venture deeper into the park, with opportunities for multi-day backpacking trips that take you into the heart of Denali's remote wilderness.

To get to Denali National Park, most visitors fly into Anchorage and then drive or take a shuttle bus along the George Parks Highway. The drive from Anchorage to the park entrance takes about five hours and offers stunning views of the Alaskan landscape. For those without a vehicle, shuttle services and guided tours are available from Anchorage. Once in the park, the park's bus system provides transportation along the Denali Park Road, with access to various trailheads and viewpoints.

Another must-visit hiking destination in Alaska is the Kenai Peninsula, known for its stunning coastal scenery, abundant wildlife, and diverse hiking trails. The Kenai Peninsula is home to the Kenai Fjords National Park, which offers some of the most dramatic hiking in Alaska, with trails that take you past glaciers, through temperate rainforests, and along rugged coastlines. One of the most popular hikes in the park is the Harding Icefield Trail, a challenging 8.2-mile round-trip hike that climbs over 3,500 feet in elevation. The trail begins at the Exit Glacier Nature Center and takes hikers up through a series of switchbacks, offering incredible views of Exit Glacier along the way. At the top of the trail, hikers are rewarded with a sweeping view of the Harding Icefield, a vast expanse of ice and snow that stretches as far as the eye can see. The Harding Icefield is one of the largest icefields in North America, and standing at its edge is a humbling experience that leaves many hikers in awe.

In addition to the Harding Icefield Trail, the Kenai Peninsula offers numerous other hiking opportunities. The Lost Lake Trail, located near the town of Seward, is a beautiful 14-mile hike that takes you through lush forests, alpine meadows, and past pristine lakes. The trail can be done as a day hike or an overnight backpacking trip, with several campsites along the way. For those looking for a shorter hike, the Tonsina Point Trail near Seward offers a 2-mile round-trip hike through forested areas to a scenic beach along Resurrection Bay, where you can watch for sea otters, seals, and even whales in the distance.

To get to the Kenai Peninsula, most visitors start in Anchorage and drive or take the Alaska Railroad along the scenic Seward Highway. The drive from Anchorage to Seward takes about two and a half hours, and the route offers spectacular views of mountains, rivers, and fjords. Alternatively, the Alaska Railroad provides a comfortable and scenic way to travel, with daily service between Anchorage and Seward during the summer months.

For those looking to experience the wild and remote beauty of Alaska's interior, the Wrangell-St. Elias National Park and Preserve is a hidden gem that offers incredible hiking and backpacking opportunities. Wrangell-St. Elias is the largest national park in the United States, covering over 13 million acres of glaciers, mountains, and rivers. Despite its size, the park remains relatively undeveloped, with few roads and even fewer visitors, making it an ideal destination for those seeking solitude and adventure.

One of the best ways to explore Wrangell-St. Elias is by hiking the Root Glacier Trail, located near the historic town of McCarthy. The trail is a relatively easy 4-mile round-trip hike that takes you to the edge of the Root Glacier, where you can walk on the glacier's surface and explore its crevasses and ice formations. Guided glacier hikes are available for those who want to learn more about the glacier and safely navigate its terrain. For more experienced hikers, Wrangell-St. Elias offers countless opportunities for multi-day backpacking trips into the park's rugged backcountry, where you can explore alpine meadows, glacial valleys, and remote mountain ranges.

Getting to Wrangell-St. Elias requires a bit more effort, as the park is remote and not connected to the main road system. Most visitors fly into Anchorage or Fairbanks and then take a small plane to the town of McCarthy or Chitina, both of which serve as gateways to the park. From there, visitors can access the park's hiking trails and backcountry areas.

In addition to the famous hiking destinations, Alaska is also home to countless lesser-known trails and wilderness areas that offer incredible hiking and backpacking experiences. For example, the Chilkoot Trail, located near the town of Skagway in Southeast Alaska, is a historic 33-mile trail that follows the route used by gold prospectors during the Klondike Gold Rush. The trail takes hikers through a variety of landscapes, from coastal rainforests to alpine tundra, and offers a fascinating glimpse into Alaska's gold rush history. The Chilkoot Trail is a multi-day hike that typically takes three to five days to complete, with designated campsites along the way. Hikers need to obtain permits to hike the Chilkoot Trail, and reservations are recommended, as the trail is limited to a certain number of visitors each year.

When hiking and backpacking in Alaska, safety should always be a top priority, as the state's wilderness can be both beautiful and dangerous. Alaska's weather is notoriously unpredictable, and hikers should be prepared for sudden changes in temperature, rain, and even snow, even during the summer months. Dressing in layers is essential, as is bringing waterproof gear to stay dry. In addition to weather concerns, wildlife safety is another important consideration. Alaska is home to a variety of large animals, including bears, moose, and wolves, and hikers should always be aware of their surroundings. Carrying bear spray and making noise while hiking are important precautions to avoid surprising wildlife. When camping, storing food in bear-proof containers and cooking away from your sleeping area are essential for keeping bears and other animals at a safe distance.

In terms of gear, hikers and backpackers in Alaska should be prepared for rugged terrain and long distances. A sturdy pair of hiking boots is a must, as many of Alaska's trails are rocky, muddy, or uneven. Trekking poles can also be helpful for navigating steep ascents and descents, especially in areas with loose rock or scree. For those planning multi-day trips, a well-fitting backpack and a quality tent are essential, as are a good sleeping bag and pad to stay warm and comfortable in the often chilly Alaskan nights. Water purification tablets or a filtration system are also important, as clean drinking water may not always be readily available in the backcountry.

Finally, a good map and compass (or GPS device) are crucial for navigation, especially in areas without established trails. Many of Alaska's hiking areas are remote, and cell phone service is often limited or non-existent, so it's important to be self-sufficient and have the skills needed to navigate the wilderness safely.

Northern Lights: Best places and times to witness the aurora borealis

The Northern Lights, or aurora borealis, are one of the most awe-inspiring natural phenomena that can be witnessed on Earth. Alaska, with its vast open skies and remote wilderness, offers some of the best opportunities in the world to experience this magical display of light and color. The aurora occurs when electrically charged particles from the sun collide with gases in Earth's atmosphere, creating vivid patterns of light that dance across the night sky. These lights can appear in shades of green, purple, red, and even pink, forming waves, curtains, and spirals that shift and change in intensity. For many travelers, seeing the Northern Lights is a once-in-a-lifetime experience, and Alaska's location in the northern hemisphere makes it an ideal destination for witnessing this spectacular phenomenon. However, there are certain times of year and specific locations where you are more likely to have a successful viewing, and careful planning can significantly increase your chances of seeing the lights.

One of the most important things to know about viewing the Northern Lights is that they are best seen during the darker months of the year, from late August to early April. The long winter nights provide the darkness needed for optimal viewing, and the best time to catch the lights is typically between 10 p.m. and 2 a.m. It's also important to note that clear skies are essential for a good aurora sighting. Cloud cover can obscure the lights, so checking the weather forecast and aurora activity before heading out is crucial. Fortunately, Alaska's cold, dry winters often bring clear skies, particularly in the interior and northern parts of the state, where some of the best aurora viewing locations are found.

One of the top destinations for seeing the Northern Lights in Alaska is the city of Fairbanks, located in the interior of the state. Fairbanks is widely regarded as one of the best places in the world to view the aurora borealis due to its location under the "auroral oval," a ring-shaped zone over the Earth's geomagnetic poles where auroral activity is most likely to occur. Fairbanks' location, combined with its long winter nights and frequent clear skies, makes it a prime spot for aurora viewing. In fact, it's not uncommon for visitors to see the Northern Lights multiple times during a week-long stay in Fairbanks, especially between September and March, when auroral activity is at its peak.

There are several ways to get to Fairbanks, depending on where you are starting your journey. For most visitors, the easiest way to reach Fairbanks is by flying into Fairbanks International Airport, which offers regular flights from major cities like Anchorage, Seattle, and Denver. Once in Fairbanks, many hotels and lodges offer aurora viewing packages, where guests can stay in accommodations specifically designed for aurora watching. Some lodges even have heated outdoor viewing areas or glass-roofed cabins, allowing visitors to watch the lights from the comfort of their rooms.

For a truly memorable Northern Lights experience, many visitors to Fairbanks choose to book an aurora viewing tour. These tours take travelers away from the city lights and into the remote wilderness, where the dark skies offer the best conditions for viewing the aurora. Popular tour options include dog sledding trips, snowmobile excursions, and trips to hot springs, where you can soak in warm mineral waters while watching the lights overhead. Chena Hot Springs Resort, located about 60 miles northeast of Fairbanks, is one of the most popular destinations for aurora viewing. The resort offers a unique experience where visitors can relax in natural hot springs while gazing up at the night sky, making it a truly unforgettable way to witness the Northern Lights.

Another excellent location for viewing the aurora borealis is the small town of Coldfoot, located in the Brooks Range about 250 miles north of Fairbanks. Coldfoot is one of the most remote places in Alaska that offers regular aurora viewing tours, and its far-northern location means that visitors here are often treated to some of the brightest and most vivid auroras in the state. Coldfoot is located along the Dalton Highway, a rugged road that stretches from Fairbanks to Prudhoe Bay, and it's accessible by car, though the drive can be challenging, especially in winter. Alternatively, many visitors choose to take a flight from Fairbanks to

Coldfoot, which offers stunning aerial views of Alaska's vast wilderness.

Coldfoot Camp, a former gold mining camp turned wilderness lodge, is the main hub for aurora viewing in the area. The camp offers guided tours that take visitors into the Brooks Range to watch the Northern Lights away from any artificial light pollution. The tours typically include transportation, meals, and overnight accommodations in rustic cabins, providing a true wilderness experience. For those interested in combining aurora viewing with outdoor adventure, Coldfoot Camp also offers activities such as dog sledding, snowshoeing, and ice fishing, allowing visitors to fully immerse themselves in the Alaskan winter landscape.

Further north, the village of Utqiaġvik (formerly known as Barrow), located on the northern coast of Alaska, offers another excellent opportunity for viewing the Northern Lights. Utqiaġvik is the northernmost town in the United States, and its location above the Arctic Circle means that it experiences nearly 24 hours of darkness during the winter months, providing ample opportunities for aurora viewing. The long, dark nights, combined with the town's isolation, make Utqiaġvik one of the best places in Alaska to see the Northern Lights, especially during the peak aurora season from November to January.

Reaching Utqiaġvik requires a bit more effort, as the town is not connected to the rest of Alaska by road. Most visitors fly into Utqiaġvik from Fairbanks or Anchorage on small regional airlines, and the flight itself offers incredible views of Alaska's Arctic landscape. Once in Utqiaġvik, visitors can explore the town's unique Inupiat culture and history while waiting for the aurora to appear. Local guides offer aurora viewing tours that take visitors to some of the best spots outside of town for unobstructed views of the night sky. Watching the Northern Lights in such a remote and starkly beautiful location as Utqiaġvik is an experience unlike any other.

For those looking for a more accessible aurora viewing experience, the city of Anchorage also offers excellent opportunities to see the Northern Lights, especially during the fall and winter months. While Anchorage is Alaska's largest city and has some light pollution, there are several spots just outside the city where the skies are dark enough for good aurora viewing. One popular location is Glen Alps, located about 20 minutes from downtown Anchorage. The Glen Alps Trailhead offers stunning views of the city and the surrounding mountains, and on clear nights, the Northern Lights can often be seen dancing above the horizon.

Another great spot near Anchorage for aurora viewing is Eklutna Lake, located about an hour north of the city in Chugach State Park. The lake's remote location and wide-open skies make it a prime spot for catching the aurora, and the surrounding mountains provide a beautiful backdrop for photos. Visitors can drive to Eklutna Lake on their own or join an aurora viewing tour that departs from Anchorage. These tours often include transportation, warm drinks, and blankets to keep you comfortable while you wait for the lights to appear.

In addition to the locations mentioned above, there are countless other places in Alaska where the Northern Lights can be seen, including remote lodges, national parks, and wilderness areas. Some travelers choose to embark on multi-day aurora viewing tours that take them to various locations throughout the state, maximizing their chances of seeing the lights. These tours often include transportation, lodging, and guided activities, providing a hassle-free way to experience the best of Alaska's Northern Lights.

When planning a trip to see the Northern Lights in Alaska, it's important to remember that the aurora is a natural phenomenon and can be unpredictable. While Alaska offers some of the best chances in the world to see the lights, there are no guarantees, as auroral activity depends on solar storms and geomagnetic conditions. However, by visiting during the right time of year, staying in areas with dark skies, and keeping an eye on aurora forecasts, visitors can greatly increase their chances of seeing the Northern Lights.

In terms of making the experience even more memorable, there are a few things to keep in mind. First, dressing warmly is essential, as aurora viewing often involves standing outside for extended periods in cold temperatures. Layering is key, and bringing a warm coat, hat, gloves, and insulated boots will help keep you comfortable while you wait for the lights to appear.

Many tour operators provide heated shelters or warm drinks to help keep guests cozy during their aurora viewing experience.

Another tip for enhancing your Northern Lights experience is to bring a camera with a tripod to capture the lights. The aurora is often too faint to be captured with a smartphone, but a DSLR camera with manual settings can capture stunning images of the lights, especially with a long exposure. Many aurora viewing tours offer photography tips and guidance to help you get the perfect shot.

National Parks and Wilderness Areas: Overview of Alaska's most breathtaking parks

Alaska's national parks and wilderness areas are some of the most breathtaking and remote natural treasures in the world. With over 54 million acres of national parkland and even more untouched wilderness, Alaska offers visitors a chance to experience landscapes that are rugged, wild, and largely unspoiled by human development. Whether you're looking to explore towering mountain ranges, massive glaciers, vast tundra, or dense forests, Alaska's national parks provide a unique opportunity to immerse yourself in the grandeur of nature. These parks aren't just places of beauty; they are home to diverse ecosystems, rich cultural histories, and some of the most incredible wildlife viewing in North America. From Denali's towering peaks to Glacier

Bay's icy fjords, these parks offer something for every nature enthusiast.

One of Alaska's most famous and visited national parks is Denali National Park and Preserve, home to North America's tallest mountain, Denali, which rises to an impressive 20,310 feet. Located in central Alaska, Denali National Park spans over six million acres of wilderness, encompassing everything from lowland forests to alpine tundra and glaciers. The park is renowned not only for its stunning landscapes but also for its abundant wildlife, including grizzly bears, wolves, moose, caribou, and Dall sheep. Visitors come from around the world to experience Denali's untouched wilderness, whether it's through hiking, wildlife viewing, or simply soaking in the awe-inspiring views of the mountain itself.

Getting to Denali National Park is relatively straightforward for those traveling from Anchorage or Fairbanks. The park is accessible via the George Parks Highway, which runs between Anchorage and Fairbanks, making it a convenient stop for those road-tripping through the state. The park's main entrance is located about 240 miles north of Anchorage and about 120 miles south of Fairbanks, making it roughly a five-hour drive from Anchorage and a two-hour drive from Fairbanks. Visitors can also take the Alaska Railroad from either city, a scenic and relaxing way to travel while enjoying stunning views of the Alaskan wilderness.

Once inside the park, there are plenty of activities to keep visitors busy. Wildlife viewing is one of the main draws, and the park's shuttle bus system offers access to the park's interior, where visitors can see animals in their natural habitat. For those looking for a more immersive experience, Denali offers numerous hiking opportunities, ranging from short, easy trails near the park entrance to more challenging backcountry treks. One of the most popular hikes is the Mount Healy Overlook Trail, which offers a moderately difficult 5-mile round-trip hike with sweeping views of the surrounding mountains. For those seeking solitude and adventure, backcountry permits are available for camping in the park's vast wilderness, where you can experience true isolation and connection with nature.

Another iconic national park in Alaska is Glacier Bay National Park and Preserve, located in the southeastern part of the state near the town of Gustavus. Glacier Bay is known for its dramatic fjords, towering glaciers, and rich marine life, making it one of the best places in the world to experience the awe of glacial landscapes. The park covers over 3 million acres of mountains, glaciers, forests, and coastline, and it is a designated UNESCO World Heritage Site due to its unique geological features and ecological significance. One of the highlights of visiting Glacier Bay is the chance to witness massive tidewater glaciers calving into the sea, a sight that leaves a lasting impression on all who witness it.

Getting to Glacier Bay National Park is a bit more challenging, as it is not connected to the state's road system. Most visitors fly into Gustavus via small planes from Juneau, which is about 50 miles southeast of the park. From Gustavus, visitors can take a short shuttle ride to the park's main visitor area. Alternatively, some visitors arrive in Glacier Bay via cruise ships, which travel through the Inside Passage and provide a front-row view of the park's glaciers and wildlife. Once inside the park, visitors can explore the bay by boat, kayak, or on guided tours, all of which offer stunning views of the glaciers, mountains, and wildlife. For those interested in marine life, Glacier Bay is home to humpback whales, orcas, sea otters, and seals, providing excellent wildlife viewing opportunities.

Another breathtaking national park in Alaska is Wrangell-St. Elias National Park and Preserve, the largest national park in the United States. Covering an astonishing 13.2 million acres, Wrangell-St. Elias is a vast wilderness of towering peaks, glaciers, and wild rivers, making it a paradise for outdoor enthusiasts and adventurers. The park is home to nine of the 16 tallest mountains in North America, including Mount St. Elias, which rises to 18,008 feet, and it contains some of the largest glaciers in the world. Despite its size, Wrangell-St. Elias is one of the least-visited national parks in Alaska, offering a true sense of isolation and unspoiled beauty.

Reaching Wrangell-St. Elias requires some planning, as the park is remote and lacks the infrastructure of more popular parks. The main entrance to the park is near the small town of McCarthy, which is accessible via the

McCarthy Road, a 60-mile gravel road that begins in Chitina. The road itself is an adventure, winding through forests and along the banks of the Copper River, with stunning views of the surrounding mountains. For those not comfortable driving the rugged road, shuttle services are available from Chitina, or visitors can fly into McCarthy from Anchorage via small planes.

Once inside Wrangell-St. Elias, visitors can explore the historic Kennicott copper mine, take guided glacier hikes, or venture into the park's vast backcountry for backpacking and camping. The Root Glacier, located near McCarthy, is one of the most accessible glaciers in the park and offers excellent opportunities for ice hiking and glacier exploration. For those seeking a more remote adventure, Wrangell-St. Elias is a prime destination for mountaineering, with opportunities to climb some of the tallest and most challenging peaks in North America.

In addition to the national parks, Alaska is home to numerous designated wilderness areas that offer incredible opportunities for outdoor recreation and wildlife viewing. One such area is the Arctic National Wildlife Refuge (ANWR), located in the far northeastern corner of the state. Covering over 19 million acres, ANWR is one of the largest and most ecologically diverse wilderness areas in the United States. The refuge is home to a wide variety of wildlife, including polar bears, caribou, wolves, and migratory birds, making it a must-visit destination for wildlife enthusiasts.

Reaching the Arctic National Wildlife Refuge requires careful planning, as there are no roads or established trails in the refuge. Most visitors fly into the small town of Kaktovik, located on the northern coast of Alaska, and from there, they take guided tours into the refuge. Kaktovik is a popular destination for polar bear viewing, especially in the fall when the bears gather along the coast to wait for the sea ice to form. Visitors to ANWR can also embark on multi-day rafting trips along the refuge's rivers, offering a unique way to experience the vastness of the Arctic wilderness.

Another wilderness area worth exploring is the Tongass National Forest, the largest national forest in the United States, covering over 16 million acres of temperate rainforest in Southeast Alaska. The Tongass is home to towering old-growth trees, misty fjords, and abundant wildlife, including bald eagles, bears, and salmon. One of the best ways to explore the Tongass is by hiking along the many trails that wind through the forest, offering stunning views of waterfalls, glaciers, and dense forests. The Mendenhall Glacier, located just outside of Juneau, is one of the most popular attractions in the Tongass and offers easy access to hiking trails and scenic viewpoints.

Getting to the Tongass National Forest is relatively easy, as much of the forest is located near the towns of Juneau, Ketchikan, and Sitka, all of which are accessible by air or ferry. Visitors can explore the forest on their own or join guided tours that offer insight into the area's ecology and cultural history. In addition to hiking, the

Tongass offers excellent opportunities for kayaking, wildlife viewing, and camping.

Chapter 12

Free and Paid Attractions

Museums, scenic views, and parks that don't cost a dime

One of the most well-known free attractions in Alaska is the Tony Knowles Coastal Trail, located in Anchorage, the state's largest city. This 11-mile trail stretches along the coastline, providing breathtaking views of Cook Inlet, the Chugach Mountains, and, on clear days, even Denali. The trail is paved, making it accessible for walkers, bikers, and runners, and it winds through scenic parks, forests, and open spaces, offering plenty of opportunities for wildlife viewing along the way. Moose are commonly spotted along the trail, and it's not unusual to see bald eagles soaring overhead. In the winter, the trail transforms into a popular spot for cross-country skiing and snowshoeing, making it a year-round attraction.

Getting to the Tony Knowles Coastal Trail is easy, as it begins right in downtown Anchorage at West 2nd Avenue. The trailhead is within walking distance of many of Anchorage's hotels and attractions, and for those driving, there are parking areas at several points along the trail. While walking or biking the full 11 miles may take a few hours, many visitors opt to explore shorter sections of the trail, stopping at popular viewpoints like Earthquake Park, which commemorates the 1964 earthquake that devastated Anchorage. At Earthquake Park, interpretive signs explain the impact of the earthquake, making it a fascinating stop for anyone interested in Alaska's natural history.

Another must-see free attraction in Anchorage is the Anchorage Museum's Alaska Native Heritage Gallery, located inside the Anchorage Museum at Rasmuson Center. While the main museum charges an entry fee, the heritage gallery is free to the public and offers a deep insight into Alaska's Native cultures. The gallery showcases a rotating selection of traditional and contemporary Native art, including sculptures, masks, and carvings, providing visitors with an appreciation of the cultural richness that defines Alaska. In addition to the gallery, visitors can explore the museum's public spaces, which often host temporary exhibitions and community art projects that are also free to view.

For travelers looking to escape the city and enjoy the natural beauty surrounding Anchorage, the Flattop Mountain Trail offers a rewarding hike with stunning panoramic views of the city, Cook Inlet, and the surrounding mountains. Flattop is one of the most popular hikes in Alaska due to its proximity to Anchorage and relatively easy access. The hike is about 3 miles round trip, with an elevation gain of 1,280 feet, making it moderately challenging but well worth the effort. At the summit, hikers are rewarded with 360-degree views that stretch for miles, offering a true sense of Alaska's vastness. The trailhead is located in

Chugach State Park, about a 20-minute drive from downtown Anchorage. While parking at the trailhead costs a small fee, walking or biking to the trailhead from nearby neighborhoods is free, and many locals take advantage of this option for a no-cost adventure.

Moving south from Anchorage, the town of Seward offers several free attractions that highlight the beauty of the Kenai Peninsula. One of the best-known free sites in Seward is the Seward Waterfront Park, which runs along the shores of Resurrection Bay. This picturesque park is perfect for a leisurely stroll, offering incredible views of the bay and the surrounding mountains. It's also a great spot to watch for wildlife, as sea otters, seals, and even whales are frequently seen swimming in the bay. The park is dotted with picnic tables, benches, and interpretive signs that explain the area's natural and cultural history, making it a relaxing and informative stop.

Seward is also home to the Alaska SeaLife Center, a popular attraction that requires an entrance fee. However, you don't need to pay to enjoy the wildlife viewing areas along the center's exterior. The facility is located right on the waterfront, and from the outside decks and nearby walkways, visitors can often see sea otters, seabirds, and even seals lounging on the rocks. The SeaLife Center's location along Resurrection Bay offers prime views of marine wildlife, giving you a taste of Alaska's abundant coastal ecosystems without spending any money.

Further up the coast, Exit Glacier in Kenai Fjords National Park is one of the few glaciers in Alaska that is accessible by road and free to visit. The glacier is a short drive from Seward, and visitors can park at the Exit Glacier Nature Center, which offers free parking and restroom facilities. From the nature center, several trails lead to viewpoints overlooking the glacier, with the shortest trail being less than a mile long. For those looking for more of a challenge, the Harding Icefield Trail offers a longer and more strenuous hike, climbing over 3,500 feet to offer breathtaking views of the massive Harding Icefield that stretches for miles beyond the glacier. The trail is free to hike, and along the way, interpretive signs provide information about the area's geology and natural history.

For those interested in Alaska's history, a visit to the Alaska State Capitol in Juneau is a free and educational experience. The Capitol building, located in the heart of downtown Juneau, offers guided tours that take visitors through the halls of Alaska's government, providing insight into the state's political history and its journey to statehood. The tours are free, and visitors can learn about the legislative process, see historical exhibits, and explore the art and architecture of the building. Juneau itself offers several other free attractions, including the scenic Mount Roberts Trail, which begins near downtown and climbs through forests to offer stunning views of the city and Gastineau Channel.

Another fantastic free attraction in Juneau is the Mendenhall Glacier Visitor Center. While the visitor center itself charges a small fee for entry, the surrounding area offers several free hiking trails and viewpoints that provide excellent views of the glacier and the surrounding wilderness. The Photo Point Trail is a short, easy walk that leads to a prime viewpoint overlooking the glacier, while the Nugget Falls Trail takes hikers to the base of a towering waterfall that cascades down near the glacier. Visitors can also explore the nearby forest and wetlands, where they may spot wildlife such as black bears, beavers, and eagles.

For travelers venturing further into the interior of Alaska, Fairbanks offers a wealth of free attractions that highlight the region's cultural history and natural beauty. One of the best free attractions in Fairbanks is the Morris Thompson Cultural and Visitors Center, located on the banks of the Chena River. The center offers interactive exhibits on the history, culture, and wildlife of Interior Alaska, providing visitors with a comprehensive overview of the region's indigenous peoples, gold rush history, and natural environment. The center is also a great place to pick up free maps and guides for exploring the surrounding area.

Another must-visit free attraction in Fairbanks is Pioneer Park, a 44-acre historical theme park that celebrates Alaska's pioneer history. The park features restored historic buildings, including a gold rush-era riverboat and a mining town, as well as museums, playgrounds, and picnic areas. While some of the park's attractions charge admission, many of the buildings and exhibits are free to explore, making it a fun and affordable way to learn about Alaska's past.

Fairbanks is also a gateway to the stunning wilderness of the Arctic Circle, and visitors looking to explore Alaska's remote north can do so without spending a fortune. The Dalton Highway, also known as the "Haul Road," runs from Fairbanks to the Arctic Ocean and offers a unique opportunity to experience Alaska's rugged interior landscapes. The highway is free to travel, and along the way, travelers can stop at scenic viewpoints, wildlife viewing areas, and historic sites, including the Yukon River and the Arctic Circle sign. While driving the entire highway requires careful planning and preparation, even a short drive from Fairbanks offers incredible views of the surrounding wilderness.

Paid Experiences Worth Every Penny: Guided tours, boat cruises, and wilderness safaris

Alaska is a place of unparalleled natural beauty, and while many of its wonders can be explored on your own, there are certain experiences that are truly worth every penny when you take advantage of guided tours, boat cruises, and wilderness safaris. These paid experiences allow visitors to access remote areas, gain expert insights from knowledgeable guides, and immerse themselves fully in the landscapes, wildlife, and culture that make Alaska such a special destination. For those who want to make the most of their trip and create lasting memories, these curated adventures offer an elevated experience, where convenience, expertise, and once-in-a-lifetime sights come together.

One of the most sought-after paid experiences in Alaska is a boat cruise through Kenai Fjords National Park, located near the town of Seward. This stunning park is known for its dramatic coastal scenery, where towering glaciers meet the ocean, and rugged fjords stretch out into the distance. A boat cruise through the park provides visitors with the opportunity to witness massive tidewater glaciers calving into the sea, as well as the chance to see marine wildlife up close, including orcas, humpback whales, sea otters, and puffins. The guided narration on these cruises enhances the experience, as the crew provides fascinating insights into the geology and wildlife of the area.

Most visitors access Kenai Fjords by first traveling to Seward, which is a scenic two-and-a-half-hour drive from Anchorage along the Seward Highway. Alternatively, you can take the Alaska Railroad, which offers a beautiful journey along the same route. Once in Seward, several companies offer half-day and full-day boat cruises, with the longer trips providing deeper access into the park's remote and untouched areas. Some cruises include meals served onboard, often with locally sourced ingredients such as fresh salmon or halibut, adding to the overall experience. For those wanting to make the trip even more memorable, many cruises are timed to coincide with the peak of wildlife activity in the spring and summer, providing the best chance of spotting whales and other marine animals.

For a more intimate encounter with Alaska's wildlife, a guided wilderness safari to see bears in their natural habitat is another paid experience that is well worth the cost. Katmai National Park and Preserve, located in southwestern Alaska, is world-renowned for its population of brown bears, particularly at Brooks Falls, where bears gather to catch salmon in the rushing waters. The sight of bears standing in the river, mouths open to catch leaping salmon, is one of the most iconic images of Alaska, and experiencing it in person is truly unforgettable.

Getting to Katmai is part of the adventure, as the park is only accessible by plane or boat. Most visitors fly to King Salmon from Anchorage, and then take a smaller floatplane to Brooks Camp, where the guided bear-watching tours take place. These tours are led by experienced guides and park rangers who ensure visitors' safety while providing a deep understanding of bear behavior and the ecosystem. The viewing platforms near the falls offer excellent vantage points, and because the bears are accustomed to human presence, they often come quite close, allowing for incredible photo opportunities.

For those looking to experience Alaska's wilderness in a different way, a flightseeing tour over Denali National Park offers a bird's-eye view of North America's tallest peak, Denali, as well as the park's glaciers, rivers, and valleys. These tours are typically done in small planes or helicopters, providing an up-close view of Denali's rugged slopes, vast icefields, and the untouched expanses of wilderness below. Some flightseeing tours even include glacier landings, where visitors can step out onto the ice and experience the vastness of the park from a completely different perspective.

Flightseeing tours depart from a variety of locations, including Anchorage, Talkeetna, and Denali Park, making it easy to incorporate this experience into your travel itinerary. Talkeetna, a charming town located about two hours north of Anchorage, is one of the most popular departure points for Denali flightseeing. The town is known for its laid-back vibe and serves as a gateway to many Denali-related adventures. For travelers without a vehicle, the Alaska Railroad offers service to Talkeetna, making it easy to reach from Anchorage or Fairbanks. Once airborne, the breathtaking views of Denali's snowy summit, coupled with expert narration from the pilot, make for an awe-inspiring experience that leaves a lasting impression.

Another paid experience that offers great value is a guided kayaking tour through the waters of Prince William Sound. This remote and beautiful area, located near the town of Whittier, is known for its calm, protected waters, where glaciers, fjords, and wildlife come together to create a paddler's paradise. Kayaking offers a quiet and immersive way to explore the sound, allowing visitors to glide past towering icebergs, float beneath waterfalls, and observe sea otters, seals, and bald eagles in their natural environment.

Most kayaking tours depart from Whittier, a small town located about an hour's drive from Anchorage. The town is accessible by car via the Anton Anderson Memorial Tunnel, the longest highway tunnel in North America, or by train on the Alaska Railroad. Kayaking tours range from half-day trips to multi-day excursions, with guides providing all the necessary gear and instruction. Whether you're a seasoned paddler or a first-time kayaker, these tours offer an incredible way to experience the untouched beauty of Alaska's coastal wilderness.

For those interested in Alaska's rich indigenous culture, a guided tour of the Alaska Native Heritage Center in Anchorage is a paid experience that provides invaluable insight into the traditions, history, and contemporary life of Alaska's Native peoples. The center features exhibits on Alaska's diverse indigenous groups, including the Inupiat, Tlingit, Haida, and Athabascan peoples, among others. Visitors can explore traditional dwellings, watch demonstrations of Native art and crafts, and attend performances of traditional songs and dances. The knowledgeable guides at the center offer in-depth explanations of the cultural significance of each exhibit, providing a deeper understanding of Alaska's Native heritage.

The Alaska Native Heritage Center is located just outside downtown Anchorage and is easily accessible by car or public transportation. Many hotels in Anchorage also offer shuttle services to the center, making it convenient for visitors without their own transportation. The admission fee includes access to all exhibits and performances, and the experience is both educational and enriching, offering visitors a chance to connect with Alaska's indigenous cultures in a meaningful way.

Another unique paid experience in Alaska is a dog sledding tour, a quintessential Alaskan adventure that allows visitors to experience the thrill of mushing through the wilderness. During the summer months, many dog sledding tours take place on glaciers, where visitors are flown by helicopter to remote camps high in the mountains. Once there, you can meet the sled dogs, learn about the history of mushing, and take a ride on a sled pulled by a team of eager dogs. These tours offer a rare chance to experience a piece of Alaskan tradition while surrounded by stunning glacier landscapes.

Dog sledding tours are offered in various locations throughout Alaska, with many departing from popular destinations such as Anchorage, Girdwood, and Seward. Helicopter flights to the glacier camps provide spectacular aerial views of the surrounding mountains and valleys, adding to the overall adventure. For visitors traveling in the winter, traditional dog sledding tours are available in places like Fairbanks and Denali, where teams of sled dogs pull guests through snow-covered forests and across frozen lakes, offering a magical and authentic Alaskan experience.

Finally, for those seeking a true wilderness adventure, a guided backpacking or camping trip into Alaska's remote backcountry is a paid experience that offers both solitude and immersion in the state's untamed landscapes. Wrangell-St. Elias National Park, the largest national park in the United States, offers countless opportunities for guided backpacking trips, where visitors can explore glaciers, valleys, and mountain ranges far from the crowds. These trips are led by experienced wilderness guides who ensure that visitors have a safe and rewarding experience while navigating the park's rugged terrain.

Backpacking trips in Wrangell-St. Elias typically begin in the town of McCarthy, which is accessible by car via the McCarthy Road or by small plane from Anchorage. Once in the park, visitors embark on multi-day hikes through some of the most remote and pristine wilderness in Alaska. The guided trips often include all necessary gear, as well as meals and transportation, making it easy for visitors to focus on the adventure. Whether you're trekking across glaciers, camping under the stars, or watching wildlife in the distance, a guided wilderness trip offers a deep connection to the land and a sense of accomplishment that is hard to match.

How to Book Activities: Booking tips, best times, and operator recommendations

Booking activities in Alaska requires some careful planning, especially given the state's vast geography and the remote nature of many of its most popular attractions. Whether you're looking to book a scenic flightseeing tour, a glacier hike, a wildlife cruise, or an adventure into Alaska's backcountry, knowing how to book, when to book, and which operators to trust can make all the difference in ensuring your experience is both smooth and memorable. Alaska's tourism season is relatively short, with peak travel times during the summer months of June, July, and August, and many activities filling up quickly. Thus, understanding the best time to book and securing reservations well in advance can be crucial to enjoying the full Alaskan experience.

The first step to booking activities in Alaska is determining what experiences are most important to you and then deciding on the best timing. Because of Alaska's size and diversity of landscapes, activities can vary dramatically depending on where you are. For example, coastal towns like Seward and Juneau are famous for glacier cruises and marine wildlife tours, while interior destinations like Fairbanks and Denali are better known for hiking, wildlife viewing, and Northern Lights tours in the colder months. It's also important to consider the weather and seasonal availability. Certain activities, such as dog sledding on glaciers, are only available in the summer, while others, like aurora borealis viewing, are best done during the long winter nights.

For most visitors, booking ahead of time is strongly recommended, especially if you're visiting during the peak summer months. Many popular tours and activities, particularly those involving flightseeing, guided wildlife tours, and glacier experiences, can book up weeks or even months in advance. The best way to secure your spot is to book directly with tour operators online, although booking through a travel agency or an Alaskan tour company can also simplify the process by offering bundled packages that include multiple activities, transportation, and accommodations.

If you're looking to book a glacier cruise, one of Alaska's top experiences, operators like Kenai Fjords Tours, based in Seward, are among the best. Kenai Fjords National Park is a stunning area known for its towering glaciers and marine wildlife. Cruises depart daily from Seward during the summer months, and options range from shorter half-day tours to full-day adventures. It's best to book as early as possible, as spaces can fill up fast, particularly on weekends and during holiday periods. The best time for a glacier cruise is generally between June and early September when the weather is more predictable, and wildlife is most active. You can get to Seward by driving from Anchorage along the scenic Seward Highway or by taking the Alaska Railroad, which offers daily service during the summer months.

Another iconic Alaskan experience is flightseeing over Denali, North America's tallest mountain. Talkeetna Air Taxi and K2 Aviation are two of the most reputable operators offering flightseeing tours of Denali National Park. These tours depart from Talkeetna, a small town located about two hours north of Anchorage, and provide breathtaking views of Denali, as well as the park's glaciers, valleys, and wildlife. Many of these flights also include an option to land on a glacier, allowing passengers to step out and take in the majesty of the surrounding mountains. Flights are weather-dependent, and it's recommended to book your flight at the beginning of your trip to allow for flexibility in case of cancellations due to poor visibility or inclement weather. Most companies offer full refunds or rescheduling options if flights are canceled due to weather conditions, so it's important to keep an eye on the forecast and be flexible with your itinerary. To get to Talkeetna, you can drive from Anchorage or take the Alaska Railroad, which offers a beautiful scenic route.

For visitors traveling to the southeastern part of the state, whale-watching tours from Juneau are another must-do activity. Juneau, accessible only by air or sea, is one of the best places in Alaska to see humpback whales, as they migrate through the area's waters during the summer months. Operators like Harv and Marv's Outback Alaska and Alaska Whale Watch offer guided tours that take visitors out into the rich marine waters of the Inside Passage, where whale sightings are almost guaranteed during the peak season from May through September. These tours typically last about three hours, and along the way, you may also spot orcas, sea lions, and bald eagles. While it's possible to book whale-watching tours once you arrive in Juneau, it's highly recommended to reserve your spot in advance, especially if you plan to visit during the busy months of July and August. You can reach Juneau via a short flight from Anchorage or Seattle, or by taking the Alaska Marine Highway ferry system, which connects Juneau with other towns in Southeast Alaska.

For more adventurous travelers, guided wilderness safaris or bear-watching tours in remote parts of Alaska offer an unforgettable experience. Katmai National Park, famous for its large population of brown bears, is a prime destination for bear viewing, particularly at Brooks Falls, where bears gather to catch salmon during the summer months. Katmai is remote and requires a flight from Anchorage or Homer, and many bear-watching tours include both the flight and guided experience. Companies like Katmai Air and Alaska Bear Adventures offer full-day or multi-day tours that include transportation, meals, and expert guidance. It's essential to book these tours well in advance, as spaces are limited and demand is high during the peak bear-watching season, which typically runs from June to September. Bear viewing is a bucket-list experience for many travelers, and the opportunity to see these magnificent animals up close in their natural habitat is worth every penny.

When it comes to booking activities in Alaska, timing is everything. Booking your tours early, ideally several months before your trip, is the best way to ensure you get the activities you want. If you're traveling during the off-season, you may find more last-minute availability, but it's still a good idea to secure your spots ahead of time to avoid disappointment. Additionally, many operators offer discounts for booking early or bundling multiple tours together, so it's worth exploring package deals, especially if you're planning to do several activities during your stay.

One of the key considerations when booking activities in Alaska is the weather. Because of Alaska's location and climate, weather conditions can be unpredictable, especially in the coastal areas where rain, fog, and wind are common. Many outdoor activities, such as flightseeing, glacier hiking, and boat tours, are weather-dependent, and cancellations due to weather are not uncommon. It's a good idea to build some flexibility into your itinerary so that you can reschedule if necessary. For example, if you're planning to do a flightseeing tour in Denali, book it early in your trip so that you have extra days available in case it needs to be rescheduled. Most operators are very accommodating when it comes to rescheduling due to weather, but having a backup plan will help ensure you don't miss out on your dream adventure.

Another important tip when booking activities in Alaska is to research your tour operators carefully. Alaska is home to many reputable tour companies, but it's always a good idea to check reviews, ask for recommendations, and ensure that the operators are experienced and prioritize safety. Websites like TripAdvisor, Google Reviews, and Alaska tourism boards are great resources for finding reliable operators. Additionally, many tour companies are members of the Alaska Travel Industry Association (ATIA), which sets high standards for service and professionalism, so choosing an ATIA member can provide extra peace of mind.

If you're looking to book more niche or specialized activities, such as photography tours, fishing charters, or Northern Lights viewing trips, there are several operators that cater to these interests. For example, photography tours in places like Denali or the Arctic Circle are designed to take you to the most scenic and remote locations at the best times of day for capturing stunning images. These tours are led by professional photographers who offer tips on technique and composition, ensuring you return home with incredible photos of Alaska's landscapes and wildlife. Fishing charters, particularly in places like Homer, Seward, or Kodiak Island, provide a chance to fish for some of the world's best salmon and halibut, with guides who know the best spots and can help you maximize your chances of a great catch.

If you're traveling during the winter months, booking a Northern Lights tour in Fairbanks or the surrounding areas is a fantastic way to experience Alaska's dark winter skies. Northern Lights viewing is best from September to April, and many tour companies in Fairbanks offer guided trips to remote locations where light pollution is minimal, increasing your chances of seeing the aurora borealis. Some tours even include overnight stays in remote cabins or yurts, allowing you to relax by a fire while waiting for the lights to appear. Companies like Northern Alaska Tour Company and Aurora Borealis Lodge are highly recommended for Northern Lights tours, and booking early is essential, as these tours fill up quickly, especially during peak aurora season.

Chapter 13

Day Trips and Excursions

From Anchorage

Anchorage, Alaska's largest city, is not only a destination filled with its own vibrant culture, but it also serves as a perfect base for some of the most breathtaking day trips in the state. For travelers looking to explore the beauty and diversity of Alaska without venturing too far from the city, three fantastic options include day trips to Whittier, Girdwood, and Turnagain Arm. These destinations offer stunning natural landscapes, outdoor adventures, and unique cultural experiences that can easily be accessed from Anchorage, either by car or train. Each of these locations provides a glimpse into the variety of Alaskan landscapes, from coastal fjords and towering glaciers to picturesque mountain towns and scenic drives. Whether you're an outdoor enthusiast, a wildlife lover, or someone simply looking to escape into nature for a day, these destinations offer unforgettable experiences that can easily fit into any itinerary.

Located just about 60 miles southeast of Anchorage, Whittier is a small coastal town that serves as the gateway to Prince William Sound. Despite its small size, Whittier is a popular destination for day trips due to its incredible access to marine wildlife, stunning fjords, and pristine glaciers. One of the most interesting aspects of Whittier is its remote nature – the town is accessible by only two means: a one-lane tunnel that is shared by both cars and trains, or by sea. The Anton Anderson Memorial Tunnel, which stretches 2.5 miles through a mountain, is the longest highway tunnel in North America, making the journey to Whittier a unique adventure in itself. The tunnel operates on a schedule that alternates between cars and trains, so timing your trip through the tunnel is an important part of planning a visit to Whittier.

Once you've arrived in Whittier, there are numerous activities to enjoy that showcase the natural beauty of the area. The most popular option for day-trippers is to take a glacier and wildlife cruise through Prince William Sound. These boat tours take visitors deep into the fjords, where they can see massive tidewater glaciers calving into the ocean, creating thunderous crashes and waves. Along the way, you're likely to spot marine wildlife, including seals, sea lions, sea otters, and even humpback whales or orcas. Many cruises also include opportunities to see bald eagles soaring above and puffins nesting on rocky cliffs. The cruises typically last between three to five hours, making them the perfect length for a day trip. During the summer months, the long daylight hours provide plenty of time to explore Whittier's coastal beauty before heading back to Anchorage.

For those interested in staying on land, Whittier also offers several hiking opportunities that allow visitors to experience the area's wilderness up close. The Portage Pass Trail is a moderately easy hike that offers incredible views of Portage Glacier and Portage Lake. The trail is about four miles round trip, and the climb to the pass provides stunning panoramic views of the surrounding mountains and glaciers. On a clear day, the vista from the pass is absolutely breathtaking, with the massive ice field stretching out in front of you and the lush greenery of the valley below.

To get to Whittier, you can drive from Anchorage along the scenic Seward Highway, which is one of the most beautiful drives in Alaska. The journey takes about an hour and a half, and along the way, you'll pass through the stunning Turnagain Arm, which is known for its dramatic tidal changes and frequent wildlife sightings. The Alaska Railroad also offers a train service between Anchorage and Whittier, making it an easy and scenic option for those who prefer not to drive.

Another excellent day trip option from Anchorage is Girdwood, a charming mountain town located just 40 miles southeast of the city. Girdwood is best known for its year-round outdoor recreation opportunities, including skiing, hiking, and mountain biking. It's home to the famous Alyeska Resort, which is Alaska's largest ski area and a popular destination for both winter and summer activities. The drive to Girdwood along the Seward Highway takes about 45 minutes, and the scenic route offers stunning views of the Chugach Mountains, Turnagain Arm, and the occasional glimpse of wildlife such as beluga whales or Dall sheep along the cliffs.

Once in Girdwood, there are plenty of activities to fill your day. One of the highlights is the Alyeska Aerial Tram, which takes visitors from the base of Alyeska Resort up to the 2,300-foot-high Mount Alyeska. From the top, you'll be treated to panoramic views of the surrounding mountains, glaciers, and Turnagain Arm. On a clear day, you can even see all the way to Prince William Sound. During the summer months, the tram provides access to several hiking trails, including the popular North Face Trail, which is the steepest hiking trail in North America. For those looking for a less strenuous option, the upper station of the tram offers a restaurant and observation deck, where you can relax and take in the views while enjoying a meal or a drink.

Girdwood is also known for its outdoor adventures. During the summer, visitors can explore the many hiking trails that wind through the nearby Chugach National Forest. One of the most popular hikes in the area is the Winner Creek Trail, which takes you through a lush rainforest and over a hand tram that crosses a deep gorge. The trail is about five miles round trip and offers a peaceful walk through the forest, with opportunities to spot wildlife such as moose and black bears.

In addition to its outdoor activities, Girdwood has a thriving arts and food scene. The town is home to several local galleries, where you can find works by Alaskan artists, as well as unique handcrafted goods. When it comes to dining, Girdwood offers some of the best food in the state, with a range of restaurants serving everything from fresh seafood to hearty Alaskan comfort food. One of the most popular spots is the Bake Shop, known for its delicious homemade soups, sandwiches, and cinnamon rolls.

For visitors looking to explore the area without a car, Girdwood is accessible by the Alaska Railroad, which offers a daily train service between Anchorage and Girdwood. The train ride is a scenic journey along Turnagain Arm and provides a relaxing and convenient way to reach the town. Whether you arrive by train or car, a day trip to Girdwood offers a perfect mix of outdoor adventure, stunning scenery, and small-town charm.

The third option for a fantastic day trip from Anchorage is a drive along the scenic Turnagain Arm, one of the most beautiful coastal drives in the world. Turnagain Arm is a narrow body of water that stretches about 50 miles from Anchorage to the town of Portage, and the drive along the Seward Highway offers breathtaking views of the water, mountains, and wildlife. The arm is famous for its dramatic tidal changes, which can result in a tidal bore, a large wave that travels up the inlet, creating a unique spectacle. Visitors driving along the highway often pull over to watch the bore tide or to spot beluga whales, which are frequently seen in the waters of Turnagain Arm during the summer months.

One of the highlights of a day trip along Turnagain Arm is the chance to visit several scenic viewpoints and natural attractions along the way. Beluga Point is a popular stop where visitors can enjoy panoramic views of the inlet and the surrounding mountains. On clear days, you can see across the water to the Kenai Peninsula and the Alaska Range beyond. Beluga Point is also one of the best spots to watch for beluga whales, which often swim close to shore as they follow the tides.

Further along the highway, the Alaska Wildlife Conservation Center is a must-visit attraction for anyone interested in Alaska's wildlife. The center is located near the town of Portage and is home to a wide range of native Alaskan animals, including bears, moose, caribou, bison, and more. Visitors can take a self-guided driving or walking tour through the center, where they can see these animals up close and learn about conservation efforts to protect Alaska's wildlife. The center is especially popular with families, as it provides an opportunity to see animals in a naturalistic setting while also supporting important wildlife rehabilitation and education programs.

For those looking for a more active adventure, the Portage Glacier is another highlight of a day trip along Turnagain Arm. The glacier is located about an hour's drive from Anchorage, and while it is no longer visible from the road, visitors can take a short boat tour across Portage Lake to get an up-close view of the glacier's blue ice. The 60-minute cruise is a fantastic way to experience one of Alaska's many glaciers and to learn about the region's glacial history from knowledgeable guides. For visitors who prefer to stay on land, there are several hiking trails in the area that offer scenic views of the glacier and the surrounding mountains.

To make the most of a day trip along Turnagain Arm, it's best to start early in the morning to allow plenty of time for stops along the way. The drive itself is relatively short, but with so many beautiful viewpoints, wildlife sightings, and outdoor activities to enjoy, a full day is easily spent exploring this stunning part of Alaska.

From Juneau: Excursions to Mendenhall Glacier and nearby islands

Juneau, Alaska's picturesque capital, is a unique destination with its rich combination of natural wonders and cultural heritage. Nestled between towering mountains and the waters of Gastineau Channel, Juneau is both remote and easily accessible by air or sea. It is one of the few U.S. state capitals that is not accessible by road, and this isolation has preserved much of its pristine natural beauty. Whether you're visiting for a few days or just passing through on a cruise, Juneau serves as the perfect starting point for unforgettable excursions that showcase Alaska's glaciers and nearby islands. The most iconic of these is a visit to Mendenhall Glacier, one of the region's most easily accessible glaciers, and a trip to the nearby islands, where visitors can experience the wildlife, scenery, and adventure that define Southeast Alaska.

Mendenhall Glacier is located just 12 miles from downtown Juneau, making it an easy half-day or full-day excursion for visitors of all ages and abilities. The glacier is part of the Tongass National Forest, the largest national forest in the United States, and it stretches 13 miles from the Juneau Icefield down to Mendenhall Lake. This massive river of ice is one of the most popular attractions in the area due to its proximity to the city and the stunning views it offers. Whether you're looking for a leisurely day trip with scenic vistas or an active adventure on the ice, Mendenhall Glacier has something for everyone.

Getting to Mendenhall Glacier from Juneau is straightforward. Visitors can either rent a car, take a taxi, or book a shuttle service from downtown Juneau to the Mendenhall Glacier Visitor Center. The shuttle is the most convenient and popular option for those without a car, as it runs frequently during the summer tourist season. The drive to the glacier takes about 20 minutes, and once you arrive, you're greeted by the stunning sight of the glacier flowing into the lake, with towering mountains framing the scene. Parking is available for those who prefer to drive themselves, and the visitor center is open year-round, offering exhibits about the glacier, as well as educational programs and guided tours during the summer months.

For those interested in a relaxing experience, the Mendenhall Glacier Visitor Center offers several short, accessible trails that lead to various viewpoints overlooking the glacier and Mendenhall Lake. One of the most popular trails is the Photo Point Trail, a short, paved path that takes visitors to a scenic overlook where you can get an up-close view of the glacier and its surrounding landscape. Another excellent option is the Nugget Falls Trail, a two-mile round-trip hike that leads to the base of Nugget Falls, a massive waterfall that tumbles into Mendenhall Lake. The trail is relatively flat and suitable for families, and the views of both the glacier and the waterfall are absolutely stunning.

For more adventurous visitors, guided glacier hikes and ice cave tours offer an unforgettable way to explore the glacier itself. Several local tour companies offer guided hikes that take visitors onto the ice, where they can walk on the glacier's surface and explore the dramatic ice formations, crevasses, and even ice caves that form within the glacier. These tours require a moderate level of fitness, as they involve some hiking over uneven terrain, but the experience of standing on a glacier and peering into its deep blue ice is well worth the effort. Some of the tours also include a short kayak or canoe trip across Mendenhall Lake, adding an extra element of adventure. It's important to note that glacier conditions can change rapidly, so booking a guided tour with an experienced operator ensures both safety and access to the best routes and features.

If you prefer to see Mendenhall Glacier from a different perspective, flightseeing tours offer a bird's-eye view of the glacier and the surrounding Juneau Icefield. These tours typically depart from Juneau International Airport and involve a short helicopter ride that takes passengers over the glacier, offering spectacular aerial views of the ice, mountains, and valleys below. Many flightseeing tours also include the option to land on the glacier itself, allowing visitors to step out onto the ice for a guided walk. These helicopter tours are an unforgettable way to experience the scale and beauty of Mendenhall Glacier, and they provide access to areas of the glacier that are otherwise inaccessible on foot.

In addition to visiting Mendenhall Glacier, Juneau offers a variety of excursions to nearby islands, where visitors can explore even more of Southeast Alaska's stunning landscapes and wildlife. One of the most popular destinations is Admiralty Island, located just a short boat ride from Juneau. Admiralty Island is home to the highest concentration of brown bears in North America, making it a prime destination for wildlife viewing. The island is part of the Admiralty Island National Monument, a protected wilderness area that also includes Tongass National Forest. Visitors to the island can take guided bear-watching tours, where they have the chance to see these magnificent animals in their natural habitat as they fish for salmon in the island's streams. The tours are typically led by experienced naturalists who provide insights into bear behavior and the island's ecosystem, making for an educational and thrilling experience.

To get to Admiralty Island from Juneau, visitors can take a floatplane or a boat tour. Floatplane tours depart from the Juneau waterfront and offer a scenic flight over the surrounding waterways before landing on the island. Boat tours, which are often combined with whale-watching trips, depart from Auke Bay, located about 15 minutes north of downtown Juneau. The journey to the island is an adventure in itself, as the waters surrounding Juneau are rich with marine wildlife, including humpback whales, orcas, sea lions, and bald eagles. A trip to Admiralty Island provides a true wilderness experience, where visitors can immerse themselves in the untouched beauty of Alaska's wild landscapes.

Another nearby island that offers a memorable day trip from Juneau is Douglas Island, located just across Gastineau Channel from downtown Juneau. Douglas Island is connected to Juneau by the Juneau-Douglas Bridge, making it easily accessible by car or bike. The island offers a quieter, more relaxed alternative to the hustle and bustle of downtown Juneau, and it's a great place to explore for those looking to escape into nature for a few hours. One of the island's highlights is the Treadwell Mine Historic Trail, which takes visitors through the ruins of the Treadwell gold mine, one of the largest and most productive gold mines in the world during the late 19th and early 20th centuries. The trail offers a fascinating glimpse into Alaska's gold rush history, and interpretive signs along the way provide information about the mine's operations and its eventual collapse in 1917.

For those interested in outdoor recreation, Douglas Island also offers several hiking trails that provide stunning views of the surrounding mountains and waterways. The Mount Jumbo Trail, a challenging hike that climbs to the summit of Mount Jumbo, offers panoramic views of Gastineau Channel, Juneau, and the surrounding islands. On clear days, the views from the top are absolutely breathtaking, and the hike provides a rewarding challenge for experienced hikers. For a more leisurely walk, the Dan Moller Trail is a popular option that takes visitors through alpine meadows and forests, with the possibility of spotting wildlife such as deer and black bears.

For those looking to explore the waters around Juneau and its islands, kayaking is another fantastic option. Guided kayaking tours are available from both downtown Juneau and Auke Bay, and they offer a peaceful and immersive way to experience Alaska's coastal beauty. Paddling through the calm waters of Gastineau Channel or the nearby islands, visitors can explore secluded coves, spot marine wildlife, and take in the stunning scenery of the surrounding mountains and forests. Some tours even include a stop at a remote beach for a picnic lunch, adding to the adventure. Kayaking is suitable for all skill levels, and the experienced guides provide all the necessary equipment and instruction to ensure a safe and enjoyable experience.

In addition to its natural beauty, Juneau and its surrounding islands offer plenty of opportunities to learn about Alaska's indigenous cultures. The Sealaska Heritage Institute in downtown Juneau is a great place to start, as it offers exhibits on the art, history, and culture of the Tlingit, Haida, and Tsimshian peoples who have lived in the region for thousands of years. The institute also hosts traditional performances and cultural demonstrations, providing visitors with a deeper understanding of Alaska's Native heritage. For those interested in indigenous art, the Walter Soboleff Building, also located in downtown Juneau, features stunning contemporary Native artwork, including large-scale totem poles and murals that reflect the rich traditions of the region's indigenous peoples.

For travelers planning a day trip to Mendenhall Glacier or the nearby islands, it's important to plan ahead and book activities in advance, especially during the summer months when Juneau sees an influx of visitors. Many of the guided tours, including glacier hikes, wildlife excursions, and kayaking trips, can fill up quickly, so reserving your spot ahead of time is recommended. Additionally, weather in Southeast Alaska can be unpredictable, so it's a good idea to dress in layers and be prepared for rain, even during the summer. Bringing a waterproof jacket and sturdy shoes will ensure that you stay comfortable while exploring the outdoors.

From Fairbanks: Exploring the Arctic Circle, Chena Hot Springs, and more

Fairbanks serves as the perfect base for some of the most extraordinary day trips and excursions in the region. From its unique position, visitors can easily venture north to the Arctic Circle, soak in the therapeutic waters of Chena Hot Springs, and explore vast wilderness areas that showcase the beauty and isolation of Alaska's rugged landscape. These experiences provide a deeper connection to the state's natural wonders and remote beauty, offering a sense of adventure that is hard to match elsewhere. Each destination around Fairbanks holds its own special appeal, making the journey as memorable as the destination.

One of the most iconic and sought-after trips from Fairbanks is a visit to the Arctic Circle, the invisible line that marks the boundary of the Earth's northern polar region. The Arctic Circle is located about 200 miles north of Fairbanks, and reaching this remote destination is a badge of honor for many travelers. The trip offers a true sense of adventure as it takes you deep into Alaska's untouched wilderness, far from the hustle and bustle of modern life. There are a few different ways to make the journey to the Arctic Circle, with the most popular options being by road or by air, each offering its own distinct experience.

For those looking to experience the journey overland, the Dalton Highway is the main route to the Arctic Circle. This 414-mile gravel road, also known as the "Haul Road," was originally built to support the Trans-Alaska Pipeline and runs from Fairbanks to Prudhoe Bay, crossing through some of the most remote and scenic landscapes in North America. While the entire highway is a formidable drive, most visitors make the trip as far as the Arctic Circle, where a sign marks the symbolic crossing into the northernmost region of the world. The Dalton Highway offers incredible opportunities to see Alaska's wild beauty up close, with sweeping views of the Brooks Range, tundra, and the Yukon River along the way. Wildlife sightings are common, with moose, caribou, and even bears often spotted along the road.

Traveling the Dalton Highway is not for the faint of heart, as the road is mostly unpaved and passes through extremely remote areas with few services. Because of this, many visitors opt to join a guided tour that departs from Fairbanks. Several local tour operators offer full-day or multi-day trips to the Arctic Circle, with experienced guides who provide insight into the region's history, geology, and wildlife. These guided tours also include stops at key points of interest along the way, such as the Yukon River Bridge and the Finger Mountain viewpoint, where visitors can take in the vastness of the surrounding wilderness. Reaching the Arctic Circle by road offers a sense of achievement and connection to the raw beauty of Alaska's interior that few other experiences can match.

For those looking for a quicker or more comfortable way to reach the Arctic Circle, flightseeing tours are another excellent option. These tours depart from Fairbanks and offer a bird's-eye view of the rugged landscape below, including the winding Yukon River, expansive tundra, and the distant peaks of the Brooks Range. Flightseeing tours typically include a landing at a remote location north of the Arctic Circle, where visitors can step out and experience the quiet solitude of this far northern region. The aerial perspective provides a unique appreciation of the scale and remoteness of Alaska's wilderness, and the chance to visit such a remote area in just a few hours makes flightseeing a popular choice for those short on time. Whether by air or by land, a trip to the Arctic Circle is a truly memorable experience, providing a deeper understanding of the vastness and isolation that define Alaska's northern reaches.

While the Arctic Circle may be the ultimate goal for many travelers to Fairbanks, the Chena Hot Springs, located just 60 miles northeast of the city, offers a more relaxing and easily accessible destination that is equally rewarding. Chena Hot Springs is famous for its natural mineral waters, which have been used for therapeutic purposes for over a century. The hot springs are nestled in a beautiful valley surrounded by the rolling hills of the Chena River State Recreation Area, making it an ideal place to unwind and soak in the soothing waters while surrounded by Alaska's natural beauty.

Getting to Chena Hot Springs is easy, with a well-maintained road leading directly from Fairbanks to the resort. The drive takes about an hour and a half, and along the way, you'll pass through the scenic Chena River State Recreation Area, which offers plenty of opportunities for outdoor activities such as hiking, fishing, and wildlife viewing. Once you arrive at the hot springs, you can spend the day enjoying the resort's many amenities, including the outdoor rock-lined hot spring lake, indoor pools, and Jacuzzis. The mineral-rich waters are said to have healing properties, making them a popular spot for those looking to relax and rejuvenate.

In addition to soaking in the hot springs, visitors can also explore the Aurora Ice Museum, which is located on-site at Chena Hot Springs. This unique attraction is the largest year-round ice environment in the world, and it features stunning ice sculptures created by world-renowned ice carvers. The museum is kept at a constant temperature of 25 degrees Fahrenheit, allowing visitors to experience the beauty of ice art even during the summer months. For an extra special treat, you can enjoy a drink at the ice bar, where the glasses themselves are made of ice.

Chena Hot Springs is also one of the best places in Alaska to view the Northern Lights, thanks to its remote location away from city lights. During the winter months, from September to April, the resort offers Northern Lights viewing tours and packages that include accommodations and guided aurora viewing. The resort's open-air hot springs provide a unique opportunity to watch the aurora borealis while soaking in the warm waters – an experience that is truly magical and unforgettable.

For those looking to combine relaxation with adventure, Chena Hot Springs offers a variety of outdoor activities year-round. In the summer, visitors can hike the many trails in the surrounding Chena River State Recreation Area, with options ranging from easy walks to more challenging hikes that offer panoramic views of the valley. The area is also home to an abundance of wildlife, including moose, beavers, and bald eagles, making it a great destination for nature lovers and photographers. In the winter, the resort offers dog sledding, snowmobiling, and snowshoeing, allowing visitors to experience Alaska's snowy landscapes in a fun and exciting way.

Another fantastic day trip from Fairbanks is a visit to the nearby Creamer's Field Migratory Waterfowl Refuge. Located just a few miles from downtown Fairbanks, this 2,200-acre refuge is a haven for birdwatchers and nature enthusiasts. Creamer's Field is best known for its role as a stopover for thousands of migratory birds, including sandhill cranes, Canada geese, and various species of ducks and swans, which pass through the area each spring and fall. The refuge's network of walking trails and viewing platforms makes it easy to observe these birds in their natural habitat, and interpretive signs along the trails provide information about the refuge's history and the birds that visit.

In addition to birdwatching, Creamer's Field offers year-round opportunities for outdoor recreation, including hiking, cross-country skiing, and wildlife viewing. The refuge's forests, wetlands, and open fields are home to a variety of animals, including moose, foxes, and beavers, making it a great place for wildlife photography. The refuge also hosts several events throughout the year, including the popular Sandhill Crane Festival, which celebrates the annual migration of these majestic birds with guided walks, educational programs, and family-friendly activities.

For visitors interested in Alaska's gold rush history, a visit to the Gold Dredge 8 or the El Dorado Gold Mine offers a fun and educational experience. Located just outside of Fairbanks, these historic sites provide a glimpse into the state's gold mining past and offer visitors the chance to try their hand at gold panning. The tours include a ride on a replica of the Tanana Valley Railroad, which takes visitors through scenic mining country, and a guided tour of the dredges and mining equipment used during Alaska's gold rush. Both Gold Dredge 8 and the El Dorado Gold Mine offer hands-on gold panning experiences, where visitors can pan for gold and keep any nuggets they find, making it a fun and memorable activity for the whole family.

For those interested in exploring Alaska's vast wilderness, the nearby White Mountains National Recreation Area offers endless opportunities for outdoor adventure. Located about an hour's drive north of Fairbanks, the White Mountains are known for their rugged beauty and extensive trail system, which provides access to remote backcountry areas. The area is popular with hikers, mountain bikers, and backpackers in the summer, and it offers some of the best cross-country skiing and snowmobiling in the state during the winter months. The White Mountains National Recreation Area is also home to several public-use cabins, which can be rented for overnight trips, providing a true wilderness experience for those looking to escape into Alaska's backcountry.

Multi-Day Excursions: Guided trips for those looking for extended adventures

Multi-day excursions in Alaska offer some of the most immersive and rewarding experiences for travelers seeking to explore the state's wild and remote landscapes in a deeper and more meaningful way. Alaska's vast size and diverse ecosystems mean that even with a few days, travelers can access areas that are otherwise too distant or challenging for a single-day trip. These guided multi-day trips provide the opportunity to experience the grandeur of Alaska at a slower pace, whether it's trekking through mountain ranges, paddling down rivers, cruising past glaciers, or camping in the wilderness under the midnight sun or the northern lights. The multi-day format allows for greater exploration, more interaction with local guides, and a deeper understanding of the natural world and its incredible ecosystems.

One of the most popular options for a multi-day guided adventure is a wildlife and glacier-focused cruise through Alaska's Inside Passage. Located in the southeastern part of the state, the Inside Passage is famous for its dramatic fjords, towering glaciers, and abundant marine wildlife. Multi-day cruises typically depart from towns like Juneau, Sitka, or Ketchikan, and sail through the protected waters of the passage, allowing travelers to experience the region's breathtaking scenery without the crowds. Unlike large cruise ships, these guided trips are often aboard smaller, more intimate vessels that provide a more personalized experience.

During a multi-day cruise in the Inside Passage, travelers can expect to see some of Alaska's most famous wildlife up close. Humpback whales and orcas are commonly spotted in the area, along with sea otters, sea lions, and seals. Onshore excursions often include visits to tidewater glaciers, where travelers can watch as massive chunks of ice calve off into the water below, creating an awe-inspiring display of nature's power. The smaller size of the boats allows access to hidden coves, remote islands, and quiet bays that larger ships cannot reach, providing a sense of tranquility and solitude in one of the world's most remote regions. Many of these trips include opportunities for kayaking, paddleboarding, or hiking in the temperate rainforest, allowing travelers to fully immerse themselves in the beauty of the area.

To book a multi-day cruise through the Inside Passage, travelers typically start their journey in Juneau, which is accessible by air or sea. From there, tour operators such as Alaskan Dream Cruises, UnCruise Adventures, and Lindblad Expeditions offer a range of itineraries, ranging from three-day to week-long adventures. These trips are all-inclusive, meaning that accommodations, meals, and guided excursions are provided, allowing travelers to focus entirely on the experience. The best time to take a multi-day cruise through the Inside Passage is during the summer months, from May to September, when the weather is mild, the wildlife is active, and the daylight hours are long.

For those looking to explore Alaska's rugged interior, a guided backpacking or trekking trip through Denali

National Park is an unforgettable multi-day experience. Denali, home to North America's tallest peak, offers some of the most dramatic and pristine landscapes in the world. Multi-day guided trips in the park allow travelers to access remote backcountry areas, far from the main tourist routes, where they can experience the true solitude and majesty of Alaska's wilderness. These excursions typically involve several days of hiking and camping in the park's backcountry, with opportunities to spot wildlife such as grizzly bears, caribou, wolves, and Dall sheep along the way.

Backpacking trips in Denali are led by experienced guides who are familiar with the park's terrain, wildlife, and weather conditions. These guides ensure that travelers are safe and well-prepared for the challenges of hiking in remote areas. Most guided backpacking trips are suitable for intermediate to experienced hikers, as they involve carrying a pack and navigating uneven terrain. The reward, however, is the chance to explore Denali's untouched wilderness, where the vastness of the landscape and the quiet stillness of nature create an experience that is both humbling and exhilarating.

To join a guided backpacking trip in Denali, travelers typically fly into Anchorage or Fairbanks and then take the Alaska Railroad or drive to the park's entrance. Several tour operators, including Alaska Alpine Adventures and Camp Denali, offer multi-day trekking trips that range from three to seven days. These trips are all-inclusive, with guides providing gear, food, and permits for camping in the backcountry. The best time for backpacking in Denali is during the summer months, from June to September, when the weather is mild and the park's wildlife is most active.

For those seeking a more luxurious but equally adventurous multi-day trip, a stay at a wilderness lodge is an excellent option. Alaska is home to several remote lodges that offer multi-day packages, where guests can enjoy a mix of outdoor activities, such as fishing, hiking, and wildlife viewing, while staying in comfortable accommodations surrounded by nature. These lodges are typically located in some of the most remote and beautiful parts of the state, providing a true escape from the modern world.

One such destination is Tutka Bay Lodge, located in Kachemak Bay State Park, just across the water from the town of Homer. The lodge is accessible only by boat or floatplane, and it offers guests a unique opportunity to explore the rugged beauty of Kachemak Bay and the Kenai Peninsula. Multi-day stays at the lodge include guided activities such as sea kayaking, wildlife watching, and hiking through the nearby rainforest. Guests can also take part in cooking classes, led by the lodge's renowned chefs, who use locally sourced ingredients such as fresh seafood and wild berries to create gourmet meals. The lodge's remote location, combined with its luxurious amenities, makes it an ideal destination for travelers looking to experience Alaska's wilderness in comfort.

To reach Tutka Bay Lodge, travelers typically fly into Anchorage and then take a short flight to Homer, where they can board a boat or a floatplane for the final leg of the journey. The lodge operates seasonally, from May to September, and multi-day packages are available for stays ranging from two to seven days.

For a truly unique multi-day adventure, travelers can embark on a dog sledding expedition through Alaska's vast wilderness. These trips, which are available year-round, allow travelers to experience the thrill of mushing their own team of sled dogs through snow-covered landscapes, with options ranging from short overnight trips to week-long expeditions. Dog sledding is a quintessential Alaskan experience, and these guided excursions provide an opportunity to learn about the sport's history, the bond between mushers and their dogs, and the incredible endurance required to travel long distances in the wilderness.

One of the best places to embark on a dog sledding expedition is in the Matanuska-Susitna Valley, located just north of Anchorage. Several tour operators, including EarthSong Lodge and Outback Kennels, offer multi-day dog sledding trips that take travelers deep into the backcountry, where they can experience the quiet solitude of Alaska's winter landscapes. These trips are led by experienced mushers who teach travelers how to handle a dog sled team, care for the dogs, and navigate through the wilderness. Multi-day trips typically involve camping in remote areas, with opportunities to see the northern lights during the long winter nights. For those visiting during the summer months, some operators also offer glacier dog sledding trips, where travelers are flown by helicopter to a remote glacier for a dog sledding experience on the ice.

To join a dog sledding expedition, travelers can fly into Anchorage and then take a shuttle or drive to the Mat-Su Valley. Multi-day trips are available year-round, with the winter season offering the best conditions for traditional dog sledding, while summer trips provide the unique experience of mushing on glaciers.

Chapter 14

Food and Dining

Must-Try Alaskan Dishes

When traveling to Alaska, one of the most memorable parts of the experience is undoubtedly the food. Alaskan cuisine is as unique and diverse as the state's landscapes, with a strong emphasis on locally sourced ingredients and traditional dishes that have been influenced by Native Alaskan, Russian, and American cultures. From fresh-caught seafood to reindeer sausage, Alaska offers a culinary adventure that perfectly complements its rugged natural beauty. While visiting, you'll have the chance to taste flavors that are deeply rooted in the land and sea, with many ingredients sourced straight from Alaska's vast wilderness and coastal waters. Exploring Alaskan cuisine is more than just satisfying your hunger—it's an immersive experience that offers insight into the state's rich history, natural resources, and local culture.

Seafood is at the heart of Alaskan cuisine, and with good reason. The state's cold, pristine waters are home to some of the best seafood in the world, and no visit to Alaska would be complete without sampling its famous catches. One of the most prized and sought-after seafood dishes is wild Alaskan salmon. Whether grilled, smoked, or cured, Alaskan salmon is known for its rich flavor and high-quality texture. There are five species of salmon native to Alaska—king, sockeye, coho, chum, and pink—and each has its own distinct taste and characteristics. King salmon, also known as chinook, is the largest and most flavorful, prized for its buttery, succulent flesh. Sockeye salmon, with its deep red color and bold flavor, is another favorite that is often smoked or grilled. Throughout the summer months, salmon is plentiful, especially during the annual salmon runs when fish migrate upstream to spawn. Restaurants and local markets in cities like Anchorage, Juneau, and Ketchikan often feature salmon prominently on their menus, and many offer it freshly caught and prepared with minimal seasoning to let the natural flavors shine.

For a true Alaskan experience, don't miss the chance to try salmon prepared in a traditional Native Alaskan style. Native communities have been smoking and curing salmon for thousands of years, using methods passed down through generations. In many coastal villages, you'll find fish camps where families still preserve salmon using ancient techniques, curing it over alder wood fires to impart a deep, smoky flavor. This process produces what is known as "salmon candy"—thin strips of salmon that have been cured, smoked, and sometimes glazed with a sweet coating of honey or maple syrup. The result is a chewy, flavorful treat that is both savory and sweet, and it's a must-try for anyone looking to taste Alaska's culinary heritage.

If you're traveling to Southeast Alaska, Juneau is a fantastic place to sample fresh seafood, including salmon, halibut, and Dungeness crab. Several restaurants in Juneau specialize in local seafood, such as Tracy's King Crab Shack, which is famous for its oversized crab legs and rich, buttery crab bisque. Located right on the waterfront, Tracy's is a casual, no-frills spot where visitors can enjoy freshly steamed crab while taking in views of the harbor. Another popular option is The Hangar on the Wharf, which offers a menu featuring both seafood and hearty American dishes, all served in a historic airplane hangar overlooking Gastineau Channel. Juneau is also home to several seafood markets where you can buy fresh or smoked salmon, halibut, and other local fish to take home.

Another Alaskan seafood delicacy you won't want to miss is halibut. Alaska is home to some of the largest halibut in the world, and the firm, white flesh of this flatfish is prized for its mild flavor and versatility. Halibut can be prepared in a variety of ways, from grilling and baking to frying and poaching, making it a favorite on menus throughout the state. One of the most popular ways to enjoy halibut in Alaska is in the form of halibut fish and chips, where chunks of the fish are battered and fried until crispy and served with a side of fries. This simple but satisfying dish is a staple at seafood shacks and restaurants throughout Alaska, especially in coastal towns like Homer, Seward, and Valdez. Homer, in particular, is known as the "Halibut Fishing Capital of the World," and visitors can even join a fishing charter to catch their own halibut and have it cooked fresh at a local restaurant.

While seafood is undoubtedly the star of Alaskan cuisine, there are several other local flavors that are just as worth exploring. One of the most iconic and unique foods you'll encounter is reindeer sausage. Reindeer, also known as caribou in North America, have been an important source of food for Alaska's indigenous peoples for centuries, and today, reindeer sausage is a popular snack found at food stands, markets, and restaurants across the state. This flavorful sausage is typically made from a blend of reindeer meat and pork or beef, seasoned with a mix of spices, and then smoked or grilled. It's commonly served in a hot dog bun with mustard, onions, and sauerkraut, making it a convenient and hearty meal on the go. In Anchorage, you can find reindeer sausage at the famous Tiki Pete's Alaskan Sausage stand, located downtown, where locals and visitors alike line up for a taste of this savory treat. If you prefer a sit-down meal, many Alaskan diners and pubs offer reindeer sausage as part of a breakfast plate, paired with eggs and hash browns for a truly Alaskan start to the day.

For those who have a sweet tooth, Alaskan cuisine also offers a few unique desserts that are worth trying. One such treat is fireweed honey, made from the nectar of fireweed flowers, which bloom in abundance across Alaska during the summer months. Fireweed honey has a light, floral flavor that is perfect for drizzling over biscuits, pancakes, or even salmon. In the town of Talkeetna, located near Denali National Park, you'll find several local producers of fireweed honey, and visitors can often purchase jars of this sweet delicacy at local farmers' markets or specialty shops. Fireweed jelly is another popular product made from the same vibrant pink flowers and can be found at many of the same markets.

Alaska is also known for its wild berries, which grow in abundance across the state during the late summer and early fall. Blueberries, lingonberries (known locally as lowbush cranberries), and salmonberries are just a few of the native berries that Alaskans harvest each year. These berries are often used in a variety of dishes, from jams and jellies to pies and cobblers. One of the most traditional ways to enjoy wild berries is in the form of akutaq, also known as "Eskimo ice cream." Akutaq is a unique dish made by mixing wild berries with animal fats, such as seal or reindeer fat, along with snow or water. This dish has been a staple of Native Alaskan diets for centuries, providing a high-energy, nutrient-rich food source in the harsh Arctic environment. While traditional akutaq may be an acquired taste, modern versions made with Crisco or butter instead of animal fat are more palatable to most visitors and can be found at cultural festivals and Native Alaskan gatherings.

In addition to seafood and game, Alaska is home to a growing farm-to-table movement, with many chefs and restaurants embracing locally sourced ingredients to create innovative and sustainable dishes. The state's short but intense growing season allows for the production of fresh, organic vegetables such as kale, carrots, potatoes, and rhubarb. In recent years, several farm-to-table restaurants have opened in cities like

Anchorage and Fairbanks, offering menus that highlight the best of Alaska's seasonal produce, along with locally sourced meats and fish. For example, in Anchorage, the renowned restaurant 229 Parks serves a menu that changes with the seasons, featuring dishes made with fresh Alaskan seafood, wild game, and farm-grown vegetables. Another excellent option is the Saltry Restaurant in Halibut Cove, accessible by boat from Homer, where guests can enjoy a gourmet meal while overlooking the serene waters of Kachemak Bay.

For those looking to explore Alaskan cuisine through hands-on experiences, several food tours and cooking classes are available in various parts of the state. In Anchorage, the "Alaska's Harvest" food tour takes visitors to local markets, restaurants, and specialty shops, where they can sample everything from smoked salmon to locally brewed craft beers. Meanwhile, in Sitka, visitors can participate in cooking classes that focus on traditional Native Alaskan recipes, learning how to prepare dishes such as smoked fish, reindeer stew, and bannock bread. These tours and classes provide a deeper understanding of Alaska's culinary traditions and allow visitors to engage with local chefs and food producers.

Best Restaurants for Every Budget: Fine dining, casual eateries, and budget-friendly spots

When it comes to dining in Alaska, the diversity of options ensures that travelers can find a delicious meal, whether they are seeking a fine dining experience, a casual bite to eat, or a budget-friendly spot. Alaska's restaurant scene is a reflection of its unique blend of cultures and natural bounty, featuring fresh seafood, locally sourced ingredients, and hearty comfort food that fits the state's rugged atmosphere. From luxurious multi-course meals to laid-back diners, Alaska offers a culinary experience that caters to every type of traveler and budget. Whether you're in bustling cities like Anchorage or Juneau or venturing into smaller towns, the dining opportunities are as varied and memorable as the landscapes themselves.

Starting with fine dining, Alaska's top-tier restaurants showcase the state's finest seafood, wild game, and seasonal ingredients, prepared with creativity and sophistication. Anchorage, the largest city in Alaska, offers some of the most renowned fine dining options in the state. One of the most notable restaurants is **Crow's Nest**, located at the top of the Hotel Captain Cook in downtown Anchorage. This award-winning restaurant offers breathtaking panoramic views of the city, the Chugach Mountains, and Cook Inlet, making it the perfect setting for a special meal. The menu focuses on fresh Alaskan seafood, including king crab legs, halibut, and wild-caught salmon, paired with locally sourced produce and expertly prepared game meats such as reindeer and elk. With an extensive wine list and elegant atmosphere, Crow's Nest is a must-visit for those looking to indulge in an unforgettable dining experience. To reach the restaurant, visitors can take a short walk or taxi from any point in downtown Anchorage, and reservations are highly recommended due to its popularity.

Another top fine dining establishment in Anchorage is **Seven Glaciers**, located at Alyeska Resort in the nearby town of Girdwood, about 40 miles south of Anchorage. This mountain-top restaurant is accessible by a scenic tram ride that adds to the overall experience, offering diners stunning views of the surrounding glaciers and the Chugach Mountains. Seven Glaciers is known for its focus on locally sourced ingredients, including fresh seafood, wild game, and organic vegetables from Alaskan farms. The seasonal menu changes frequently to highlight the best local products, with dishes like seared halibut, braised venison, and Alaskan king crab being common favorites. In addition to the food, Seven Glaciers offers an impressive wine list and expertly crafted cocktails, making it a top choice for those looking to experience fine dining in one of the most beautiful settings in Alaska.

For travelers visiting Juneau, **Salt** is another excellent fine dining option. Located in the heart of downtown Juneau, Salt offers a contemporary menu featuring modern interpretations of classic Alaskan dishes. The restaurant prides itself on using sustainably sourced seafood and locally harvested ingredients, and its menu showcases dishes like roasted black cod, grilled octopus, and pan-seared scallops. The stylish, minimalist décor of the restaurant creates an upscale yet relaxed atmosphere, making it an ideal spot for a romantic dinner or a celebration. Salt also features a thoughtfully curated wine and cocktail menu, with many drinks highlighting local flavors such as spruce tips and wild berries. The restaurant is easily accessible by foot from any downtown Juneau hotel, and reservations are recommended, especially during the busy summer tourist season.

For those seeking a more casual dining experience, Alaska has plenty of mid-range eateries that offer excellent food without the formality of fine dining. In Anchorage, **49th State Brewing Company** is a favorite among locals and visitors alike. Located downtown, this brewpub offers a relaxed atmosphere with an extensive menu featuring Alaskan comfort food and craft beer brewed on-site. The menu includes dishes such as beer-battered halibut and chips, reindeer sausage, and the famous Yak Burger, made from locally sourced yak meat. The outdoor patio is a great spot to enjoy a meal during the warmer months, with views of the city and the mountains in the distance. 49th State Brewing Company is also known for its lively atmosphere, with live music and events taking place regularly. Whether you're looking to try Alaskan beer or enjoy a hearty meal after a day of exploring the city, this brewpub offers a great combination of quality food and a fun, laid-back environment.

In Fairbanks, **Lavelle's Bistro** is a popular choice for those seeking a casual yet elevated dining experience. Located in downtown Fairbanks, Lavelle's offers a diverse menu that blends local ingredients with international flavors. Diners can enjoy dishes such as Alaskan king crab mac and cheese, grilled salmon with lemon beurre blanc, or a perfectly cooked ribeye steak. The bistro also features a well-stocked wine bar, making it a great place to relax with a glass of wine after a day of sightseeing. Lavelle's is known for its friendly service and warm atmosphere, making it a favorite spot for both locals and visitors. The restaurant is easy to reach from most downtown Fairbanks hotels, either by foot or a short taxi ride, and it's a great choice for travelers looking for a satisfying meal without breaking the bank.

For a casual dining experience with a focus on local seafood, **Ray's Waterfront** in Seward is a must-visit. Located right on the harbor, Ray's offers stunning views of Resurrection Bay and the surrounding mountains, making it an ideal spot for lunch or dinner after a day of exploring Kenai Fjords National Park. The menu features a wide range of seafood dishes, including grilled halibut, blackened salmon, and Dungeness crab, as well as steaks and pasta for those who prefer land-based options. The relaxed atmosphere and friendly service make Ray's a favorite among locals and tourists alike. Seward is located about two hours south of Anchorage, and visitors can reach the town by car or by taking the Alaska Railroad. Ray's is conveniently located near the harbor, making it an easy stop after a boat tour or a day of sightseeing.

For budget-conscious travelers, Alaska also offers plenty of affordable dining options that don't compromise on quality. In Anchorage, **Lucky Wishbone** is a beloved local institution that has been serving up fried chicken and burgers since 1955. This retro diner offers a no-frills, family-friendly atmosphere and a menu that focuses on comfort food classics. The fried chicken, in particular, is a standout, with crispy skin and juicy meat that has earned the restaurant a loyal following. Lucky Wishbone is located just outside of downtown Anchorage, and it's easily accessible by car or public transportation. The prices are budget-friendly, making it a great option for families or travelers looking for a quick, satisfying meal without spending a lot.

In Juneau, **Pel'meni** offers a unique and budget-friendly dining experience with its simple menu of Russian dumplings. Located in downtown Juneau, this tiny eatery specializes in just two types of dumplings—beef and potato—served with a variety of toppings such as butter, sour cream, and curry powder. The dumplings are filling, flavorful, and affordable, making Pel'meni a popular spot for both locals and tourists. The restaurant's casual vibe and late-night hours make it a great stop after an evening of exploring downtown Juneau. Pel'meni is located just a short walk from most downtown attractions, and it's a great option for a quick, inexpensive meal that still feels unique to the area.

In Fairbanks, **Sam's Sourdough Café** is a favorite among budget-conscious travelers looking for a hearty breakfast or lunch. This no-frills diner offers generous portions of classic American comfort food, with an emphasis on breakfast items such as pancakes, omelets, and biscuits with gravy. The café's namesake sourdough pancakes are a local favorite, and the casual, friendly atmosphere makes it a great place to start the day. Sam's Sourdough Café is located just a short drive from downtown Fairbanks, and it's easily accessible by car or public transportation.

Cafes and Breweries: Where to grab a coffee or local brew

Alaska's rugged landscapes and natural beauty are often associated with outdoor adventures, but one of the most delightful ways to relax after a day of exploration is to sit back and enjoy a cup of freshly brewed coffee or a pint of locally crafted beer. From cozy mountain cafés to bustling urban breweries, Alaska offers an abundance of charming spots where you can enjoy the local flavors and atmosphere. Whether you're in the heart of Anchorage, the quieter corners of Juneau, or the vibrant community of Fairbanks, Alaska's cafés and breweries reflect the state's unique culture and offer a perfect blend of comfort, warmth, and innovation.

Starting with coffee, Alaska's café culture is strong, and locals take their coffee seriously. Given the long, cold winters, coffee has become a staple in Alaskan life, and you'll find numerous cafés and roasteries dedicated to brewing top-quality coffee, often with locally roasted beans. Anchorage, as the largest city in the state, boasts a thriving coffee scene with a variety of independent cafés that offer not just great coffee but also welcoming spaces to unwind or plan your next adventure.

One of the standout cafés in Anchorage is **Kaladi Brothers Coffee**, a local chain that has become an institution across Alaska. With multiple locations throughout the city, Kaladi Brothers is known for its commitment to ethically sourced, high-quality coffee beans, many of which are roasted in-house. The café offers a range of drinks, from rich espresso to perfectly brewed drip coffee, and also features a selection of pastries and light bites. What makes Kaladi Brothers particularly special is the laid-back and friendly vibe that permeates its locations. Whether you're looking for a place to relax with a good book, meet up with friends, or get some work done, Kaladi Brothers provides a welcoming environment for locals and visitors alike. One of its most popular locations is on Brayton Drive, which is easily accessible by car or public transportation from downtown Anchorage.

Another great spot for coffee in Anchorage is **Black Cup**, a café that takes coffee roasting to a new level. Known for its dedication to crafting the perfect cup, Black Cup roasts its own beans and focuses on single-origin coffees from around the world. The atmosphere is more intimate than some of the larger cafés, with a focus on quality over quantity. You can expect expertly made pour-overs, cold brews, and espresso drinks that showcase the nuances of different beans. The café's interior is cozy yet modern, with large windows that let in plenty of natural light, making it a great spot to relax or people-watch. Located on Tudor Road, Black Cup is a short drive from downtown Anchorage and is well worth a visit for coffee lovers seeking a more refined coffee experience.

For those traveling to Juneau, **Heritage Coffee Roasting Co.** is the go-to spot for locals and visitors looking for a great cup of coffee. With several locations around town, Heritage Coffee has been serving the Juneau community since the 1970s and is known for its high-quality roasts and comfortable cafés. The downtown location on Front Street is especially popular, thanks to its central location near many of Juneau's main attractions, including the Alaska State Capitol and the Juneau-Douglas City Museum. Visitors can enjoy a variety of coffee drinks, from lattes and mochas to drip coffee, along with a selection of baked goods and light snacks. The café's warm and inviting atmosphere makes it the perfect place to take a break after exploring Juneau's historic downtown. Whether you're stopping by for a quick pick-me-up or spending a leisurely afternoon, Heritage Coffee offers a true taste of Juneau's local flavor.

Moving north to Fairbanks, **Venue** is a standout café that combines great coffee with a vibrant, artistic atmosphere. Located on Cushman Street in downtown Fairbanks, Venue offers a wide range of coffee drinks made with locally roasted beans, as well as an extensive selection of teas, smoothies, and light meals. What sets Venue apart is its dedication to supporting local artists and musicians, with rotating art exhibits and live music performances taking place regularly. The café's spacious interior and community-focused vibe make it a popular gathering place for locals, and it's an ideal spot to relax after a day of sightseeing or exploring the nearby Chena River. Venue is easily accessible by foot from most downtown hotels and attractions, making it a convenient stop for visitors looking to experience Fairbanks' coffee culture.

For those venturing into smaller towns or more remote areas, Alaska's café scene extends far beyond its larger cities. In Homer, a charming town on the Kenai Peninsula, **Two Sisters Bakery** offers both exceptional coffee and mouthwatering baked goods. Located on Bunnell Street, just a short walk from Homer's picturesque harbor, Two Sisters is a beloved local spot where travelers can enjoy freshly brewed coffee, along with a wide variety of homemade pastries, bread, and desserts. The café's warm, rustic interior and friendly staff make it a welcoming place to start the day, whether you're preparing for a hike in Kachemak Bay State Park or simply taking in the views of Homer's iconic Spit. Two Sisters also serves lunch, with a menu featuring sandwiches, soups, and salads made from locally sourced ingredients. The bakery is an easy stop if you're exploring Homer on foot, and there is ample parking nearby for those arriving by car.

Now shifting gears to breweries, Alaska is home to a burgeoning craft beer scene that reflects the state's adventurous spirit and rugged landscapes. Whether you're a seasoned beer enthusiast or just looking to try something new, Alaska's breweries offer a wide range of locally crafted beers that showcase the creativity and passion of the state's brewers. Many breweries also serve food and offer tours, making them great places to spend an afternoon or evening while learning more about the brewing process and tasting some of the best beers in the region.

One of the most iconic breweries in the state is **Alaskan Brewing Co.**, located in Juneau. Founded in 1986, Alaskan Brewing Co. is known for its flagship Alaskan Amber, a smooth, malt-forward beer that has won numerous awards and remains a favorite among locals and visitors alike. In addition to Alaskan Amber, the brewery produces a wide range of seasonal and specialty beers, including Alaskan Smoked Porter, which is made using alder-smoked malt to create a rich, complex flavor. The brewery offers tours and tastings at its facility on Shaune Drive, where visitors can learn about the brewing process, sample a variety of beers, and purchase limited-edition brews that are only available at the brewery. To get to Alaskan Brewing Co., visitors can take a short taxi ride or hop on a local bus from downtown Juneau. The brewery also operates a tasting room in downtown Juneau, which is conveniently located near many of the city's main attractions.

In Anchorage, **49th State Brewing Company** is one of the most popular breweries in the city, offering not just great beer but also a full menu of delicious food and stunning views of Cook Inlet and the surrounding mountains. The brewery's downtown location on West 3rd Avenue is a favorite among both locals and tourists, thanks to its spacious outdoor patio and lively atmosphere. 49th State Brewing Company is known for its wide selection of craft beers, including the award-winning Solstice IPA and Denali Gold, as well as seasonal brews that showcase local ingredients such as spruce tips and wild berries. The brewery also serves hearty pub fare, including burgers, pizzas, and fish and chips, making it a great place to grab a meal after a day of exploring Anchorage. Whether you're enjoying a pint on the patio during the summer or cozying up inside during the winter, 49th State Brewing Company offers a quintessential Alaskan beer experience. The brewery is easily accessible by foot from downtown hotels or by car, with plenty of parking available nearby.

For those visiting Fairbanks, **HooDoo Brewing Co.** is a must-stop destination for craft beer lovers. Located just a few minutes from downtown Fairbanks, HooDoo is a small, independent brewery that has earned a loyal following for its carefully crafted, European-style beers. The brewery's taproom is a laid-back space where visitors can sample a rotating selection of beers, including the popular HooDoo Kolsch, IPA, and Stout. While HooDoo doesn't serve food, there is often a food truck parked outside the brewery offering tasty bites to pair with your beer. The brewery also offers tours, where visitors can learn about the brewing process and the history of HooDoo. To get to HooDoo Brewing Co., visitors can either drive or take a short taxi ride from downtown Fairbanks, and the brewery is open year-round.

In the town of Homer, **Grace Ridge Brewing** is another fantastic spot to enjoy locally brewed beer in a relaxed, friendly setting. This small, family-owned brewery is located on Ocean Drive, just a short distance from Homer's harbor, and offers a range of beers that reflect the town's coastal character. Grace Ridge Brewing is known for its small-batch brews, including the popular Kayak Beach Blonde and Sadie Peak IPA. The brewery's taproom features large windows that offer views of Kachemak Bay, and visitors can often be found sipping a beer while watching the boats come and go from the harbor. Grace Ridge Brewing also hosts regular events, including live music and food truck nights, making it a fun and lively spot to spend an evening in Homer.

Local Markets and Food Trucks: Tasting Alaska's best street food and market finds

Exploring Alaska's vibrant local markets and food trucks is one of the most authentic and enjoyable ways to experience the state's diverse culinary landscape. Unlike a formal restaurant, these spots offer a more casual, interactive, and dynamic experience, giving you the chance to sample a variety of foods that reflect the state's cultural and natural richness. From fresh seafood to wild berries, reindeer sausages to homemade jams, these markets and food trucks provide a gateway to

Alaska's incredible bounty. Whether you're wandering through a farmers' market in Anchorage or grabbing a quick bite from a food truck in Fairbanks, each of these experiences tells the story of Alaska through its flavors.

One of the most well-known markets in the state is the **Anchorage Market & Festival**, which operates on weekends during the summer months. Located in downtown Anchorage, this open-air market is a hub for locals and tourists alike, with dozens of vendors selling everything from local produce to handcrafted goods, and of course, a wide array of Alaskan street food. Walking through the market, you'll encounter stalls selling freshly caught seafood, Alaskan honey, jams made from wild berries, and traditional smoked salmon. The market is also a great place to try some of Alaska's more unique dishes, like reindeer sausage, which is often served in hotdog form and topped with mustard and onions. The reindeer sausage stands are a crowd favorite, and the rich, slightly gamey flavor of the meat gives you a true taste of Alaska's wilderness.

Anchorage Market & Festival is also home to several food trucks, which offer a wide variety of cuisine from around the world. You'll find everything from Thai curries to Mexican tacos, but the star of the show is often the Alaskan seafood. Some of the most popular food trucks at the market specialize in fish tacos, which are made with fresh halibut or salmon and served with cabbage, lime, and a tangy sauce. Another favorite is the fried halibut sandwich, which features a thick piece of crispy, golden halibut on a soft bun with tartar sauce and pickles. The market's bustling atmosphere and the diverse range of food options make it a must-visit destination for anyone spending time in Anchorage during the summer.

Getting to the Anchorage Market & Festival is easy, as it is centrally located in downtown Anchorage, near the intersection of 3rd Avenue and E Street. If you're staying at a hotel in the downtown area, the market is within walking distance, making it a convenient stop during a day of exploring the city. For those coming from outside downtown, there are several public transportation options, including buses, or you can drive and find parking nearby.

In addition to the Anchorage Market, another great spot to explore the local food scene is the **South Anchorage Farmers' Market**, which is located in the parking lot of the Subway Sports Centre on weekends during the summer. This market focuses on locally grown produce, with vendors selling everything from fresh vegetables and fruits to homemade baked goods and artisan cheeses. While the market is smaller and more low-key than the downtown Anchorage Market, it offers a great opportunity to connect with local farmers and sample farm-to-table products that are unique to Alaska's short but bountiful growing season. In addition to the fresh produce, there are often food trucks at the South Anchorage Farmers' Market serving up local specialties, such as grilled salmon sandwiches and reindeer chili. The market is a bit farther from the city center, but it's well worth the drive for those looking to experience a more local, community-oriented market.

In Fairbanks, the **Tanana Valley Farmers' Market** is another fantastic spot to immerse yourself in Alaska's local food culture. Operating from late spring through fall, this market is located on College Road, just a few miles from downtown Fairbanks. The Tanana Valley Farmers' Market is the oldest farmers' market in Alaska, and it features a wide variety of vendors selling fresh produce, handmade crafts, and ready-to-eat foods. Here, you can sample everything from locally grown vegetables and herbs to homemade jams and pickles. One of the highlights of the market is the opportunity to try freshly harvested berries, such as blueberries and lingonberries, which are often sold by the pint during the summer months.

The Tanana Valley Farmers' Market also features a number of food trucks and stalls that offer a range of delicious, locally inspired dishes. Reindeer sausage is a popular option, as is freshly grilled salmon served on skewers or in sandwiches. For those with a sweet tooth, the market offers a variety of baked goods, including berry pies, sourdough bread, and cinnamon rolls, many of which are made using traditional Alaskan recipes. The market's relaxed, friendly atmosphere makes it a great place to spend a morning or afternoon sampling local foods and chatting with vendors about their products. The market is easy to reach by car from downtown Fairbanks, and there is plenty of parking available on-site.

For travelers visiting Juneau, the **Juneau Public Market** is a lively event that takes place over Thanksgiving weekend at Centennial Hall in downtown Juneau. While the market only operates once a year, it draws vendors and visitors from all over Southeast Alaska and offers an incredible selection of local foods, arts, and crafts. In addition to handmade goods and gifts, the market is a great place to sample some of Alaska's most iconic foods, including smoked salmon, reindeer sausage, and wild berry preserves. Local food producers often set up booths where you can taste their products and learn about how they are made. While it's a bit different from the outdoor farmers' markets, the Juneau Public Market provides a unique opportunity to discover local flavors, especially for those visiting Juneau during the winter.

For a more casual, everyday food experience, Juneau's food truck scene offers some excellent options for grabbing a quick and tasty bite. One of the most popular food trucks in Juneau is **Deckhand Dave's Fish Tacos**, located near the downtown cruise ship docks. Known for its fresh and flavorful fish tacos, Deckhand Dave's serves up some of the best seafood in town, with options that include halibut, salmon, and rockfish. The tacos are made to order and topped with a variety of fresh ingredients, including cabbage, pico de gallo, and a zesty house-made sauce. Deckhand Dave's is a favorite among both locals and tourists, and its convenient location near the docks makes it an easy stop for anyone exploring downtown Juneau. The food truck is open seasonally, typically from late spring through fall, and is a great place to grab a quick meal before heading out on an excursion or taking a stroll along the waterfront.

Moving back to Anchorage, another standout in the local food truck scene is **Yeti Dogs**, a small but beloved food truck that specializes in gourmet hot dogs. Located on the corner of West 4th Avenue and D Street, Yeti Dogs offers a variety of Alaskan-inspired hot dogs, including reindeer sausage topped with caramelized onions and spicy mustard. The menu also includes classic beef hot dogs and bratwursts, all of which are served on freshly toasted buns and loaded with toppings. Yeti Dogs has gained a loyal following thanks to its high-quality ingredients and friendly service, making it a must-try spot for anyone looking to sample a local twist on a classic American favorite.

For those who prefer a more adventurous food experience, Anchorage is also home to **International Street Food**, a food truck that offers a rotating menu of globally inspired dishes, with an emphasis on using local ingredients. The menu changes frequently, but you can expect to find dishes like Thai-style salmon curry, Alaskan seafood paella, and reindeer gyros. The fusion of international flavors with local ingredients makes International Street Food a unique and exciting addition to Anchorage's food truck scene, and it's a great option for those looking to try something new and different.

Exploring Alaska's local markets and food trucks provides not only a taste of the state's diverse culinary offerings but also a deeper connection to its culture and people. These experiences allow visitors to interact with local farmers, chefs, and artisans, and to learn more about the state's rich agricultural and culinary traditions. Whether you're sampling fresh seafood from a food truck in downtown Juneau or buying wild berry preserves at a farmers' market in Fairbanks, Alaska's local food scene offers something for everyone, from adventurous eaters to those seeking familiar comfort foods with a local twist.

Chapter 15

Festivals and Seasonal Events

Winter Festivals

Winter in Alaska is a time of celebration, filled with unique festivals and events that embrace the cold, the snow, and the state's rich cultural heritage. From the world-famous Iditarod dog sled race to intricate ice sculptures that glow under the Northern Lights, Alaska's winter festivals provide a deep connection to the state's history, traditions, and wild landscape. Despite the cold and long nights, winter in Alaska is anything but dull. These festivals bring together locals and visitors for a chance to enjoy the season, celebrate resilience, and witness the beauty of Alaska in winter. Whether you are an outdoor enthusiast, an art lover, or simply someone looking to experience something new, Alaska's winter festivals offer unforgettable experiences.

One of the most iconic winter events in Alaska is the **Iditarod Trail Sled Dog Race**, often referred to as "The Last Great Race." Every March, this world-renowned event begins in Anchorage and runs over 1,000 miles to Nome, commemorating the historic sled dog route used in the early 20th century to deliver life-saving serum during a diphtheria outbreak. The Iditarod is more than just a race—it's a symbol of Alaskan culture and the endurance of both humans and animals in one of the world's harshest environments.

The race officially kicks off with a ceremonial start in downtown Anchorage, where you can witness the teams of mushers and their dogs as they prepare to embark on this incredible journey. The excitement in Anchorage during the start of the Iditarod is palpable, with thousands of spectators lining the streets to cheer on their favorite teams. Visitors have the opportunity to meet the mushers, take photos with the dogs, and learn about the deep connection between Alaskans and sled dogs. If you're lucky enough to be in Anchorage during the race's kickoff, be sure to check out the associated events, such as meet-and-greets with former race champions, dog-sledding demonstrations, and downtown festivities that keep the energy buzzing.

After the ceremonial start, the official timed start takes place the following day in Willow, a town located about 80 miles north of Anchorage. Visitors can drive up to Willow to watch the mushers take off on the first leg of the journey, marking the true beginning of the race. The race then travels through some of the most remote and rugged parts of Alaska, passing through small villages, mountain ranges, and frozen rivers before finally ending in Nome. For those who can't follow the race in person, many locals and tourists alike keep up with the progress of the mushers through live updates and GPS tracking, making the Iditarod a statewide event that captures the hearts of everyone in Alaska during the winter season.

Getting to Anchorage for the start of the Iditarod is fairly straightforward, with regular flights available from most major U.S. cities. Once in Anchorage, downtown hotels are the most convenient option for staying close to the action. Public transportation and shuttles are available to get to key locations during the race, and if you're planning to head to Willow or beyond, renting a car is the best way to travel.

Another winter festival that draws attention to Alaska's artistic side is the **World Ice Art Championships**, held annually in Fairbanks. This international event showcases the incredible talent of ice sculptors from around the world who come to Alaska to create stunning, larger-than-life sculptures out of blocks of ice. The competition runs throughout the month of March, and during this time, visitors can wander through a winter wonderland filled with intricate ice carvings illuminated by colorful lights that make the sculptures glow under the night sky. Some of the sculptures are massive, rising over 20 feet tall, while others feature delicate details that highlight the craftsmanship involved in creating art from ice.

One of the most impressive aspects of the World Ice Art Championships is the **Multi-Block Competition**, in which teams of artists work together to create massive ice installations using multiple blocks of ice. These sculptures often depict mythical creatures, towering castles, and other fantastical scenes that transport viewers into a dreamlike world of frozen beauty. In addition to the multi-block category, there are also single-block and abstract categories, as well as a special section for children's ice sculptures, making the event accessible and enjoyable for all ages.

The Ice Park in Fairbanks, where the event is held, is not just about viewing the sculptures. It also features interactive ice slides, mazes, and even ice bowling, providing fun activities for families and children. The atmosphere in the park is magical, especially at night when the colorful lights illuminate the sculptures and the Northern Lights often dance in the sky above. Fairbanks is known for being one of the best places in the world to view the aurora borealis, so attending the World Ice Art Championships offers a double treat—stunning ice art and the chance to see the Northern Lights.

Fairbanks can be reached by air, with regular flights from Anchorage and other major Alaskan cities, as well as from Seattle and other parts of the U.S. Once in Fairbanks, the Ice Park is easily accessible by car or public transportation. The event runs for several weeks, so visitors have flexibility in planning their trip around other winter activities in Fairbanks, such as dog sledding, snowmobiling, or taking a soak in the nearby Chena Hot Springs.

For a truly unique and authentic Alaskan winter experience, the **Fur Rendezvous Festival** in Anchorage, affectionately known as "Fur Rondy," is another must-see event. This long-running festival, which dates back to 1935, was originally a way for miners and trappers to come into town to trade fur and celebrate the end of a long winter. Today, it's a massive winter carnival that lasts for two weeks in late February and early March, offering everything from traditional Alaskan sports to quirky contests and cultural events.

One of the highlights of Fur Rondy is the **Running of the Reindeer**, a playful event that is akin to Spain's Running of the Bulls. Participants dress in colorful costumes and sprint down the snow-covered streets of Anchorage while being chased by a herd of reindeer. The event is all in good fun and attracts thousands of spectators who cheer on the runners as they dodge the friendly reindeer.

Fur Rondy also features classic Alaskan competitions such as the **World Championship Sled Dog Races**, where teams of mushers race through the streets of Anchorage, showcasing their speed and skill in navigating urban environments. Other traditional activities include the blanket toss, an event with roots in Native Alaskan culture, where participants are launched into the air on a large animal skin, often reaching incredible heights. The festival also includes carnival rides, parades, and the crowning of the Fur Rondy Queen, making it a celebration that blends Alaska's historical roots with modern-day fun.

Anchorage is the hub of all Fur Rondy activities, and most of the events take place in and around the downtown area, making it easy to get around on foot or by using public transportation. For visitors, staying in downtown Anchorage ensures you'll be close to the action, and many hotels offer special rates during the festival. Getting to Anchorage is simple, with daily flights from major cities, and once there, you can easily fill your days with both Fur Rondy activities and other winter adventures like skiing or snowshoeing.

Beyond these major festivals, Alaska's smaller towns and communities also host a variety of winter events that provide a glimpse into local traditions and celebrations. In the town of Talkeetna, the **Talkeetna Winterfest** kicks off in December and features a mix of activities, from holiday markets and live music to the famous Oosik Classic Ski Race, a quirky cross-country ski race that draws participants from across the state. The event embodies the laid-back, fun-loving spirit of Talkeetna, a town known for its artistic community and its position as a gateway to Denali National Park.

Winterfest events take place throughout the town, with many happening at the Talkeetna Historical Society and various local businesses. Visitors can explore the town's charming shops, grab a bite to eat at one of the cozy cafés, or simply enjoy the snowy landscape. Talkeetna is located about two hours north of Anchorage and can be reached by car or train. Many visitors make a day trip or weekend trip out of Winterfest, enjoying the festivities as well as the town's proximity to outdoor winter activities like snowshoeing or snowmobiling.

Summer Festivals: Music festivals, cultural fairs, and events celebrating Alaskan heritage

Summer in Alaska is a season of celebration, where the long, sunlit days give way to a variety of festivals that showcase the state's vibrant cultural scene, musical talent, and deep connection to its heritage. As the snow melts and the state's dramatic landscapes are illuminated by nearly 24 hours of daylight, locals and visitors alike come together to enjoy a range of events, from outdoor music festivals to fairs that celebrate Alaska's indigenous cultures and history. Each festival offers a unique opportunity to experience Alaska's distinct identity, with a mix of local and international influences that reflect the diversity and pride of the people who call this state home.

One of the most anticipated events of the summer is the **Anchorage Folk Festival**, which takes place in Alaska's largest city. This music festival celebrates folk music traditions, both local and international, with a focus on acoustic performances. Musicians from around the world come to Anchorage to participate, creating a dynamic mix of sounds and styles that include bluegrass, old-time music, and folk-inspired jazz. The festival is known for its open, welcoming atmosphere, encouraging both professional musicians and amateurs to join in jam sessions, workshops, and community events. For those who enjoy live music in a relaxed setting, Anchorage Folk Festival is an excellent way to experience the collaborative and creative spirit of the state.

The festival is held at various venues across Anchorage, with many performances taking place outdoors to take full advantage of Alaska's summer weather. These performances are often free, making them accessible to all. A central hub of the festival is typically at the Alaska Center for the Performing Arts, located in downtown Anchorage. Visitors can explore other parts of the city as they move from one venue to another, allowing them to experience Anchorage's vibrant cultural scene while enjoying the music. Anchorage is easily accessible by air, with daily flights from major cities across the U.S. and abroad. For those already in the city, public transportation and taxis make it easy to navigate the festival venues.

For travelers interested in experiencing indigenous Alaskan culture, the **Celebration Festival** in Juneau is a must-see event. Held every two years, this large gathering celebrates the heritage and traditions of the Tlingit, Haida, and Tsimshian peoples, who have inhabited Southeast Alaska for thousands of years. The festival is a vibrant, colorful affair that includes traditional dance performances, art exhibitions, and storytelling sessions, all of which highlight the rich cultural legacy of Alaska's indigenous communities. One of the most striking aspects of the Celebration Festival is the **Grand Entrance**, in which hundreds of dancers dressed in traditional regalia parade through the streets of Juneau, singing and drumming as they go.

The festival also includes workshops and educational events that allow visitors to learn more about indigenous arts and crafts, including totem pole carving, weaving, and beading. For those looking to take home a piece of Alaska, the Celebration Market offers handmade jewelry, clothing, and artwork created by local indigenous artisans. The festival creates a sense of unity and pride among participants, and it is a moving experience for anyone interested in learning more about the deep history of the region.

Juneau, Alaska's capital city, is located in the Southeast and can be reached by air or ferry, as it is not connected to the mainland road system. Flights to Juneau are available from Anchorage, Seattle, and other major cities, while the Alaska Marine Highway System provides ferry service to Juneau from various locations along the coast. Once in Juneau, visitors can explore the city's museums, hike its scenic trails, or take a day trip to nearby Mendenhall Glacier when they are not attending festival events.

For those who prefer outdoor music festivals, the **Seward Music and Arts Festival** is another excellent option. Held in the charming coastal town of Seward on the Kenai Peninsula, this annual event draws both local and regional musicians, offering a diverse lineup that includes everything from rock and indie music to bluegrass and jazz. In addition to live music performances, the festival also features an array of art displays, craft vendors, and food trucks, making it a fun and lively community gathering. One of the highlights of the Seward Music and Arts Festival is its family-friendly atmosphere, with activities for children, interactive art installations, and opportunities for festival-goers to join in creative workshops.

Seward itself is a popular summer destination, known for its proximity to **Kenai Fjords National Park**, where visitors can take boat tours to see glaciers and marine wildlife. During the festival, many attendees choose to combine the event with outdoor adventures, including hiking, kayaking, or taking a scenic drive along the Seward Highway, one of the most beautiful roadways in the U.S. Getting to Seward is relatively simple, with regular bus and train service from Anchorage, which is about 120 miles to the north. The drive takes around 2.5 hours, and many visitors take advantage of the Alaska Railroad's Coastal Classic route, which provides stunning views of mountains, forests, and the coastline as it makes its way from Anchorage to Seward.

Alaska is also home to several cultural fairs and festivals that celebrate the state's rich agricultural heritage and frontier spirit. One of the largest of these events is the **Alaska State Fair**, held every summer in Palmer, a small town located about an hour's drive northeast of Anchorage. The fair is a quintessential summer event, with a mix of agricultural displays, carnival rides, food vendors, and live entertainment. Visitors can wander through the fairgrounds to see prize-winning livestock, marvel at enormous vegetables grown in Alaska's long summer days, and sample a wide variety of food, from traditional Alaskan dishes to fair favorites like funnel cakes and corn dogs.

One of the highlights of the Alaska State Fair is the live music performances, which feature both local bands and national acts. The fair has hosted concerts by artists ranging from classic rock bands to contemporary country stars, making it a draw for music lovers of all genres. In addition to the entertainment, the fair offers educational exhibits that showcase Alaska's farming industry, including workshops on sustainable agriculture and homesteading. The fair's family-friendly activities, including petting zoos, pony rides, and interactive exhibits, make it an ideal destination for visitors of all ages.

Palmer can be reached by car from Anchorage, and there are also shuttle services available for those who prefer not to drive. The fair typically runs for two weeks, giving visitors plenty of time to explore the event and the surrounding area, which includes scenic hiking trails and the nearby **Matanuska Glacier**, a popular spot for glacier trekking and ice climbing.

For those who want to experience Alaska's artistic side, the **Sitka Summer Music Festival** offers a unique blend of world-class classical music in a stunning natural setting. Held in the coastal town of Sitka, located on Baranof Island in Southeast Alaska, this festival brings together renowned musicians from around the world for a series of chamber music performances. The festival takes place throughout June, with concerts held in a variety of venues, including the historic Harrigan Centennial Hall and the Sitka Fine Arts Campus.

One of the special aspects of the Sitka Summer Music Festival is the intimate setting, which allows attendees to get up close to the performers and experience the music in a personal, engaging way. In addition to the main concerts, the festival offers free public performances, educational workshops, and opportunities for attendees to meet and interact with the musicians. Sitka itself is a charming town with a rich history, including its role as the capital of Russian America before Alaska was sold to the United States. Visitors to Sitka can explore its historic sites, such as **Sitka National Historical Park**, hike the town's scenic trails, or take a boat tour to see the region's abundant marine wildlife.

Sitka is accessible by air, with flights available from Anchorage, Juneau, and Seattle, or by ferry via the Alaska Marine Highway. Once in Sitka, the town is easily navigable on foot or by using the local bus system, making it convenient to attend the festival's events while also enjoying everything else Sitka has to offer.

For visitors looking for an eclectic and artistic celebration, the **Fairbanks Summer Arts Festival** is another exciting event. Held in Alaska's second-largest city, this two-week festival offers workshops and performances in a wide range of disciplines, including music, dance, theater, visual arts, and culinary arts. The festival attracts artists from across the U.S. and around the world, making it an ideal destination for those who want to immerse themselves in Alaska's artistic community. In addition to attending performances, visitors can participate in hands-on workshops, learning everything from watercolor painting to ballroom dancing.

Fairbanks is located in the Interior of Alaska and is easily reached by air, with regular flights from Anchorage, Seattle, and other major cities. Once in Fairbanks, the festival's events take place at various venues around the city, many of which are within walking distance of downtown hotels and attractions. In addition to the festival, Fairbanks offers a variety of summer activities, including riverboat tours, visits to local museums, and opportunities to see the midnight sun, which shines nearly 24 hours a day during the peak of summer.

Autumn and Spring Events: Smaller festivals and off-season events worth attending

Autumn and spring in Alaska are often considered the off-season for tourism, but these transitional months offer a quieter, more intimate view of the state. With smaller crowds, milder weather, and beautiful seasonal landscapes, these periods are ideal for those who want to explore Alaska's charm without the hustle and bustle of peak summer and winter activities. In addition to the natural beauty of fall colors or spring blooms, Alaska's communities host a variety of smaller festivals and events during these seasons, offering unique cultural experiences that are worth planning a trip around. Whether you are interested in art, food, wildlife, or local traditions, Alaska's autumn and spring events provide something for everyone, making these off-season periods just as magical as the high seasons.

One of the notable events in the fall is the **Sitka Whalefest**, which takes place in early November in the picturesque town of Sitka, located on Baranof Island in Southeast Alaska. This festival is a celebration of marine life, particularly the whales that migrate through the region during the fall months. Sitka Whalefest is unique in that it combines scientific presentations with community celebrations, offering visitors the chance to learn from marine biologists and researchers while also enjoying art, music, and food that reflect Sitka's coastal culture. The scientific symposiums cover topics like whale migration, marine ecosystems, and ocean conservation, but the festival is not all about academics. There are also whale-watching tours, seafood feasts, art exhibits, and storytelling sessions, which provide a more relaxed and enjoyable way to connect with the natural world.

The best way to get to Sitka is by air, with daily flights available from Anchorage, Juneau, and Seattle. The Alaska Marine Highway System also provides ferry service to Sitka, offering an alternative for those who prefer a more scenic route through the Inside Passage. Once in Sitka, most of the Whalefest activities are centered around downtown, which is easily walkable. Visitors can take part in organized whale-watching boat trips, where knowledgeable guides help spot humpback whales, orcas, and other marine wildlife. The festival offers a perfect blend of education and entertainment, allowing you to experience Alaska's wildlife in a way that's both informative and deeply engaging.

Another wonderful event to experience during the fall is the **Anchorage Harvest Festival**, which typically takes place in late September. As summer draws to a close, this festival celebrates the bounty of Alaska's short but productive growing season. The Anchorage Harvest Festival features farmers' markets, local artisans, and food vendors offering a taste of Alaska's harvest. You'll find everything from locally grown vegetables and fresh seafood to homemade jams, honey, and baked goods made with Alaskan ingredients. There are also cooking demonstrations, where chefs show how to make the most of local produce, as well as workshops on gardening and sustainable farming.

In addition to the food offerings, the Anchorage Harvest Festival also includes live music, family-friendly activities, and craft booths selling handmade goods like knitwear, pottery, and jewelry. The festival is held at various locations around Anchorage, but a central hub is typically at the Alaska Botanical Garden or one of the city's larger parks. These venues offer beautiful backdrops of fall foliage, making the festival a lovely way to enjoy the crisp autumn air while sampling local flavors. Anchorage is the most accessible city in Alaska, with regular flights from major U.S. cities, and the festival locations are easily reachable by car or public transportation.

For those who enjoy the arts, the **Juneau Jazz & Classics Festival** is an excellent event to experience in the spring. Held annually in May, this music festival brings world-class jazz, blues, and classical musicians to Alaska's capital city, offering concerts in both formal venues and more casual settings like local pubs and outdoor stages. The festival is a celebration of music and community, with performances that range from intimate chamber music recitals to lively jazz jams that invite the audience to dance along.

One of the unique aspects of Juneau Jazz & Classics is the variety of venues where performances are held. You can attend a classical concert at the **Alaska State Capitol**, watch a jazz band perform in a cozy café, or enjoy a blues performance on a scenic boat cruise through the Inside Passage. The festival also offers workshops and masterclasses, where attendees can learn from the visiting musicians and hone their own skills. Juneau is easily accessible by air, with flights from Anchorage and Seattle, or by ferry. Once in Juneau, the festival's venues are spread throughout the downtown area, making it easy to walk from one performance to the next.

In addition to the musical performances, the festival coincides with the arrival of spring in Southeast Alaska, meaning visitors will also have the chance to witness the region's natural beauty as the trees begin to bloom and the days grow longer. Many visitors take advantage of the festival's timing to explore Juneau's outdoor attractions, such as Mendenhall Glacier or the nearby hiking trails, making it a perfect combination of culture and nature.

Springtime in Alaska also brings the **Hummingbird Festival** in Ketchikan, which is held in April to celebrate the return of the migratory Rufous hummingbirds to Southeast Alaska. Ketchikan, known for its rich native culture and stunning coastal scenery, hosts this festival at the Southeast Alaska Discovery Center, where visitors can participate in birdwatching tours, educational presentations, and art exhibits dedicated to the tiny but vibrant birds. The Hummingbird Festival is a more intimate and nature-focused event, ideal for birdwatchers, nature lovers, and anyone looking to experience the quieter, more peaceful side of Alaska in the off-season.

The event also includes a children's art contest, photography workshops, and guided walks where local experts explain the importance of migratory birds to the region's ecosystems. Ketchikan can be reached by air or ferry, with regular flights from Seattle, Juneau, and Anchorage. The town itself is small and walkable, with the Southeast Alaska Discovery Center located in the heart of downtown. Many visitors combine their trip to the festival with visits to Ketchikan's totem pole parks or a day cruise to the nearby Misty Fjords National Monument.

Another noteworthy off-season event is the **Winter Arts Faire** in Homer, held annually in late November, which is a testament to the artistic talent found in this coastal town on the Kenai Peninsula. While this event technically takes place just before winter, it serves as an ideal way to transition from the calm of autumn into the festive holiday season. The Winter Arts Faire showcases the work of local artists, craftspeople, and makers, offering everything from handmade pottery and glassware to paintings, textiles, and jewelry. The event is a great opportunity to purchase one-of-a-kind Alaskan gifts and support local artisans.

The Winter Arts Faire is held at the **Homer High School Commons**, with artists setting up booths to display their work. Live music, food vendors, and art demonstrations add to the lively atmosphere, making it a fun and engaging event for both locals and visitors. Homer is about a 4.5-hour drive from Anchorage, and many visitors use the event as an opportunity to explore the town's scenic beauty, which includes views of **Kachemak Bay** and the surrounding mountains. The town is also known for its art galleries and excellent restaurants, making a trip to Homer for the Winter Arts Faire a well-rounded experience.

For outdoor enthusiasts, the **Copper Basin 300 Sled Dog Race** is a spring event worth attending. Held every January in Glennallen, this race is considered one of the most challenging mid-distance dog sled races in Alaska. While it takes place at the end of winter, it marks the transition into spring with milder weather and longer days. The Copper Basin 300 attracts top mushers from around the state, offering visitors the chance to witness the excitement of competitive sled dog racing in a more intimate setting than the famous Iditarod.

Glennallen, located in the Copper River Valley, is a small community about 185 miles northeast of Anchorage, accessible by car via the Glenn Highway. The race follows a rugged 300-mile course through some of the state's most beautiful wilderness, and visitors can watch the start and finish of the race, as well as follow the mushers at checkpoints along the route. In addition to watching the race, visitors can explore the stunning scenery of the Copper River Valley, which is known for its wildlife, glaciers, and opportunities for outdoor recreation like snowshoeing and snowmobiling.

Chapter 16

Off-the-Beaten-Path Adventures

Remote towns, secret trails, and unique experiences

One of the true hidden treasures of Alaska is the **small town of McCarthy**, located deep within the heart of Wrangell-St. Elias National Park, the largest national park in the United States. This remote town, with a population of fewer than 100 residents, is a fascinating relic of Alaska's copper mining past, offering visitors a chance to step back in time while surrounded by some of the most stunning mountain scenery in the world. McCarthy's history is tied to the nearby **Kennecott Copper Mine**, a now-abandoned mining town that once produced massive amounts of copper. Today, Kennecott is a well-preserved ghost town, and visitors can explore the old mining buildings and equipment that tell the story of the copper boom in Alaska's early 20th century.

Getting to McCarthy is part of the adventure, as the town is only accessible via a long, gravel road—the **McCarthy Road**—which stretches 60 miles from Chitina to McCarthy. The drive is rough, but the views along the way are spectacular, with rugged mountains, rivers, and glaciers framing the landscape. For those who prefer not to drive, there are air taxi services available from Chitina and other nearby towns. Once in McCarthy, visitors can explore the Kennecott Mill, take a guided tour of the old copper mine, or hike in Wrangell-St. Elias National Park, which offers some of the most pristine and remote hiking trails in Alaska. Glacier hiking and ice climbing on the **Root Glacier** are particularly popular activities, offering a chance to walk on ancient ice and take in the vast, untouched wilderness that surrounds the area.

For those seeking solitude and a true escape from civilization, the small island community of **Seldovia** is another hidden gem worth exploring. Located across Kachemak Bay from the bustling town of Homer, Seldovia is a quaint and peaceful village that can only be reached by boat or small plane. This isolation has preserved the town's quiet charm, making it a perfect destination for travelers looking to experience Alaska at a slower pace. With fewer than 300 year-round residents, Seldovia offers a glimpse of small-town Alaskan life, where fishing and subsistence living remain central to the local culture.

Once in Seldovia, visitors can explore the town's historic boardwalk, which runs along the waterfront and offers picturesque views of the bay and surrounding mountains. The boardwalk is lined with charming homes, local shops, and art galleries, many of which showcase works by local artisans. The town's peaceful atmosphere makes it an ideal place to relax, but for those looking for adventure, Seldovia is also surrounded by beautiful hiking trails, such as the **Otterbahn Trail**, which leads to a secluded beach with stunning views of the bay and the open ocean. The nearby **Seldovia Bay Ferry** offers daily service to and from Homer, making it easy to combine a visit to Seldovia with other activities on the Kenai Peninsula.

For those interested in discovering Alaska's hidden hiking trails, the **Skookum Volcano Trail** in the Wrangell Mountains is one of the state's best-kept secrets. This remote trail, located near Nabesna in the northern part of Wrangell-St. Elias National Park, offers a challenging yet rewarding hike that takes you through some of Alaska's most dramatic volcanic landscapes. The trail leads to the summit of an ancient volcano, offering breathtaking views of the surrounding mountains, glaciers, and valleys. Along the way, hikers can see remnants of volcanic activity, such as lava flows and ash deposits, as well as a variety of wildlife, including Dall sheep, caribou, and golden eagles.

The Skookum Volcano Trail is off the beaten path, and getting there requires some planning. The trailhead is located about 42 miles down the Nabesna Road, a gravel road that runs through Wrangell-St. Elias National Park. While the road is drivable in most vehicles during the summer months, it can be rough in places, so it's important to check road conditions before setting out. For those looking for a truly remote hiking experience, the Skookum Volcano Trail offers solitude, stunning scenery, and a chance to explore one of Alaska's lesser-known natural wonders.

Another hidden gem worth discovering is the **village of Talkeetna**, a quirky and artistic town located at the confluence of three rivers: the Susitna, Chulitna, and Talkeetna. Talkeetna serves as the gateway to Denali for climbers and adventurers, but it's also a wonderful destination in its own right, offering a charming blend of outdoor adventure and small-town culture. Talkeetna's historic downtown is filled with colorful shops, galleries, and restaurants, many of which showcase local art and crafts. The town is known for its laid-back atmosphere and friendly residents, making it a welcoming place for visitors.

One of the highlights of Talkeetna is the opportunity to take a **flightseeing tour** of Denali and the surrounding mountain ranges. These small plane tours offer breathtaking views of North America's tallest peak, and many tours include the option to land on a glacier, giving visitors the chance to step out onto the ice and experience the rugged beauty of the Alaska Range up close. For those who prefer to stay on the ground, Talkeetna offers plenty of outdoor activities, including rafting on the Talkeetna River, hiking in the nearby **Talkeetna Mountains**, or simply enjoying the stunning views of Denali from the town's riverfront park. Talkeetna is located about two hours north of Anchorage and is accessible by car, train, or small plane.

One of the most unique experiences in Alaska can be found in the **ghost town of Port Chatham**, located on the southern tip of the Kenai Peninsula. Port Chatham was once a thriving fishing and canning community, but it was abandoned in the 1950s under mysterious circumstances, with residents fleeing the town due to unexplained phenomena and reports of strange creatures in the nearby forests. Today, the town remains abandoned, and its remote location and eerie history have made it a destination for adventurous travelers and paranormal enthusiasts. Reaching Port Chatham requires either a boat or a plane, as there are no roads that lead to the town. For those willing to make the journey, exploring the abandoned buildings and hiking through the surrounding wilderness offers a rare glimpse into Alaska's forgotten past.

Port Chatham's isolation and haunting atmosphere make it one of Alaska's most intriguing hidden gems. Visitors can explore the remains of the old cannery, walk through the overgrown streets, and take in the haunting beauty of the town's surroundings. The area is also known for its abundant wildlife, including bears, moose, and eagles, making it a great destination for those interested in both history and nature. Port Chatham is best visited as part of a guided tour, as its remote location and lack of infrastructure make it difficult to navigate without local knowledge.

For travelers looking for a unique and remote adventure, **Adak Island** in the Aleutian Islands is one of the most remote places you can visit in Alaska. Once a military outpost during World War II and the Cold War, Adak is now home to fewer than 100 residents and offers visitors a chance to experience Alaska's wild and windswept frontier. The island is known for its stark beauty, with rolling hills, volcanic landscapes, and an abundance of wildlife, including sea otters, puffins, and bald eagles. Adak is also one of the few places in Alaska where you can hike to the remains of military bunkers and abandoned buildings, providing a fascinating glimpse into the island's history.

Getting to Adak requires a flight from Anchorage, and the island's remoteness means that services are limited, so visitors should come prepared with everything they need for their stay. Once on the island, there are a variety of outdoor activities to enjoy, including hiking, birdwatching, and fishing in the island's many lakes and streams. For those seeking solitude and a true escape from civilization, Adak offers an unparalleled opportunity to experience Alaska's wild, untamed beauty.

Backcountry Adventures: How to plan your wilderness explorations

The first step in planning a backcountry adventure in Alaska is deciding which region you want to explore. Alaska is divided into several distinct geographical areas, each offering its own unique wilderness experiences. One of the most popular destinations for backcountry adventurers is **Denali National Park**, home to North America's tallest peak, Denali (formerly known as Mount McKinley). The park spans six million acres of rugged wilderness, with no marked trails in much of the backcountry, providing an ideal setting for those looking for an unstructured and immersive experience in nature. For those seeking high-altitude mountaineering, hiking, or multi-day backpacking trips, Denali's backcountry offers some of the best opportunities in the world.

Denali National Park is accessible by road, with the **Park Road** extending 92 miles into the park. However, private vehicles are only allowed to travel the first 15 miles; beyond that, visitors must use park buses, or in some cases, special permits for backcountry camping. To access the more remote parts of Denali, many adventurers choose to fly in via small bush planes that can land on the glaciers. These flights are typically arranged from Talkeetna, a small town north of Anchorage, where local air taxis offer trips into the park's deeper wilderness areas. For those planning to explore the backcountry on foot, Denali's wilderness is known for its unpredictability, with challenging terrain, rapid changes in weather, and the potential for encounters with wildlife, such as bears and moose.

Another exceptional destination for backcountry adventures is **Wrangell-St. Elias National Park**, the largest national park in the U.S., covering an area larger than nine U.S. states combined. The park is located in southeastern Alaska and is famous for its massive glaciers, mountain ranges, and volcanic landscapes. It's also one of the least-visited national parks in the country, making it an ideal spot for those looking to experience true solitude. Wrangell-St. Elias offers everything from glacier hiking and ice climbing to rafting on wild rivers and multi-day backpacking excursions through untouched wilderness. The park is vast and remote, with access points primarily through the small towns of **McCarthy** and **Kennecott**, or by bush plane from larger cities like Anchorage or Fairbanks.

Once you've chosen your destination, it's essential to be well-prepared for the logistics of traveling in the backcountry. Alaska's wilderness is known for being rugged and unforgiving, so having the right gear is crucial. When packing for a backcountry adventure, start by ensuring you have proper clothing. Layering is key in Alaska, where temperatures can vary significantly throughout the day. Moisture-wicking base layers, insulated mid-layers, and waterproof outerwear are all essential for staying dry and warm. Even in the summer, nighttime temperatures can dip below freezing in some areas, especially at higher elevations, so be sure to bring cold-weather gear, including a warm hat, gloves, and a sleeping bag rated for cold temperatures.

In addition to clothing, you'll need a reliable tent, preferably a four-season or three-season tent that can withstand high winds and potential snowfall. A good quality backpacking stove and fuel are also essential for cooking meals in the backcountry, as open fires are not always permitted, and fuel sources can be scarce in some areas. Pack enough lightweight, high-calorie food to sustain you for the duration of your trip, and always bring extra in case of delays or unexpected challenges. Freeze-dried meals, energy bars, and dehydrated fruits and vegetables are excellent choices for long trips.

Navigation tools are another critical component of any backcountry adventure. While GPS devices can be helpful, it's essential to have a topographic map and compass as backups, as GPS signals may be unreliable in remote areas. Knowing how to read maps and navigate through unmarked wilderness is a valuable skill when exploring Alaska's backcountry. Many areas have no cell service, so it's important to rely on your own navigational abilities and to have a clear understanding of your route before setting out.

Another important consideration for backcountry adventurers is safety. Alaska's wilderness is home to a variety of wildlife, including black and brown bears, wolves, and moose. While wildlife encounters can be an exciting part of your adventure, they can also pose a serious risk if not handled properly. Always carry bear spray and know how to use it effectively. Store food in bear-proof containers and hang your food away from your campsite to avoid attracting bears. If you're traveling in areas with a high bear population, it's also a good idea to travel in groups and make noise while hiking to avoid surprising any wildlife.

In addition to wildlife safety, the remote nature of Alaska's backcountry means that you need to be self-sufficient and prepared for any emergencies. Carry a well-stocked first aid kit, and know basic wilderness first aid, such as treating cuts, sprains, or hypothermia. It's also wise to bring a satellite communication device, such as a **SPOT** or **Garmin InReach**, which allows you to send distress signals or communicate with the outside world in case of an emergency. These devices can be lifesaving in the event of an injury or if you become lost.

One of the great joys of backcountry exploration in Alaska is the opportunity for multi-day backpacking trips. One such popular trek is the **Kesugi Ridge Trail**, located in **Denali State Park**. This 29-mile trail offers panoramic views of Denali and the Alaska Range, along with diverse terrain that includes alpine meadows, forests, and rocky ridges. It's a challenging hike, but the rewards are incredible, with endless vistas, the chance to spot wildlife, and a true sense of isolation. The trail is usually done in three to five days, with several campsites along the way. It's accessible by car, with trailheads located along the **Parks Highway** between Anchorage and Denali National Park.

Another exciting backcountry option is **Gates of the Arctic National Park**, which is one of the most remote and wild parks in the United States. Located in the northern part of Alaska, above the Arctic Circle, Gates of the Arctic is known for its rugged mountains, vast river valleys, and the complete lack of roads or trails. This park is for experienced adventurers who are comfortable navigating without the support of established paths. Most visitors to Gates of the Arctic arrive by bush plane, and once in the park, they are entirely on their own. Popular activities include rafting on the **Noatak River**, backpacking in the **Brooks Range**, and wildlife watching for caribou, wolves, and grizzly bears. Exploring this park offers a true sense of wilderness adventure, but it also requires thorough preparation and a high level of self-reliance.

Planning a backcountry adventure in Alaska also involves understanding the weather conditions you're likely to encounter. Alaska's weather can be unpredictable, with sudden storms, strong winds, and rapidly dropping temperatures. Summer months, from June to August, generally offer the most favorable conditions for hiking and camping, with long daylight hours and milder temperatures. However, even during the summer, rain is common, and snow can fall at higher elevations. Always check the weather forecast before setting out, and be prepared for rain, wind, and cold temperatures.

In addition to summer adventures, the fall months offer a beautiful time to explore the backcountry, as the landscape turns golden with the changing colors of the tundra and trees. However, fall also brings shorter days and colder nights, so it's important to be prepared for more challenging conditions. Winter backcountry adventures, such as snowshoeing, skiing, or winter camping, offer another way to experience Alaska's wilderness in its most extreme form. Winter travel requires specialized gear, such as avalanche safety equipment, and it's essential to have experience traveling in snowy and icy conditions.

Whether you choose to explore the mountains of Denali, the glaciers of Wrangell-St. Elias, or the untouched wilderness of Gates of the Arctic, a backcountry adventure in Alaska promises to be an unforgettable experience. The solitude, beauty, and challenge of these remote areas allow you to connect with nature in a way that few other places can offer. With careful planning, the right gear, and respect for the wilderness, your Alaskan backcountry journey will be both safe and rewarding.

Small Town Charms: Discovering Alaska's quaint villages and their local flavor

One of the most charming small towns to explore in Alaska is **Talkeetna**, located about 115 miles north of Anchorage. Talkeetna is a quirky, vibrant village known for its bohemian atmosphere and its role as the gateway to **Denali National Park**. The town itself is small, with fewer than 900 residents, but it has a big personality. Talkeetna's historic downtown features rustic log cabins, colorful art galleries, cozy cafés, and craft shops that showcase the work of local artisans. One of the town's most famous attractions is **Nagley's Store**, a historic general store that has been serving the community for over a century. This small-town institution sells everything from groceries to souvenirs and is a gathering place for both locals and visitors.

Talkeetna is also the starting point for many climbers attempting to summit Denali, and as a result, it attracts adventurers from all over the world. Visitors can take a **flightseeing tour** to view Denali and the Alaska Range from above, or for the more adventurous, there are glacier landings where you can step out onto the ice and experience the majesty of the mountains up close. In the summer months, Talkeetna offers a range of outdoor activities, including rafting on the Talkeetna River, hiking the **Talkeetna Lakes Trail**, or enjoying a lazy afternoon at the riverfront park, which offers stunning views of Denali on clear days. The town also hosts the **Talkeetna Bluegrass Festival**, a lively summer event filled with music, dancing, and local food.

Getting to Talkeetna is easy, as the town is accessible by car via the **Parks Highway**, or by the **Alaska Railroad**, which runs between Anchorage and Fairbanks, stopping in Talkeetna along the way. Many visitors choose to take the train, which offers panoramic views of the surrounding wilderness as you travel through the Matanuska-Susitna Valley. Once in Talkeetna, the town is walkable, with most of the main attractions located within a few blocks of the train depot.

For those interested in history, **Skagway** is another small town that should not be missed. Located in Southeast Alaska, Skagway was once a booming Gold Rush town and played a central role in the Klondike Gold Rush of the late 1800s. Today, the town's historic downtown has been carefully preserved, with many buildings from the Gold Rush era still standing, giving visitors a glimpse into what life was like during one of the most exciting periods in Alaska's history. Walking down **Broadway Street**, you'll see colorful wooden storefronts, saloons, and hotels that look much as they did over a century ago.

The **Klondike Gold Rush National Historical Park** is located in Skagway, and its visitor center offers exhibits, guided tours, and a wealth of information about the town's fascinating past.

One of the most popular activities in Skagway is taking a ride on the **White Pass & Yukon Route Railroad**, a scenic train that follows the path of the old gold rush stampeders as it climbs from Skagway into the mountains of the **Coast Range**. The train ride offers breathtaking views of waterfalls, glaciers, and rugged mountain peaks, making it a must-do experience for anyone visiting the town. For those who enjoy hiking, the nearby **Chilkoot Trail** offers a challenging but rewarding trek through the same terrain that gold prospectors traversed in search of fortune.

Skagway is accessible by ferry from Juneau and other towns in Southeast Alaska, or by cruise ship, as the town is a popular stop on many Alaska cruise itineraries. Visitors can also fly into **Skagway Airport**, although flight options are more limited. Once in Skagway, the town is small enough to explore on foot, with most of the attractions located within a few blocks of the ferry terminal and downtown.

Moving south to **Haines**, another small town in Southeast Alaska, visitors will find a peaceful, artistic community that sits at the head of the **Lynn Canal**, one of the longest fjords in North America. Haines is known for its natural beauty and is a haven for outdoor enthusiasts. The town is surrounded by snow-capped mountains, dense forests, and pristine waters, making it an ideal destination for activities like hiking, kayaking, and wildlife watching. In fact, Haines is one of the best places in Alaska to see bald eagles, with thousands of eagles congregating along the **Chilkat River** each fall during the **Alaska Bald Eagle Festival**.

Haines also has a rich cultural heritage, with a strong connection to the Tlingit people, who have inhabited the area for thousands of years. The **Sheldon Museum and Cultural Center** offers exhibits on the history and culture of Haines, including its Tlingit heritage, the Gold Rush era, and the early settlers who shaped the town. Another highlight of Haines is **Fort Seward**, a historic military fort that has been converted into an arts and cultural district. The fort is home to art galleries, craft shops, and studios, where visitors can watch local artists at work and purchase handmade goods.

Getting to Haines is a bit more challenging than some other towns, as it is not connected to the rest of Alaska by road. However, it is accessible by ferry from Juneau or by small plane. Once in Haines, the town is easy to navigate by foot, and there are rental options for those who want to explore the surrounding areas by car or bike.

Further north, **Nome** is a small town located on the edge of the Bering Sea in Western Alaska. Nome is famous for being the finish line of the **Iditarod Trail Sled Dog Race**, but it also has a rich history as one of the largest gold rush towns in Alaska. At its peak, Nome was home to over 20,000 prospectors, all hoping to strike it rich in the goldfields surrounding the town. Today, Nome is a quieter place, with around 3,800 residents, but it still retains its gold rush spirit.

Visitors to Nome can explore the town's history at the **Carrie M. McLain Memorial Museum**, which features exhibits on Nome's gold rush past, as well as the native Inupiat culture that has thrived in the region for thousands of years. Nome's remote location makes it an ideal spot for wildlife viewing, and visitors can see musk oxen, moose, and even polar bears in the wild. The **Bering Land Bridge National Preserve**, located near Nome, offers stunning views of the surrounding tundra and the opportunity to explore one of the most remote national parks in the United States.

Getting to Nome is typically done by air, with daily flights from Anchorage. While Nome does not have a road connecting it to other parts of Alaska, visitors can rent vehicles in town to explore the surrounding areas, including **Anvil Mountain** and the nearby gold dredges that still stand as a testament to Nome's gold rush history.

For a completely different small-town experience, **Petersburg**, located in Southeast Alaska, is known as "Little Norway" due to its strong Norwegian heritage. The town was founded by Norwegian fishermen in the late 1800s, and its Scandinavian roots are still evident today, with traditional Norwegian architecture, festivals, and cultural events. Each May, Petersburg hosts the

Little Norway Festival, a lively celebration of Norwegian culture that includes traditional music, dancing, and food.

Petersburg is also a working fishing town, and visitors can see commercial fishing boats at work in the harbor or visit one of the local fish processing plants to learn about the industry. The surrounding area is home to stunning fjords, glaciers, and wildlife, making it an excellent destination for kayaking, whale watching, and hiking. The nearby **LeConte Glacier** is one of the most impressive tidewater glaciers in Southeast Alaska, and boat tours from Petersburg offer close-up views of the glacier's towering icebergs.

Petersburg is accessible by ferry from Juneau or other Southeast Alaska towns, or by small plane. Once in Petersburg, the town is small and easy to navigate on foot, with plenty of local shops, restaurants, and cultural sites to explore.

Cultural Immersion: Visiting native villages and learning about indigenous traditions

Visiting native villages can be a life-changing experience, providing insight into the deep connection between the people and the land, the traditional practices that have been passed down through generations, and the challenges and triumphs of modern-day indigenous life in Alaska. Each village has its own story, shaped by its environment, history, and people. While Alaska's cities may offer museums and cultural centers that provide a glimpse into these cultures, there is nothing quite like visiting the villages themselves, where you can engage directly with the community, participate in traditional activities, and witness firsthand the resilience and richness of indigenous life.

One of the most accessible ways to experience cultural immersion is by visiting the **Alaska Native Heritage Center** in Anchorage, which offers a comprehensive introduction to the state's 11 distinct indigenous cultures. The center showcases the history and traditions of the Inupiat, Yupik, Aleut, Tlingit, Haida, and others through exhibits, demonstrations, and performances. Visitors can watch traditional dancing, listen to storytelling, and see artisans crafting items such as masks, baskets, and clothing using traditional methods. While this center is located in a more urban environment, it serves as a perfect starting point for anyone who wants to learn about Alaska's native peoples before venturing to more remote villages.

For those seeking a more immersive experience, visiting the **village of Kotzebue** in the northwest Arctic is a remarkable opportunity to learn about the Inupiat people. Kotzebue, located above the Arctic Circle, is a hub for the indigenous villages that dot the northern coast of Alaska. The Inupiat have lived in this region for thousands of years, relying on the sea, rivers, and tundra for sustenance. Visiting Kotzebue provides a glimpse into the traditional subsistence lifestyle that remains an integral part of the community's identity. While in Kotzebue, visitors can learn about traditional hunting, fishing, and gathering practices, as well as the importance of the bowhead whale hunt, which is a significant cultural and spiritual event for the Inupiat.

Getting to Kotzebue typically requires a flight from Anchorage, as the town is not connected to Alaska's road system. Once there, guided tours are available that introduce visitors to the local culture, including stops at the **Northwest Arctic Heritage Center**, where you can learn about the region's history and ecology. Visitors may also have the opportunity to participate in traditional crafts such as ivory carving or witness traditional dances performed by local groups. Kotzebue is also a prime location for viewing the Northern Lights in the winter months, adding an extra layer of awe to your cultural immersion experience.

For those interested in the rich maritime cultures of Southeast Alaska, the **Tlingit and Haida** peoples offer a fascinating perspective on the intersection of land and sea. The village of **Klawock**, located on **Prince of Wales Island**, is home to one of the most significant collections of totem poles in Alaska. The art of totem pole carving is a central part of Tlingit and Haida culture, with each pole telling a story that reflects the history, lineage, and beliefs of the clan that commissioned it. Visiting Klawock offers the chance to see these magnificent totems up close and to learn about the deep spiritual significance they hold for the Tlingit and Haida people.

In addition to totem poles, Klawock is known for its thriving traditional arts scene, with local artisans continuing to practice techniques passed down for generations. Visitors can tour the **Klawock Totem Park**, which features a collection of over 20 poles, or visit local workshops where master carvers and weavers create their art. Getting to Klawock requires a flight to **Ketchikan**, followed by a ferry ride to **Prince of Wales Island**, where Klawock is located. Once on the island, visitors can also explore nearby Tlingit and Haida villages, further deepening their understanding of these coastal cultures.

Further north, in **Nome**, you can experience the traditional practices of the **Yupik** and Inupiat peoples. Nome is best known as the finish line for the **Iditarod Trail Sled Dog Race**, but it is also home to a rich indigenous heritage. The Yupik people have inhabited the region for thousands of years, and their connection to the land and sea is evident in their traditional subsistence practices. While in Nome, visitors can tour the **Carrie M. McLain Memorial Museum**, which offers exhibits on the indigenous history of the region, as well as displays of traditional clothing, tools, and crafts.

Nome is accessible by air from Anchorage, and once there, guided cultural tours can introduce visitors to the ways in which the Yupik and Inupiat people have adapted to life in the harsh Arctic environment. Visitors may have the opportunity to witness traditional seal or whale hunting, depending on the season, or to learn about the intricate art of making **qiviut**, a soft wool harvested from the undercoat of the musk ox. Nome's remote location and rich indigenous culture make it a must-visit for those interested in learning about life in the Arctic and the enduring traditions of Alaska's native peoples.

For a more remote cultural experience, the **village of Bethel** in western Alaska provides an intimate look into the life of the **Yupik** people. Bethel is located on the **Kuskokwim River** and serves as a hub for the surrounding Yupik villages. The Yupik are known for their traditional dances, songs, and ceremonies, which are often performed during the **Cama-i Dance Festival**, an annual event that draws indigenous dance groups from across the state. Visitors to Bethel can attend the festival to see these powerful performances and learn about the cultural significance of the dances.

Bethel is accessible by air from Anchorage, and the village itself is small and easily navigable by foot or bike. While in Bethel, visitors can also learn about traditional Yupik subsistence practices, such as fishing, berry picking, and hunting, which remain central to the community's way of life. Bethel offers a quieter, more intimate experience than some of the larger villages, making it an ideal destination for those seeking a deep cultural connection.

Finally, the **village of Ketchikan**, located in Southeast Alaska, is home to the **Saxman Native Village** and offers a wealth of opportunities to learn about the **Tlingit** people. Saxman is known for its impressive collection of totem poles, which are displayed in the **Saxman Totem Park**. Visitors to Saxman can take part in guided tours that explain the meaning and history behind each totem, as well as learn about the traditional carving methods used to create these towering works of art.

In addition to the totem poles, Saxman offers cultural performances that include traditional Tlingit dancing, drumming, and storytelling. These performances provide insight into the spiritual and ceremonial practices of the Tlingit people, offering a deeper understanding of their connection to the land and their ancestors. Ketchikan is easily accessible by air or ferry, making it a convenient destination for those traveling in Southeast Alaska.

Visiting Alaska's native villages provides an opportunity to step back in time and experience traditions that have been passed down through generations. Each village offers a unique glimpse into the diverse cultures that have thrived in Alaska for thousands of years, and the chance to learn from the people who continue to preserve these traditions today. Whether you're witnessing traditional dances, participating in subsistence activities, or simply learning about the deep connection between Alaska's indigenous peoples and the land, a visit to these villages is an unforgettable experience that will leave a lasting impact.

Chapter 17: Practical Travel Tips

Money and Costs: Budgeting tips and what to expect in terms of cost

When planning a trip to Alaska, one of the most important considerations is budgeting and understanding the costs involved. While Alaska is a dream destination for many due to its pristine wilderness, wildlife, and outdoor adventures, it's also known for being a more expensive place to travel compared to other U.S. destinations. This is largely due to its remote location, the high cost of shipping goods, and the seasonality of tourism. However, with the right planning and budgeting strategies, you can make the most of your trip without overspending, ensuring that you have an unforgettable experience without breaking the bank.

Alaska's cost of living is higher than the national average, and this is reflected in the prices you'll encounter as a traveler. Everything from accommodations and transportation to dining and excursions tends to cost more in Alaska than in other parts of the United States. However, it's important to note that costs can vary significantly depending on the time of year, the region of Alaska you're visiting, and the type of activities you plan to do. By being aware of these factors and planning accordingly, you can better manage your travel budget and have a clearer idea of what to expect in terms of costs.

Seasonality and Travel Costs

One of the biggest factors influencing the cost of your trip to Alaska is the time of year you choose to visit. Alaska has a relatively short peak tourist season, which runs from late May through early September. During this time, prices for flights, accommodations, and tours are at their highest, as this is when most people choose to visit. The summer months offer the best weather, longer daylight hours, and a wider range of activities, but they also come with a price tag. Flights from the Lower 48 states to Alaska can be quite expensive during peak season, especially if you're flying into popular destinations like Anchorage, Juneau, or Fairbanks.

If you're looking to save on travel costs, consider visiting Alaska during the shoulder seasons, which include May (before Memorial Day) and September (after Labor Day). During these times, you can often find lower prices on flights and accommodations, while still enjoying relatively mild weather and the chance to experience many of Alaska's top attractions. Some activities, such as wildlife viewing and hiking, can be just as rewarding in the shoulder season, and you'll also encounter fewer crowds.

For the budget-conscious traveler, visiting Alaska in the winter can offer significant savings. Flights, hotels, and tours are typically much cheaper during the winter months, although the range of activities is more limited due to snow and shorter daylight hours. However, winter brings its own unique charm, with opportunities for activities like dog sledding, viewing the Northern Lights, and snowshoeing. If you're an outdoor enthusiast willing to embrace the cold, a winter trip to Alaska can be an affordable and unforgettable adventure.

Flights and Transportation Costs

Getting to Alaska is likely to be one of the biggest expenses of your trip, especially if you're flying from a distant location. The majority of travelers fly into **Ted Stevens Anchorage International Airport** in Anchorage, which is the state's largest city and a central hub for exploring other parts of Alaska. **Juneau International Airport** and **Fairbanks International Airport** are also popular entry points, depending on which region of Alaska you plan to explore. Flights to Alaska can range anywhere from $400 to $1,200 or more, depending on the season, departure city, and how far in advance you book.

To save on airfare, consider booking your flights several months in advance and keeping an eye out for deals. Airlines like Alaska Airlines, Delta, and United frequently offer sales or discounted fares to Alaska, particularly in the off-season. It's also worth considering flying into Anchorage and then taking regional flights to other parts of the state, as this can sometimes be cheaper than booking direct flights to smaller airports.

Once you've arrived in Alaska, transportation costs will depend on how you choose to get around. **Car rentals** are a popular option, especially for travelers planning to explore multiple regions or embark on road trips. Rental car prices in Alaska can range from $50 to $150 per day, depending on the vehicle type and the time of year. It's important to note that car rental prices can skyrocket during the peak summer months, so booking in advance is essential if you want to secure a vehicle at a reasonable price.

If you're traveling to more remote areas or smaller towns that are not accessible by road, such as **Kodiak Island** or **Wrangell**, you'll likely need to take a regional flight or ferry. **Alaska Airlines** and **Ravn Alaska** operate flights to many of Alaska's remote communities, but fares can be high due to the limited availability of flights. **Alaska's Marine Highway System**, the state's ferry network, is an excellent alternative for traveling between coastal towns, particularly in Southeast Alaska. While ferry prices can still be relatively expensive, they are often more affordable than flying, and the journey itself offers breathtaking views of Alaska's coastline.

Accommodation Costs

Accommodations in Alaska vary widely in terms of price and availability, ranging from luxury lodges and hotels to budget-friendly hostels and campgrounds. In popular tourist destinations like Anchorage, Juneau, and Denali National Park, hotel prices tend to be highest during the summer months, with rates averaging between $150 and $300 per night for mid-range accommodations. Luxury lodges or resorts can cost upwards of $500 per night, especially in more remote locations that offer exclusive access to Alaska's wilderness.

If you're traveling on a tighter budget, there are several ways to save on accommodation costs. **Hostels**, such as **Base Camp Anchorage** or **Juneau International Hostel**, offer dormitory-style lodging with rates as low as $30 to $50 per night, making them an excellent option for solo travelers or backpackers. **Vacation rentals** through platforms like Airbnb or Vrbo can also be a cost-effective alternative to hotels, particularly if you're traveling with a group or staying in one place for an extended period.

For outdoor enthusiasts, **camping** is one of the most affordable ways to experience Alaska's natural beauty. Alaska is home to countless campgrounds, both in state and national parks, with nightly fees ranging from $15 to $30 for tent camping. RV parks are also widely available, with prices ranging from $25 to $60 per night, depending on the location and amenities. Many campgrounds in Alaska offer stunning views and access to hiking trails, lakes, and rivers, allowing you to fully immerse yourself in the wilderness at a fraction of the cost of a hotel.

Food and Dining Costs

Dining in Alaska can be more expensive than in other parts of the U.S., due in large part to the cost of transporting food to the state. In larger cities like Anchorage and Juneau, you'll find a wide range of dining options, from casual eateries and food trucks to fine dining restaurants specializing in locally sourced ingredients like wild salmon, halibut, and game meats.

Meals at mid-range restaurants typically cost between $15 and $30 per person, while higher-end restaurants can cost $50 or more per person, especially if you're indulging in Alaska's famous seafood.

For budget travelers, there are plenty of affordable dining options, particularly in the form of **local food trucks** and casual diners. In cities like Anchorage, you can find food trucks serving up delicious reindeer sausages, fresh fish tacos, and gourmet burgers for around $10 to $15. Grocery stores are also widely available in larger towns, allowing you to save money by preparing some of your own meals, especially if you're staying in vacation rentals or campsites with cooking facilities.

In smaller towns and more remote areas, dining options may be limited, and food prices can be higher due to the cost of shipping goods. It's a good idea to stock up on non-perishable snacks and essentials before heading to these areas, especially if you're planning to spend time in the backcountry or at more isolated lodges.

Activity and Tour Costs

One of the biggest draws of visiting Alaska is the wide range of outdoor activities and guided tours available, but it's important to factor these costs into your travel budget. Popular activities like **glacier hikes**, **wildlife cruises**, and **flightseeing tours** tend to be more expensive, with prices ranging from $150 to $500 or more, depending on the duration and type of tour. For example, a half-day **Kenai Fjords National Park** wildlife cruise may cost around $160 per person, while a **flightseeing tour** of Denali with a glacier landing can cost upwards of $400 per person.

While these experiences can be pricey, they are often worth the investment for the unforgettable views and access to remote areas of Alaska that are otherwise difficult to reach. To save on tour costs, consider booking in advance, as many operators offer discounts for early reservations or for booking multiple tours at once. It's also worth looking for **combo deals** that bundle together activities like glacier hikes and wildlife cruises at a discounted rate.

For budget-friendly activities, Alaska offers plenty of free or low-cost outdoor adventures, such as hiking, fishing, and wildlife viewing. Many of Alaska's **state parks** and **national parks** have little to no entrance fees, and some of the most scenic hiking trails are free to access. For example, hiking **Flattop Mountain** in Anchorage or the **Mount Roberts Trail** in Juneau costs nothing beyond the transportation to the trailhead. Additionally, public lands offer countless opportunities for wildlife viewing, including the chance to see bears, moose, eagles, and whales in their natural habitats.

Budgeting Tips for Alaska

- **Plan in advance**: Alaska's peak season can fill up quickly, so booking flights, accommodations, and tours several months in advance can save you money and ensure availability.

- **Travel during the shoulder season**: Visiting in May or September can save you a significant amount on flights and hotels while still allowing you to experience many of Alaska's top attractions.
- **Opt for budget accommodations**: Consider staying in hostels, vacation rentals, or campgrounds to keep accommodation costs down.
- **Take advantage of free activities**: Hiking, wildlife viewing, and exploring state parks are all budget-friendly ways to enjoy Alaska's natural beauty.
- **Self-cater when possible**: Grocery stores are widely available in larger towns, and preparing your own meals can help you save on dining costs, especially in remote areas.

Traveling with Kids: Family-friendly activities and accommodations

One of the biggest draws of Alaska for families is the incredible diversity of outdoor activities that are accessible to people of all ages and abilities. From national parks to wildlife preserves, Alaska provides a vast playground where children can learn about nature firsthand. Whether it's the awe-inspiring sight of a whale breaching in the Gulf of Alaska, a hike through the lush temperate rainforests of Southeast Alaska, or a visit to a hands-on museum, there's no shortage of experiences that are sure to captivate the imagination of young explorers.

Anchorage: The Perfect Family Base

For families traveling with kids, **Anchorage** is a fantastic starting point. As Alaska's largest city, Anchorage offers a wide range of family-friendly activities, museums, parks, and accommodations, making it an ideal hub for exploring the surrounding areas. **Ted Stevens Anchorage International Airport** is easily accessible with regular flights from many major U.S. cities, and from here, you can rent a car or take public transportation to get around.

Anchorage's **Alaska Zoo** is a must-visit for families, offering kids the chance to see native Alaskan wildlife up close. The zoo is home to bears, moose, wolves, and a wide variety of other animals that children will recognize from storybooks and wildlife documentaries. The **Alaska Wildlife Conservation Center**, located just an hour's drive south of Anchorage, offers an even more immersive experience, where children can learn about efforts to protect and rehabilitate endangered species while seeing animals in a more natural setting.

For families with an interest in the natural sciences, the **Anchorage Museum** at **Rasmuson Center** offers interactive exhibits that focus on Alaska's geography, history, and indigenous cultures. The museum's **Imaginarium Discovery Center** is particularly popular with younger visitors, featuring hands-on exhibits that encourage kids to learn about science, art, and technology through play.

One of the best outdoor family activities in Anchorage is a visit to **Kincaid Park**, a massive 1,500-acre park that offers numerous hiking and biking trails, picnic areas, and playgrounds. The park is located on the western edge of Anchorage, with stunning views of **Cook Inlet** and, on clear days, the distant peaks of the **Alaska Range**. The trails at Kincaid Park are mostly flat and easy to navigate, making them perfect for families with young children. In the winter, the park transforms into a snowy wonderland, where families can enjoy sledding, cross-country skiing, and snowshoeing.

If your family enjoys biking, Anchorage's **Tony Knowles Coastal Trail** is a scenic, family-friendly trail that runs for 11 miles along the coastline, offering breathtaking views of the inlet and surrounding mountains. Bike rentals are available at various shops throughout Anchorage, making it easy to embark on this outdoor adventure.

Denali National Park: Outdoor Adventures for All Ages

A visit to **Denali National Park and Preserve** is a highlight of any trip to Alaska, and it's an especially magical experience for families. The park is home to **Denali**, North America's tallest peak, and offers a wealth of opportunities for wildlife viewing, hiking, and outdoor exploration. Located about four hours north of Anchorage by car or by train on the **Alaska Railroad**,

Denali is relatively accessible, and there are accommodations in and around the park that cater to families.

Denali is famous for its wildlife, and children will be thrilled by the chance to see animals like grizzly bears, caribou, moose, and Dall sheep in their natural habitats. Guided bus tours are a popular way for families to explore the park without needing to hike long distances. These tours are narrated by knowledgeable guides who can provide fascinating insights into the park's ecology, geology, and wildlife. The **Tundra Wilderness Tour** is especially recommended for families, as it offers great opportunities for wildlife sightings and stunning views of the park's landscapes, all from the comfort of a bus.

For families with younger children, **Denali's Savage River Loop Trail** is an easy, two-mile trail that offers beautiful views of the river and surrounding mountains. The trail is flat and well-maintained, making it perfect for strollers or little legs that may tire easily. The **Denali Visitor Center** also offers a Junior Ranger program, where kids can participate in educational activities and earn a badge, making them official Junior Rangers of Denali National Park.

Accommodations near Denali include family-friendly lodges, cabins, and campgrounds. Many of these lodges offer kid-friendly amenities, such as guided nature walks, wildlife viewing platforms, and educational programs that allow children to learn more about the park's unique ecosystem.

Kenai Peninsula: A Paradise for Nature-Loving Families

The **Kenai Peninsula** is another fantastic destination for families, offering a wide variety of activities that appeal to kids of all ages. From wildlife cruises to glacier hikes, the Kenai Peninsula provides endless opportunities for adventure and learning.

Seward, located at the edge of the **Kenai Fjords National Park**, is a great place to base your family's exploration of the region. The park is famous for its glaciers, marine wildlife, and dramatic fjords, and many family-friendly tour operators offer boat cruises that allow you to see these natural wonders up close. **Kenai Fjords Tours** and **Major Marine Tours** are two companies that offer wildlife cruises designed with families in mind. During these cruises, kids will be able to see puffins, sea otters, seals, and even whales, while learning about the park's glaciers and marine ecosystems.

For a hands-on wildlife experience, visit the **Alaska SeaLife Center** in Seward, where children can learn about marine life through interactive exhibits and see animals like sea lions, seals, and octopuses up close. The center also offers touch tanks, where kids can safely handle sea stars, sea urchins, and other marine creatures.

The **Exit Glacier** area, located just outside of Seward, offers easy hiking trails that lead to stunning views of the glacier. The **Exit Glacier Overlook Trail** is a family-friendly hike that is suitable for all ages and provides educational signage along the way, teaching visitors about the effects of climate change on Alaska's glaciers.

If your family enjoys fishing, the Kenai Peninsula is one of the best places in Alaska to try your hand at catching salmon or halibut. Many local tour operators offer fishing charters that are suitable for beginners and children, providing all the equipment and guidance you need to have a successful day on the water.

Accommodations for Families in Alaska

When it comes to accommodations, Alaska offers a variety of options that are perfect for families. Many hotels, lodges, and vacation rentals cater to families by offering larger rooms, kitchenettes, and family-friendly amenities like pools, playgrounds, and game rooms. For example, the **Alyeska Resort** in **Girdwood** is a great option for families, offering spacious rooms, an indoor pool, and easy access to outdoor activities like hiking, skiing, and tram rides.

Vacation rentals through platforms like Airbnb or Vrbo are also a popular choice for families, as they often provide more space and the ability to cook your own meals, which can be a huge money-saver. Staying in a cabin or lodge in the more remote areas of Alaska can also give your family a true wilderness experience, with opportunities for wildlife viewing and nature walks right outside your door.

Camping is another option for adventurous families, with many of Alaska's state and national parks offering campgrounds that are well-equipped for families with young children. Some campgrounds, like **Riley Creek Campground** in Denali, offer ranger-led programs for kids, which can make the camping experience even more enriching.

Traveling to and Around Alaska with Kids

Getting to Alaska with kids is relatively straightforward, with many major airlines offering direct flights to Anchorage, Fairbanks, and Juneau from cities across the United States. Once in Alaska, renting a car is one of the most convenient ways to get around, especially if you're traveling with young children and want the flexibility to stop and explore at your own pace. Many of Alaska's most popular destinations, like Denali, Seward, and Homer, are accessible by car, and the state's well-maintained highways make road-tripping a fun and scenic adventure.

If your family prefers not to drive, the **Alaska Railroad** is a fantastic alternative. The train connects Anchorage with Denali, Fairbanks, and Seward, offering a relaxing and scenic way to travel between some of Alaska's top destinations. The train offers large windows, comfortable seating, and onboard dining, making it a family-friendly mode of transportation that allows you to enjoy the journey as much as the destination.

Solo Travel in Alaska: Safety tips and how to meet fellow travelers

Traveling solo to Alaska is an adventure like no other, offering a sense of freedom, independence, and personal connection to one of the most remote and breathtaking parts of the world. Whether you are seeking solitude in the vast wilderness, hoping to meet fellow adventurers along the way, or simply testing your boundaries as a solo traveler, Alaska provides endless opportunities to explore its majestic landscapes, fascinating wildlife, and unique cultural heritage. While solo travel can sometimes feel daunting, Alaska is a safe and welcoming destination for those traveling on their own, as long as you plan carefully and follow some basic safety guidelines.

Alaska's rugged beauty is both its greatest appeal and one of the biggest challenges for solo travelers. From the towering peaks of Denali National Park to the endless miles of coastline along the Inside Passage, Alaska's vastness means that you may spend long stretches of time without seeing another soul. For some, this sense of isolation is part of the allure, offering an opportunity to truly disconnect from the outside world and immerse themselves in nature. For others, the solitude can be intimidating, especially when faced with Alaska's unpredictable weather and challenging terrain. However, with proper preparation, solo travelers can safely and confidently explore Alaska, while also finding ways to connect with fellow travelers and locals along the way.

One of the key considerations for solo travelers in Alaska is safety. Alaska's wilderness, while awe-inspiring, is also unforgiving, and it's important to be aware of the risks involved in traveling alone, particularly in remote areas. Wildlife encounters, weather changes, and the sheer vastness of the landscape can present challenges, but with the right knowledge and precautions, you can mitigate these risks and enjoy a safe and rewarding adventure.

Safety Tips for Solo Travelers in Alaska

One of the first things to keep in mind when traveling solo in Alaska is the importance of letting someone know your travel plans. Whether you're embarking on a day hike, a multi-day backpacking trip, or a road trip through the state, always inform a trusted friend or family member of your itinerary, including where you plan to go, how long you'll be gone, and when you expect to return. Alaska's remote areas often lack cell service, so it's crucial that someone knows where you are in case of an emergency.

When hiking or camping in bear country, which includes much of Alaska, solo travelers need to take extra precautions. Bears, especially brown bears (grizzlies) and black bears, are a common sight in many parts of the state, and it's important to know how to avoid encounters and what to do if you come across one. Solo hikers are more vulnerable because they tend to make less noise than groups, which can increase the risk of surprising a bear. To reduce this risk, make noise while hiking by talking, singing, or clapping, especially when walking through dense brush or along streams where bears might be feeding. Always carry bear spray, keep it easily accessible, and know how to use it. It's also important to store your food properly when camping—use bear-proof containers or hang your food high in a tree, well away from your campsite.

Another safety concern for solo travelers in Alaska is the weather, which can be unpredictable and extreme, even in the summer months. It's essential to be prepared for sudden changes in weather, including rain, snow, and cold temperatures, even if the forecast looks favorable. Always carry extra layers, waterproof gear, and a reliable map and compass (or GPS device) in case you get lost or need to take shelter unexpectedly. If you're hiking or camping, make sure you have a solid understanding of your route, and don't hesitate to turn back if the weather worsens or if you're unsure of your location.

For solo travelers driving in Alaska, it's important to keep in mind that some of the state's most scenic routes are also remote and may lack services like gas stations or food stops. Before embarking on a road trip, make sure your vehicle is in good condition, carry extra fuel, and bring plenty of water and snacks in case of delays or breakdowns. The **Alaska Highway**, which connects the Lower 48 to Alaska, and the **Denali Highway** are both stunningly beautiful but can be long and desolate stretches of road. Always keep an emergency kit in your car, including a first aid kit, blanket, flashlight, and tools for changing a tire.

Despite these challenges, solo travel in Alaska is incredibly rewarding, and there are plenty of ways to meet fellow travelers and share experiences along the way. Hostels, lodges, and tour groups are all great options for connecting with other adventurers, while Alaska's outdoor culture fosters a strong sense of camaraderie among travelers. Whether you're hiking with a group you met at a hostel, swapping stories with fellow campers around a fire, or joining a guided wildlife tour, you'll find plenty of opportunities to bond with others who share your love for the outdoors.

Meeting Fellow Travelers and Making Connections

One of the easiest ways to meet fellow travelers in Alaska is by staying at hostels, which are popular among solo adventurers and budget travelers. Hostels in cities like **Anchorage**, **Juneau**, and **Fairbanks** provide a communal atmosphere where it's easy to strike up conversations with other travelers, exchange tips, and even find companions for day trips or hikes. **Base Camp Anchorage** and the **Alaska Backpackers Inn** are two well-known hostels in Anchorage that attract a mix of international visitors and solo travelers looking to explore Alaska's wilderness. Many hostels also organize group activities, such as hiking excursions or wildlife tours, providing an easy way to meet new people while experiencing some of Alaska's best attractions.

In smaller towns and rural areas, **bed and breakfasts** and **wilderness lodges** often provide a more intimate and social atmosphere than hotels. These accommodations are typically family-run and offer opportunities to get to know both the hosts and other guests. In some cases, the hosts themselves may offer guided tours or outdoor activities, giving you the chance to explore with someone knowledgeable about the local area.

Joining group tours is another excellent way to meet fellow travelers while experiencing some of Alaska's top attractions. Whether you're interested in wildlife viewing, glacier hikes, or flightseeing tours, group excursions often attract solo travelers and provide a chance to bond over shared experiences. **Kenai Fjords Tours**, for example, offers boat tours of **Kenai Fjords National Park**, where you'll have the opportunity to see whales, sea otters, and glaciers, all while sharing the experience with other like-minded adventurers. **Denali National Park** also offers bus tours that are popular with solo travelers, as they provide an easy way to explore the park's vast wilderness while enjoying the company of other visitors.

For solo travelers looking to explore Alaska's national parks, **ranger-led programs** are a fantastic way to learn more about the environment while meeting other visitors. Many of Alaska's national parks, including Denali and **Wrangell-St. Elias National Park**, offer guided hikes, wildlife talks, and evening programs that are open to all visitors. These programs provide an opportunity to engage with the natural world alongside other travelers, while also gaining a deeper understanding of Alaska's unique ecosystems.

If you're looking to meet fellow adventurers with similar outdoor interests, consider joining a hiking or outdoor group before your trip. Platforms like **Meetup** and **Facebook** often have Alaska-based groups where locals and travelers organize hikes, camping trips, and other outdoor activities. These groups can be a great resource for finding hiking partners, especially if you're planning to venture into more remote areas where traveling alone may not be advisable.

Solo-Friendly Activities in Alaska

There are plenty of solo-friendly activities to enjoy in Alaska, whether you prefer the quiet solitude of nature or the social atmosphere of guided tours and group excursions.

Hiking is one of the best ways to experience Alaska's natural beauty as a solo traveler. With thousands of miles of trails ranging from easy walks to challenging backcountry routes, Alaska offers something for every level of hiker. Popular trails like **Flattop Mountain** near Anchorage and the **Mount Roberts Trail** in Juneau provide stunning views and are frequented by other hikers, making them ideal for solo adventurers who want the security of knowing others are nearby.

For a more structured solo adventure, consider signing up for a **multi-day tour** or guided trip. Companies like

REI Adventures and **Alaska Wildland Adventures** offer guided trips that include hiking, kayaking, and wildlife viewing, allowing solo travelers to experience the wilderness in a safe and supportive group setting. These trips are designed to provide an immersive experience in some of Alaska's most remote and pristine locations, while also offering the opportunity to meet and connect with fellow travelers.

Wildlife cruises are another excellent solo-friendly activity, offering the chance to see Alaska's iconic wildlife while enjoying the camaraderie of other passengers. From whale watching in **Juneau** to bear viewing tours in **Katmai National Park**, these cruises provide an unforgettable way to experience Alaska's natural wonders, all while being part of a group.

If you're traveling solo and want to spend time in a more social environment, Alaska's cities offer a range of cultural activities that are perfect for solo exploration. Museums, art galleries, and cultural centers in cities like Anchorage, Juneau, and Fairbanks provide insight into Alaska's history and indigenous cultures, and they're great places to meet other travelers or engage with locals. The **Alaska Native Heritage Center** in Anchorage is a must-visit for solo travelers interested in learning about the state's indigenous peoples, offering a variety of exhibits, performances, and demonstrations that provide a deeper understanding of Alaska's cultural heritage.

Sustainable Travel: How to minimize your footprint and travel responsibly in Alaska

The idea of sustainable travel is often tied to leaving a place as untouched as possible and making choices that support environmental preservation and local cultures. Alaska's diverse landscapes, which range from temperate rainforests and sprawling tundras to glaciers and vast waterways, are highly sensitive to changes. Therefore, sustainable practices are essential to maintain the integrity of these environments. Traveling responsibly in Alaska also means understanding the unique challenges of its remote communities and respecting the people who call this land home.

Whether you're hiking in Denali National Park, cruising through the Inside Passage, or exploring remote villages, there are numerous ways to reduce your environmental impact, engage in responsible tourism, and still enjoy everything Alaska has to offer.

Choosing Eco-Friendly Transportation Options

The vastness of Alaska means that most travelers will need to rely on various forms of transportation to get around the state. However, how you choose to travel can significantly influence your environmental footprint. Since air travel has a considerable carbon footprint, it's important to think carefully about how you can reduce emissions. While flying is often the only option for reaching remote locations like Juneau or Kodiak Island, you can minimize your overall travel impact by limiting the number of flights you take within the state. Instead, consider combining destinations into a single itinerary to avoid unnecessary air travel.

For those starting their journey from the continental U.S., one sustainable alternative is to take the **Alaska Marine Highway System**, the state's extensive ferry network. Ferries not only provide a scenic way to travel between coastal communities but also produce fewer emissions per passenger than airplanes. The ferry system connects key destinations, including **Ketchikan**, **Wrangell**, **Petersburg**, **Juneau**, and **Skagway**, making it a practical and environmentally responsible way to explore Southeast Alaska. Along the way, passengers are treated to stunning views of glaciers, forests, and marine life—providing a more immersive travel experience.

If you're traveling within Alaska, consider using public transportation or shared rides whenever possible. In Anchorage, the **People Mover** bus system offers reliable and affordable public transit that helps reduce the number of cars on the road. For longer distances, the **Alaska Railroad** is an eco-friendly way to see the state's stunning landscapes. The railroad connects Anchorage, **Fairbanks**, **Denali National Park**, and **Seward**, providing a scenic and sustainable alternative to driving. Train travel allows you to sit back and enjoy views of towering mountains, rushing rivers, and expansive valleys, all while reducing your carbon footprint.

Supporting Sustainable Accommodations

One of the best ways to practice sustainable travel in Alaska is by staying at eco-friendly accommodations that prioritize environmental stewardship and community engagement. Look for lodges, hotels, and campsites that have received certifications such as **LEED (Leadership in Energy and Environmental Design)** or participate in eco-labeling programs like **Green Key** or **Travel Green Alaska**. These certifications indicate that the property adheres to sustainable practices, such as energy conservation, waste reduction, and water efficiency.

Many wilderness lodges in Alaska, particularly those located in remote areas, place a strong emphasis on sustainability. For example, **Tutka Bay Lodge** on the **Kenai Peninsula** operates with a deep commitment to reducing its environmental impact by using solar power, composting organic waste, and sourcing local ingredients for meals. Similarly, **Camp Denali** in **Denali National Park** focuses on low-impact living, with renewable energy systems and a focus on wildlife preservation.

If you're camping in Alaska, take extra care to follow the **Leave No Trace** principles. These guidelines, which are designed to minimize the environmental impact of outdoor activities, include packing out all waste, respecting wildlife, and avoiding damage to natural habitats. Many campgrounds in Alaska offer recycling facilities, so be sure to dispose of your waste properly and recycle whenever possible. Additionally, if you're camping in remote areas, consider using biodegradable soap and ensuring that your campsite is set up away from water sources to avoid contamination.

Minimizing Your Waste

Alaska's remote location makes waste disposal and recycling more challenging than in many other parts of the U.S., so reducing waste is a critical component of sustainable travel. Before embarking on your trip, bring reusable items such as water bottles, shopping bags, and utensils to help cut down on single-use plastics. Many of Alaska's towns and national parks have limited waste management facilities, and even in larger cities like Anchorage or Juneau, the infrastructure for recycling can be limited.

When visiting national parks, wildlife reserves, or other protected areas, take care to pack out everything you bring in. This includes food packaging, plastic bottles, and other waste. The "Leave No Trace" philosophy encourages travelers to leave natural areas exactly as they found them, which is especially important in Alaska, where litter can have long-lasting effects on ecosystems.

You can also minimize waste by choosing sustainable tour operators who have adopted green practices. Many wildlife tours and adventure companies in Alaska prioritize sustainability, from offering eco-friendly boat cruises that reduce fuel consumption to providing reusable water bottles to guests. **Alaska Wildland Adventures**, for instance, has committed to reducing its carbon footprint by limiting single-use plastics, offsetting emissions, and supporting local conservation efforts.

Respecting Wildlife and Natural Habitats

Alaska's wildlife is one of its most iconic attractions, drawing visitors from around the world to see bears, whales, moose, and more in their natural environments. However, it's essential to observe wildlife in a way that doesn't disrupt their habitats or behavior. One of the most important rules for sustainable wildlife viewing is to keep a safe distance from animals. Approaching wildlife too closely can cause stress, disrupt feeding or mating behaviors, and even lead to dangerous encounters. In Alaska, you're likely to encounter bears, moose, and other large animals, so always give them plenty of space—at least 300 feet for bears, and more if they show signs of agitation.

Many of Alaska's national parks and wildlife refuges have strict guidelines for wildlife viewing. For example, **Katmai National Park** is famous for its brown bears, which gather at **Brooks Falls** to fish for salmon. While it's an incredible experience to witness these animals up close, it's important to follow the park's guidelines and stay within designated viewing platforms to avoid disturbing the bears. When visiting national parks, always follow the advice of rangers and respect any restrictions that may be in place to protect wildlife.

Another way to minimize your impact is by choosing wildlife tours that prioritize conservation and ethical viewing practices. Many tour operators in Alaska, such as **Kenai Fjords Tours** and **Major Marine Tours**, are certified by **Adventure Green Alaska**, a statewide program that recognizes sustainable tourism businesses. These operators adhere to strict guidelines to ensure that wildlife is observed from a safe distance and that boat engines are minimized to reduce noise pollution and disturbances to marine animals.

If you're hiking in Alaska, stick to established trails to avoid trampling fragile vegetation or disturbing wildlife habitats. Many of Alaska's ecosystems, including its tundra and coastal wetlands, are incredibly delicate, and off-trail hiking can cause irreversible damage. In some areas, like **Denali National Park**, it's common to encounter trail-less wilderness, so it's important to take extra care in these environments. Whenever possible, follow natural features like ridgelines or rocky terrain to minimize your impact on sensitive plant life.

Engaging with Local Communities and Cultures

Sustainable travel isn't just about protecting the environment—it's also about supporting local communities and respecting the cultures that make Alaska unique. Alaska's indigenous peoples have a long and rich history that is deeply intertwined with the land and its natural resources. When visiting native villages or participating in cultural tours, it's important to approach these experiences with respect and a willingness to learn.

One way to engage responsibly with local communities is by supporting native-owned businesses and tour operators. For example, **Alaska Native Heritage Tours** offers guided experiences led by Alaska Native guides, providing insight into indigenous traditions, history, and perspectives. By choosing to support these businesses, you contribute directly to the preservation of indigenous cultures and help ensure that local communities benefit from tourism.

Many small towns in Alaska, particularly those in remote areas, rely heavily on tourism for their economies. When visiting these communities, make an effort to shop at local markets, dine at family-owned restaurants, and purchase locally made crafts or souvenirs. This not only supports the local economy but also helps preserve traditional crafts and skills.

Additionally, be mindful of your behavior when visiting small communities, especially in rural or indigenous areas. Respect local customs and traditions, and ask for permission before taking photos of people, homes, or cultural sites. Remember that many Alaskan communities are close-knit, and visitors are often seen as guests—so treat your hosts and their surroundings with courtesy.

Supporting Conservation Efforts

Many organizations in Alaska are dedicated to protecting the state's natural resources and wildlife, and one way to travel sustainably is by supporting these conservation efforts. Whether through donations, volunteering, or participating in eco-friendly tours, there are numerous ways to contribute to Alaska's environmental preservation.

For example, the **Alaska Conservation Foundation** works to protect Alaska's ecosystems by supporting conservation projects, scientific research, and environmental advocacy. Similarly, the **Alaska Wildlife Conservation Center** focuses on the rescue and rehabilitation of orphaned or injured animals, providing educational programs for visitors. By visiting these organizations or contributing to their work, you can play a role in preserving Alaska's incredible wildlife and natural beauty.

Chapter 18

Resources and Apps for Travelers

From real-time weather and wildlife tracking to navigation in wilderness areas, the right technology can significantly enhance your travel experience in Alaska. Meanwhile, understanding where to access the best visitor centers and the most up-to-date maps will ensure you're well-informed and prepared for all the adventures this incredible state has to offer.

Top Apps for Alaska

Technology has become an integral part of travel, and using the right apps in Alaska can be particularly helpful given the state's unique challenges in terms of remoteness, changing weather, and limited connectivity in certain regions. Here are the top apps that every traveler should consider downloading before embarking on their Alaskan journey:

1. **Maps.me**: This app is one of the best offline mapping solutions available, especially for remote areas like Alaska. With **Maps.me**, you can download detailed maps of specific regions in Alaska and navigate without the need for a cellular connection. This is especially important when exploring national parks like **Denali** or **Wrangell-St. Elias**, where you may be far from cell towers. The app includes hiking trails,

campsites, and points of interest, which are all accessible even when you're offline.

2. **Aurora Forecast**: Alaska is famous for its northern lights, and **Aurora Forecast** helps you track the best times and locations to see the aurora borealis. This app provides real-time predictions and alerts for northern lights activity, which is especially useful if you're traveling to northern destinations like **Fairbanks**, **Coldfoot**, or **Barrow** in search of these spectacular light displays.

3. **The Alaska App**: Created by **Alaska.org**, this app is specifically designed for travelers exploring the state. It includes detailed information on attractions, tours, accommodations, and events across Alaska. It's also packed with local tips, guides to must-see destinations, and recommendations for family-friendly activities. **The Alaska App** covers everything from cultural sites in **Juneau** to outdoor adventures on the **Kenai Peninsula**.

4. **AllTrails**: Alaska is a hiker's paradise, and **AllTrails** is an excellent app for exploring the state's numerous hiking and backpacking routes. With detailed trail descriptions, difficulty ratings, and reviews from fellow hikers, **AllTrails** can help you choose the perfect route based on your fitness level and interests. Whether you're looking to hike the **Harding Icefield Trail** near **Seward** or explore **Chugach State Park**, this app will ensure you stay on track.

5. **iOverlander**: For those traveling Alaska by RV or planning to camp in remote locations, **iOverlander** is an indispensable app. It provides information on campsites, parking spots, and services like water and dump stations, often based on crowd-sourced updates from other travelers. The app is particularly helpful in areas where campgrounds may be limited, such as along the **Denali Highway** or on the outskirts of smaller towns like **Valdez** or **Homer**.
6. **Weather Underground**: Alaska's weather can change rapidly, so it's important to stay updated on local forecasts. **Weather Underground** offers hyper-localized weather data, including wind patterns, precipitation forecasts, and severe weather alerts. This app can be especially useful when planning outdoor activities like glacier hiking, wildlife viewing, or sea kayaking.
7. **MarineTraffic**: If your travel plans include coastal regions or the Inside Passage, **MarineTraffic** is an excellent app to track ferries, cruise ships, and other marine vessels in real-time. This is particularly useful for planning trips in areas like **Juneau**, **Ketchikan**, and **Skagway**, where water-based transportation plays a significant role in getting around.

Important Websites and Numbers

In addition to using travel apps, having access to key websites and phone numbers is crucial when traveling in Alaska. These resources will provide you with valuable information about everything from road conditions to emergency contacts.

1. **Alaska Department of Transportation (DOT)**: The Alaska DOT website (www.dot.alaska.gov) is an important resource for real-time road conditions, especially in the winter months when snow and ice can make travel more challenging. The DOT also offers updates on construction and ferry schedules, making it a valuable tool for road trips across the state. Their phone hotline for road conditions is 511, which is accessible from anywhere in Alaska.
2. **National Park Service (NPS)**: The NPS website (www.nps.gov/alaska) provides detailed information about Alaska's national parks, including trail maps, camping regulations, and park alerts. Whether you're visiting **Denali National Park**, **Glacier Bay**, or **Kenai Fjords**, the NPS website will help you plan your activities and ensure that you follow park guidelines to protect the environment and wildlife.
3. **Alaska Marine Highway**: For those traveling by ferry, the Alaska Marine Highway website (www.dot.alaska.gov/amhs) provides schedules, fare information, and booking options for routes connecting coastal towns. This service is essential for travelers looking to explore Southeast Alaska, as well as communities that are not accessible by road.

4. **Travel Alaska**: This official tourism website (www.travelalaska.com) is packed with information on accommodations, activities, and events throughout the state. It's an excellent resource for itinerary planning, whether you're visiting urban areas like Anchorage or rural locations like **Nome** or **Unalaska**.
5. **Alaska State Troopers**: For emergencies, the Alaska State Troopers are the primary law enforcement agency in the state. You can contact them by dialing 911 in emergencies or the non-emergency number at (907) 269-5511.

Alaska's Visitor Centers

Visitor centers are an invaluable resource for travelers, providing maps, brochures, and expert advice on the best things to see and do in each region. Alaska's visitor centers are located throughout the state and offer both logistical support and historical context for visitors looking to explore Alaska's vast and diverse landscapes.

- **Anchorage Visitor Information Center**: Located at 546 W 4th Ave, Anchorage, this iconic log cabin-style visitor center is in the heart of downtown. Here, travelers can pick up maps, get advice on the best tours, and learn about events happening in the city. The center's staff are knowledgeable about the state's various regions and can help you plan excursions to nearby attractions like **Turnagain Arm** or **Prince William Sound**.

- **Denali National Park Visitor Center**: Located just inside the park's entrance, this visitor center offers detailed maps, trail information, and exhibits on Denali's wildlife and geology. It's an essential stop for anyone planning a hike or backcountry camping trip in the park. Rangers are on hand to provide safety briefings and updates on wildlife activity.
- **Juneau Information Center**: Located at 245 Marine Way, this center is a great place to learn about Juneau's history, culture, and outdoor activities. Staff can help with planning excursions to **Mendenhall Glacier**, whale watching tours, or day trips to nearby islands.
- **Fairbanks Visitor Center**: Situated at 101 Dunkel St, this center provides visitors with information on local attractions, including the northern lights, hot springs, and dog sledding. The Fairbanks center also offers detailed maps of the Arctic Circle region for those planning to travel north.

Maps and Guides: Where to Find the Best Maps and How to Use Them in Remote Areas

While digital apps like **Google Maps** and **Maps.me** are useful, nothing beats having a physical map when traveling in Alaska's more remote areas. Many places in Alaska have limited or no cell service, making it crucial to carry a paper map as a backup.

- **National Geographic Maps**: These detailed topographic maps are perfect for hikers and outdoor enthusiasts. They are available for most of Alaska's national parks, including Denali, Glacier Bay, and Wrangell-St. Elias. You can find them at most visitor centers, outdoor gear shops, or order them online before your trip.
- **USGS Topographic Maps**: The **U.S. Geological Survey (USGS)** provides highly detailed topographic maps of Alaska's wilderness areas. These maps are essential for serious backpackers or those venturing off established trails, as they provide accurate elevation data and show natural features like rivers, mountains, and glaciers.
- **The Milepost**: This annual publication is a must-have for anyone road-tripping through Alaska. It offers mile-by-mile descriptions of highways, including the **Alaska Highway**, **Parks Highway**, and **Seward Highway**. It's packed with detailed maps, fuel stops, camping spots, and roadside attractions, making it a valuable companion for long drives.

When using maps in remote areas, it's essential to have a reliable compass and know how to read topographic features. If you plan to explore areas like **Gates of the Arctic National Park** or the **Brooks Range**, consider bringing a GPS device with preloaded maps for added security.

Chapter 19

FAQs

Common traveler concerns and expert answers

It's natural to have plenty of questions—after all, it's a unique and vast destination with its own set of challenges. To help alleviate concerns and ensure that travelers feel confident and well-prepared, we've compiled a list of frequently asked questions along with expert answers that cover a variety of common topics. Whether you're curious about what to pack, how to get around, or what to expect from the weather, these FAQs will provide the answers you need to enjoy your Alaskan adventure.

1. What is the best time of year to visit Alaska?

The best time to visit Alaska depends on what you want to experience. Most visitors travel during the summer months, from mid-May to mid-September, when the weather is warmer and most tourist attractions are open. Summer offers long daylight hours, perfect for outdoor activities like hiking, wildlife viewing, and fishing. This is also the best time to explore national parks like **Denali** and **Kenai Fjords**.

If you're interested in seeing the northern lights (aurora borealis), late fall, winter, and early spring—specifically from September to April—are the best times to visit. **Fairbanks** is a popular destination for aurora viewing during this period. Winter is also ideal for snow sports and attending Alaska's famous winter festivals, like the **Iditarod** or the **Ice Art Championships**.

2. What should I pack for a trip to Alaska?

Alaska's weather is notoriously unpredictable, so it's important to pack layers that can accommodate a wide range of temperatures and conditions. Even in summer, temperatures can range from 40°F (4°C) in the mornings and evenings to 70°F (21°C) during the day. In winter, temperatures can drop below 0°F (-18°C) in some areas.

- **Summer:** Pack lightweight, moisture-wicking base layers, a fleece or down jacket, a waterproof rain jacket, and sturdy hiking boots. Don't forget a hat, gloves, and sunglasses, as well as bug spray, since mosquitos can be prevalent in some areas.
- **Winter:** For cold-weather travel, pack insulated clothing, a heavy winter jacket, thermal layers, waterproof boots, and accessories like hats, scarves, gloves, and hand warmers.

3. How do I get around Alaska?

Alaska is a huge state with limited roadways, so getting around can require a mix of transportation methods.

- **Driving:** Renting a car or RV is a popular option for travelers, especially for those exploring

regions connected by major highways like **Anchorage**, **Denali National Park**, and **Fairbanks**. The **Alaska Highway** and **Seward Highway** offer scenic drives, but it's important to plan carefully since services like gas stations can be few and far between in remote areas.
- **Ferries:** The **Alaska Marine Highway System** is a network of ferries connecting coastal communities in Southeast and Southwest Alaska. This is a scenic and practical option if you're traveling between cities like **Juneau**, **Sitka**, and **Ketchikan**.
- **Railroads:** The **Alaska Railroad** offers a scenic way to travel between Anchorage, Fairbanks, Denali, and Seward. It's a comfortable and stress-free way to see some of Alaska's most breathtaking landscapes.
- **Flights:** Due to the lack of road infrastructure in certain areas, small planes and bush flights are common, especially if you're visiting remote areas like **Kodiak Island** or **Katmai National Park**. Major airlines fly into **Anchorage**, **Juneau**, and **Fairbanks**, while smaller regional airlines connect to more remote areas.

4. Is Alaska expensive to visit?

Alaska can be more expensive than many other U.S. destinations due to its remote location, the cost of importing goods, and the seasonality of tourism. Expect to pay higher prices for food, fuel, and accommodations, especially in more isolated areas.

That said, there are plenty of ways to travel on a budget in Alaska. Consider staying at hostels, camping, or traveling during the shoulder seasons (spring or fall) when prices are lower. Public transport, such as buses or trains, can also be more cost-effective than renting a car, and there are numerous free outdoor activities, including hiking and wildlife viewing.

5. Will I be able to see the northern lights during my visit?

The northern lights (aurora borealis) are best viewed from September through April, primarily in northern Alaska. **Fairbanks** is one of the best places to see the aurora, thanks to its location under the auroral oval (a ring-shaped zone over the polar regions where the northern lights are most visible). However, it's important to note that viewing the aurora depends on weather conditions, solar activity, and clear skies. The longer the night, the better your chances—so the peak of winter, when there are more hours of darkness, offers the best opportunity to see the lights.

6. Are there any wildlife safety tips I should know?

Yes, Alaska is home to a variety of wildlife, including bears, moose, wolves, and whales, so it's important to be cautious and respect the animals in their natural habitat.

- **Bears:** If you're hiking or camping, always carry bear spray and make noise to avoid surprising a bear. Never approach or feed bears,

and store food in bear-proof containers when camping.
- **Moose:** While moose may seem less threatening than bears, they can be aggressive, especially if they feel threatened or are protecting their young. Give them plenty of space and avoid approaching them.
- **Whales:** If you're on a whale-watching tour, your guide will follow specific regulations to keep a safe distance from the animals, ensuring minimal disturbance. For your safety, always follow the guide's instructions.

7. Can I visit Alaska without renting a car?

Absolutely. While a car offers flexibility, it's not always necessary, especially if you're visiting cities like Anchorage or Juneau. Both cities have public transportation, and many tours offer hotel pick-ups for excursions. For coastal travel, ferries connect several towns in Southeast Alaska, and the **Alaska Railroad** provides scenic routes through popular regions. If you're planning to visit national parks, consider joining a guided tour or using the park's shuttle systems, such as the one in **Denali National Park**.

8. What are some must-see attractions in Alaska?

Some of Alaska's most iconic attractions include:

- **Denali National Park**: Home to North America's tallest peak, Denali, this park offers

incredible wildlife viewing, hiking, and scenic bus tours.
- **Kenai Fjords National Park**: Famous for its glaciers and marine wildlife, this park is best explored by boat, where you can see whales, puffins, sea lions, and more.
- **Glacier Bay National Park**: Located in Southeast Alaska, this park offers breathtaking views of tidewater glaciers and is a prime location for kayaking, whale watching, and camping.
- **Mendenhall Glacier**: Just outside Juneau, this glacier is easily accessible and offers great hiking opportunities, along with spectacular ice formations and wildlife sightings.
- **Northern Lights Viewing**: As mentioned earlier, **Fairbanks** is a top spot for aurora viewing, along with winter activities like dog sledding and visiting the **Chena Hot Springs**.

9. Do I need travel insurance for my trip to Alaska?

While travel insurance is not required, it's highly recommended, especially for a destination like Alaska where weather conditions can be unpredictable and activities like hiking, fishing, or flightseeing tours carry some risk. Travel insurance can cover trip cancellations, delays, medical emergencies, and lost or damaged gear. Make sure your policy covers any adventure activities you plan to participate in, such as kayaking or glacier hiking.

10. How do I stay connected in remote areas of Alaska?

Staying connected in remote areas of Alaska can be a challenge, as cell service is often spotty or nonexistent outside of major cities. Consider downloading offline maps and guides to your phone before you leave areas with strong Wi-Fi or cellular connections. If you're spending a significant amount of time in the wilderness, you may want to consider renting a satellite phone or GPS device. Many remote lodges and national parks, such as those in **Denali** or **Wrangell-St. Elias**, offer Wi-Fi but at limited speeds.

Made in United States
Troutdale, OR
03/03/2025

29490920R00239